To Mrs. Hammon
for all your kindness

from Alison & Boo.

GW00750895

EGGS, MILK AND CHEESE

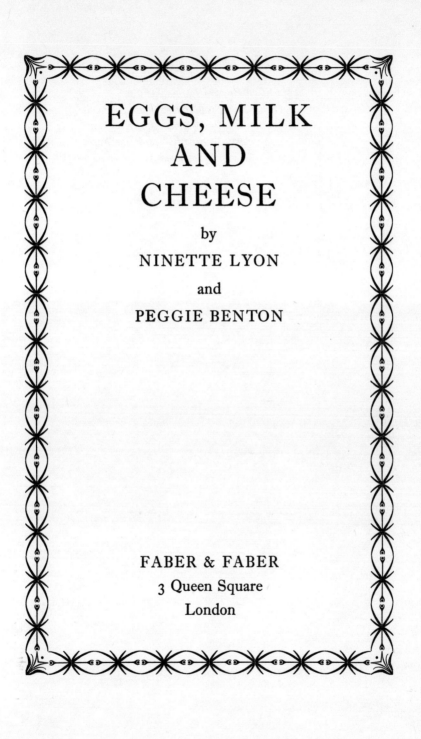

EGGS, MILK AND CHEESE

by

NINETTE LYON

and

PEGGIE BENTON

FABER & FABER
3 Queen Square
London

First published in 1971
by Faber and Faber Limited
3 Queen Square London WC1
Printed in Great Britain by
Ebenezer Baylis & Son Limited
The Trinity Press, Worcester, and London
All rights reserved

ISBN 0 571 08302 1

ACKNOWLEDGEMENTS

Thanks are due to the following for their help with the English edition: Mrs Audrey Ellison; Mr L. G. Barrow, Managing Director of Crowson & Son Ltd; Mr R. A. Ingham of J. Sainsbury's Dairy Division; Mrs Christine Johnson, Swiss Cheese Adviser at the Swiss Centre; Unigate; Express Dairy Group Services; the Milk Marketing Board; the British Country Cheese Council; the British Egg Information Service; the British Standards Institution; the Commercial Section, Irish Embassy; Auguste Noël Ltd; the New Zealand Dairy Board; and the Eggs and Poultry Branch, the Milk and Milk Products Branch, and the Food Standards Branch of the Ministry of Agriculture and Fisheries.

CONTENTS

9

CONTENTS

THE NEW MEASURES

THIS book is going to press at a difficult moment, when plans for metrication are only just beginning to crystallize. Following the advice of the British Standards Institution and of leading cookery authorities, we have adopted the system which we are told is to be generally followed.

For ease of conversion, ounces are reckoned as 25 g (or grammes). This makes ½ lb equivalent to 200 g and 1 lb equivalent to 400 g, instead of the accurate equivalents of 227 g and 455 g respectively.

Half-ounces are reckoned as 15 g, since 12·5 g is too awkward either to measure or to quote. This leads to an obvious discrepancy in that while 15 g appears as a half-ounce, 25 g is quoted as a whole one. However, since food packaging is said to be coming into line, and children are already using these measurements in many schools, people should quickly accustom themselves to the system.

The British Standards Institution is planning the introduction of the following five standard liquid measures for use in the kitchen:

⅙ measure	½ dl	(50 ml)	
¼ ,,	¾ dl	(75 ml)	
⅓ ,,	1 dl	(100 ml)	
½ ,,	1½ dl	(150 ml),	about ¼ pint
1 ,,	3 dl	(300 ml),	,, ½ pint

Whenever we mention a 'cup' or a 'glass' in this book we are referring to the full measure of 3 dl which is just under our present half-pint.

SOME COOKING TERMS USED IN
THIS BOOK

Aspic. A savoury jelly, or cold food which is set in such a jelly.

À point. The moment when a food has reached the perfect stage.

Bain-marie. A rectangular pan filled with hot water and used for keeping food warm, or in which food can be cooked at a moderate temperature in its own saucepan, either in the oven or on top of the stove.

Bouquet garni. The classic bouquet garni consists of parsley stalks, thyme and a bay leaf tied together. Other herbs may be called for in a recipe.

Chambrer. To bring something (usually wine) to room temperature.

Fines Herbes. All sorts of herbs, but usually parsley, tarragon, chives and chervil.

En ruban. Egg yolks and sugar beaten together until they are smooth and will fall from the beater like a ribbon.

Flan. An open tart, cooked in a ring. In Spain, 'flan' is rather confusingly used to describe a caramel custard.

Fondue. A dish which in Switzerland is made with melted cheese, wine, etc. The word 'fondue' literally means 'melted'.

Liaison. A substance such as egg yolk, *beurre manié*, cream, cornflour or arrowroot which is used to bind a soup, sauce or cream.

Poaching. Cooking in a liquid which is only simmering, not boiling. For poaching eggs, see p. 41.

Reducing. Boiling until the quantity of a liquid is reduced by evaporation.

Soft Peak Stage. Egg whites beaten until they form a point which curls over when held upright on the beater.

Stiff Peak Stage. At this stage, the point will remain upright.

OVEN TEMPERATURES

T HE following table, which has been issued by the Electricity
Council, shows the usual dial settings for the oven heats
which are likely to be mentioned in cookery books. It is wise
to check these with the instruction book for your cooker, as the
behaviour of ovens can vary according to how the sources of heat
are placed.

To simplify setting, the Fahrenheit scale is shown in units of
25°, and the Centigrade figures have been rounded off.

	ELECTRICITY		GAS
	Fahrenheit	*Centigrade*	
Slow	225°–300°	110°–150°	¼–2
Moderate	325°–350°	170°–180°	3–4
Fairly hot	375°–400°	190°–200°	5–6
Hot	425°–450°	220°–230°	7–8
Very hot	475°–500°	240°–260°	9

EGGS

A CRITICAL APPROACH

The egg is smooth and very pale;
It has no nose, it has no tail;
It has no ears that one can see;
It has no wit, no repartee.
Roy Bishop

WHILST we are on this rather critical note, it must be mentioned that eggs, even when fresh, have one or two disagreeable characteristics. They turn your silver black and if you have a sensitive nose you will notice that unless glass and crockery are very carefully washed and rinsed, a slight taint of egg will cling to them. If you are drinking the same wine throughout the meal, it is worth changing glasses after an egg course.

Should you drop an egg on the kitchen floor and try hastily to wipe it up, you will create a skating rink. Avoid walking on the egg until it has dried and then scrape it up with a knife.

Dickens's Mr Mantalini observed that 'an egg doesn't match any waistcoat but a yellow waistcoat, demmit'. So if you spill egg on your clothes and try to wipe it off, the resulting smear is unlikely to match. Wait until the egg has congealed, when it can be lifted off, leaving no trace.

ODD FACTS ABOUT EGGS

It is a curious fact that although words such as 'ovoid' which we use in connection with eggs are derived from the Latin word 'ovum', the word 'egg' is of Icelandic origin and appears to have come into our language before the Roman invasion of Britain.

Since earliest times eggs have played an important part in the symbolism of people all over the world, and it was even believed in some early societies that the universe was formed from a giant egg.

Philosophers took the egg to symbolize the world and its elements, the shell representing earth; the white, water; the yolk, fire, and the empty space within the egg, air.

Even before hens were domesticated, the egg was regarded as a symbol of fertility and it has always played an important part in fertility rites.

The early Christians adopted the egg as a symbol of the Resurrection and it has been associated with Easter ever since. In medieval times eggs were distributed in churches on Easter Sunday and the scholars at Oxford used to hold an egg feast on the Saturday before Shrove Tuesday, when the Lenten abstinence from eggs began.

Boys in some parts of the Midlands and the North of England still roll 'pace' eggs down the hillsides at Easter, the word 'pace' not referring to speed, but being derived from the same root as 'paschal', which refers to Easter.

Eggs are the subject of many superstitions too. The white of an egg dropped into water by a young girl on New Year's Eve is said to show from the resulting patterns her marriage prospects. The same method is sometimes used by gipsies to foretell the future of a client.

In some parts of Brazil, in order that a child may learn to speak more quickly, he is given at first light dew which has been collected in an egg shell at the full of the moon. But egg shells have been held to be witches' ware and carefully smashed and put into the hens' food pail to prevent a witch from using one as a boat. (Incidentally, this was sound husbandry since the calcium in the shells returned to the hens to form firmer shells for future eggs.) A race memory of witchcraft may cause some people to batter their empty shells down into the egg cup—to the chagrin of the washer-up.

Though such a simple everyday food, eggs still hold an element of mystery. One marvels that this small, smooth object contains everything necessary to produce a living creature. Eggs have always intrigued people and presented certain puzzling aspects, like the old conundrum—which came first, the chicken or the egg? Samuel Butler suggested that the hen was the egg's way of producing another egg.

EGG PRODUCTION

It takes one and a half hens to keep an average Englishman going, that is to say there are about 72 million hens in this country, which in 1969 produced over 14½ thousand million eggs. It is obvious that the farmer's wife, selling her eggs for pin money, can no longer cope with the demand. Without deep litter and batteries, the subject of so much protest, not only would the price of eggs be very much higher, but it would be impossible to meet the demand for them. As it is, the price of eggs, contrary to the general trend, has not risen in the past ten years.

It may be of passing interest to know that the average Englishman eats 270 eggs a year; a Frenchman only 200 and the American consumption per head is 300 eggs a year.

The Deep Litter System. Hens live and move freely in colonies of several hundred on deep layers of clean straw or shavings. They are brought into the houses when they are five months old and live there until they are sixteen months old, when they become less productive. The house is then cleared and sterilized and a new batch of hens arrives.

The Battery System. Here the hens live caged under controlled conditions of temperature and air, fed with a balanced diet and kept supplied with water. They certainly suffer neither cold, hunger nor neglected diseases, but to us their lives seem unbearably cramped and monotonous. Unfortunately no one is able to ask the hen's opinion.

Free Range. This is a modernization of the farmer's wife's method. The hens still run about in the open, but where her most scientific aid to production used to be a china egg popped into the hens' favourite nesting places to encourage them to lay, the hen-houses and diet are now carefully planned to achieve maximum output.

Disregarding poultry keepers with less than fifty hens, who are not at present obliged to register with the egg marketing authorities, the laying flock of free range hens in Britain is only about 6 per cent of the total hen population. From the number of eggs sold as 'free range' it would seem to be very much greater!

In order to run any of these systems efficiently a large amount of capital is required and the business must inevitably become concentrated in fewer and larger units.

THE DISTRIBUTION OF EGGS

The farmer collects his eggs at least once a day, and any which are dirty are immediately cleaned, either by hand or electric machine (not washed, since the shells are porous and germs could pass into the egg together with the moisture). The eggs are then collected by one of over five hundred local packing stations and carefully tested for any of twenty possible faults. This is done by 'candling'. In the old days, eggs were held up before a candle, but now machinery and powerful lights are used to expose any defects.

Perfect eggs are graded into 'large', which weigh not less than $2\frac{3}{16}$ oz; 'standard', between $1\frac{7}{8}$ and $2\frac{3}{16}$ oz; 'medium', from $1\frac{5}{8}$ to $1\frac{7}{8}$ oz and 'small', between $1\frac{1}{2}$ and $1\frac{5}{8}$ oz. Small eggs are seldom seen in the shops.

The graded eggs are then packed into boxes of 360 which are date-stamped, and any of which are not sold by a specified date may be bought back by the egg marketing organization for manufacturing purposes.

THE COMPOSITION OF THE EGG

Eggs, like bananas, are one of the most familiar forms of natural packaging. Since they contain all the nutrient necessary to transform a single cell into a complete, live, chirruping chick, it is obvious that the package contains some pretty valuable material.

A standard 2 oz egg has a yolk weighing $\frac{1}{2}$ oz which, since it contains almost all the fat in the egg, has a calorie value of 50. The white, which weighs $1\frac{1}{4}$ oz has only about a tenth of this calorie value. The protein of eggs, which is of exceptionally high quality, is about 20 per cent cheaper than that derived from other foods. The yolk of an egg contains vitamins A, D, E, and K and certain of the B group. The egg also contains valuable mineral compounds and is a rich source of iron.

The shell, which weighs about $\frac{1}{4}$ oz is composed of calcium, which is an essential component of healthy teeth and bones. Some people pulverize this in the blender whilst beating the rest of the egg, but though doubtless very healthy, the result is quite horrid unless pulverization is complete.

At the rounded end of the egg there is an air space which gradually expands as the egg loses its freshness. This is why a really stale egg will float in water while a fresh one sinks to the bottom.

The yolk of an egg is held in place by two gelatinous chalazes or threads. These should be removed when making soups and sauces. Some recipes suggest straining the eggs for this purpose, but the thread can easily be removed with a piece of the shell.

The colour of the shell, so important to some egg lovers, has nothing to do with its flavour or 'goodness', but depends on the breed of the hen which laid the egg. Whilst the majority of English people prefer a brown egg, most Americans would rather have a white one. The fact that brown eggs are more expensive does not mean that they are better than white, but simply that the breed of hens which lay them are less prolific, and so produce fewer eggs for the food which they consume.

The colour of a yolk, which has nothing to do with its freshness or food value, depends on the diet of the hen. Grass and corn produce deeper-coloured yolks, but the same result can be obtained by adding carotene to the hen's food.

In fact, whether eggs are brown or white and the birds old or young, housed in a battery or living on free range, no significant difference in the nutritional value of the eggs has yet been proved.

Eggs which have been fertilized can be recognized by a small dark speck which is easily removed with a piece of shell. They have a slightly higher nutritional value, but do not keep as well. The eggs produced by modern methods are never fertilized, so one is only likely to come across these when buying from a small producer who allows a cock to run with the hens.

EGGS AND DIET

Diet is always the subject of argument. The speed with which expert opinion changes and the tenacity with which opposite points of view are defended provide a useful let-out for those who prefer to eat what they like and damn the consequences. As Hilaire Belloc remarked, 'all the world is torn and rent by varying views on nutriment'.

Eggs used to be prescribed as a cure for melancholy. Nowadays they are recommended for many conditions. Since they are almost without carbohydrates eggs are useful for diabetics (and slimmers) and are now included in the bland high-protein diet of people with stomach ulcers. In the case of mouth and throat injuries they are one of the few natural foods which will slip down easily. They are a first-class supplement to the milk diet of babies, and ideal for old people with dental troubles.

It used to be thought that eggs were bad for the liver. It is true that people with liver complaints should avoid eggs, but those whose livers are merely delicate will suffer no harm from them.

Eggs contain traces of cholesterol, which admittedly has had a bad press recently, but some doctors say that cholesterol helps the organic action of the bile, and is beneficial to the sex hormones.

People with delicate digestions used to be advised to eat eggs very lightly cooked. Now this is considered to be an error. A hard-boiled egg digests slowly and completely, whilst a raw yolk demands an immediate effort of digestion. As for a raw white, unless it is beaten to a foam it slips through the stomach unaffected by the digestive juices and even inhibiting their secretion, and may produce allergic reactions or diarrhoea.

Slimming. Fashions in slimming diet change in a most bewildering way, but it does seem to be generally agreed that an imbalance in diet will cause one to lose weight, though it may lead to other troubles. The safest way to shed a few pounds is to eat less, and especially less sugar and starch.

So whether you go flat out on a high-protein-and-fat, no-carbohydrate diet, or just try to moderate your ways, eggs are especially valuable, since they supply so many of the vital food requirements for a comparatively low calorie count.

EGGS WHICH ARE DIFFERENT

The eggs of most birds and many fishes are edible. Although hen's eggs are the only ones to be produced on a vast commercial scale, goose, duck and bantam's eggs can all be eaten, remembering that their respective weights are about 9, 3 and 1 oz, while a hen's egg averages nearly 2 oz. Substitutions, therefore, are made by the weight and not the number of eggs.

Ducks often choose a dirty spot in which to lay their eggs and these may acquire harmful bacteria which pass through the porous shells. It is wise either to boil them for 15 minutes or to use them in baking. When boiled, the white of a duck's egg becomes blueish and slightly gelatinous and the yolk a strong reddish-orange.

A goose will lay from 15 to 30 eggs in a year against a good hen's average 250. Goose eggs may be safely used for omelettes and other briefly-cooked dishes. Bantam's eggs, which are about half the size of a hen's, can be interchanged with them. Turkey eggs were described by Mrs Beeton as 'almost as delicate as those of a hen'. Guinea fowl's eggs are considered to be more delicate. They are small, shaped like a pointed gooseberry, and have a rather muddy complexion.

Of the wild bird's eggs, those of the plover and quail are the most appreciated. The quail and its eggs, which for centuries have been a popular delicacy in Europe, have almost disappeared from our countryside and are now either imported or artificially bred. The eggs, which are the size of a cherry, can be bought fresh in springtime. They are sometimes sold ready-cooked or in the form of a pickle, which must be stored in a cool place. Quail's eggs can be served as appetizers, as a garnish for hors-d'œuvre, or accompanied by mayonnaise or tartare sauce.

Unlike the eggs of most sea birds, which have a strong fishy taste, gull's eggs are excellent. Turtle's eggs, which consist entirely of yolk inside a soft shell, are delicious. They are served in restaurants in such places as Brazil where turtles lay their eggs along the sandy beaches.

An ostrich lays an egg which is as large as twenty hen's eggs. The flavour is good, provided the egg has not been left to bake in the sun, or been partially hatched by the male, whose partner does not bother her head with such duties. The biggest eggs yet traced are those of the fossilized aepiornis of Madagascar, which had a volume of almost two gallons. And talking of size, the *Guinness Book of Records* quotes a New Jersey hen which laid an egg weighing one pound.

The French physiologist Alexis Carrel, who won the Nobel

Prize in 1912, advised eating eggs in which the chick was already partially formed, since he believed that they helped to renew the body cells. Such eggs must have been exceptionally hard to take.

A new development during the last war, when eggs were for a time rationed to one per person per month, was the 'shell egg' so named to distinguish a real egg from the 'reconstituted' ones which you made from egg powder.

The Chinese bury eggs for years until they turn black and are said to be exquisite. In the sixteenth century Gianbattista della Porta, a Neapolitan physician, invented a gigantic egg made by poaching the yolks of four or five dozen eggs in a bladder until they were firm, and then surrounding them, in a larger bladder, with the whites. The final product, with the skin removed, was served on a bed of lettuce. These giant eggs became fashionable in seventeenth-century England and France. An attempt recently made at Maxim's of Paris to re-create one of these monsters was only successful after the third or fourth try.

Easter Eggs

Ever since eggs began to be exchanged at Easter as symbols of re-birth, a great deal of ingenuity has been used to make them into attractive presents. The poorest peasant could dye an egg with onion skins or scratch a pattern on it with the point of a pin. In some parts of Europe the more sophisticated folk designs are minor works of art.

Famous artists such as Watteau and Lancret painted eggs for the delight of the French Court during the seventeenth and eighteenth centuries. In Russia, the rich and the aristocratic exchanged hand-wrought eggs made of gold and set with jewels. The most famous, perhaps, was an enamelled golden egg containing a hen covered with precious stones, sitting within an Imperial crown on a small egg encrusted with rubies.

Now, unfortunately, mass-produced chocolate and cardboard eggs have largely replaced the charmingly decorated real eggs of more leisured times.

Decorating Easter Eggs. There are so many ways of decorating eggs for Easter. One only needs patience and a little imagination.

Since the shells of eggs are porous, it is not safe to eat those which have been coloured with certain materials, but there are special dyes made for this purpose. White eggs take the dye best.

Patterns can be painted on the shells with melted candle grease. Allow the grease to set firmly before dyeing, and peel it off when the eggs are dry. Flowers, ferns and grasses, tied round the eggs, make delicate patterns. If your imagination fails you, just write or scratch a name on each egg after it is coloured.

Unless you are sure that the dye is safe, it is best to empty the egg. You can either make a hole in the broad end with a meat skewer, pierce the yolk and gently shake the egg into a basin, or make a pinhead hole in the broad end of the shell and another, twice as big, at the narrow end. Blow steadily into the smaller hole until the egg is empty.

Eggs emptied by the first method can be filled with melted chocolate and used to surprise the children who find them in their breakfast egg cup.

Another amusing surprise is made by slicing off the round end of a hard-boiled egg (preferably from a duck or goose), scooping it out and re-filling it with earth or cotton wool in which you plant grass seed. In a fortnight the seed should have grown into a mop of bright green hair and only needs a face painted beneath it. Remember to keep the grass damp as it grows.

EGG STORAGE

A fourteenth-century sage affirmed that 'hen's eggs be best, and the best be those that be fresh'. Few people would disagree with him. In order to enjoy fresh eggs it is wise not to buy too many at a time, and since the keeping quality of eggs is damaged by light, never buy from a shop where eggs are displayed in a sunny window.

Testing for Freshness. A rough test of the freshness of an egg is to drop it into a deep bowl of water. A fresh egg, having a smaller air cell, should sink to the bottom; an older one tends to stand on end, and an egg which floats is really past praying for. It must be remembered, however, that the thickness of the shell influences the behaviour of the egg.

A better test, but this involves breaking the egg, is to study its shape as it lies on a saucer. With a fresh egg the yolk will stand high and domed on a thick, compact white. As the egg becomes older the yolk flattens and the white becomes more runny until, with an elderly egg, the yolk breaks and they run into one another.

Oscar Wilde remarked, 'An egg is an adventure. It may be different', by which he probably meant stale. Nowadays, with the careful testing of eggs it needs considerable carelessness on someone's part—maybe your own—for you to encounter a stale one.

Keeping Eggs at Home. Eggs are considered to remain 'fresh' for 12 days at ordinary room temperature (about 65°F, 19°C) and for three weeks in a refrigerator at about 45°F (7–8°C). They should be kept standing with the pointed end down so that the air cell remains floating at the broad end.

Once an egg is broken, the yolk and the white should be stored separately and kept covered, since bacteria from the air can cause food poisoning. To prevent the yolks hardening, seal them with a thin layer of milk or water, or if they are to be made into mayonnaise, use oil instead. Whites should not be kept, even in the refrigerator, for more than 2–3 days.

If you are not sure whether an egg is raw or has been hard-boiled, try spinning it like a top. The raw egg will fall over at once —and if you *should* break it, at least you will be in control. We have seen the dire results of offering raw instead of hard-boiled eggs at a picnic.

Since eggs absorb odours through their porous shells they should be stored away from foods with a strong smell. Incidentally, one can take advantage of this characteristic by keeping the eggs destined for an omelette together with fresh mushrooms, truffles, aromatic herbs or Parmesan cheese for a couple of days so that the pleasant flavours are absorbed.

Preserving Eggs at Home. In the days when there were very sharp fluctuations in the price of eggs many people, during a glut, preserved them for home use. Now, the large commercial hen-houses are artificially lit so that the hens believe in a perpetual summer and lay all the year round. The supply of eggs is constant and prices vary less, whilst the storage space in modern homes tends to diminish. However, we give a brief description of four methods of home preserving. In every case, the eggs must be free from cracks and infertile. They should be at least 12 hours old.

An old-fashioned way is to rub absolutely clean, dry eggs with buttered paper, seeing that there is a complete film of grease so that all air is excluded. A coating of paraffin wax serves the same purpose.

Another method is to dip the eggs in a solution such as Oteg and allow them to dry thoroughly. With both these methods, the eggs should be stored in boxes, broad ends upwards, in a cool place. The boxes should not be airtight.

The third method is to immerse the eggs in waterglass, which can be bought at the chemist's and carries directions on the package. The eggs are placed in layers, point downwards, in earthenware crocks which can be ready-filled with the liquid; or the cold solution can be poured over the previously stacked eggs. In either case, care must be taken not to crack the shells, or cause breakage by allowing too great a weight of eggs to rest on those beneath. The crock should be covered to lessen evaporation, and the liquid topped up when necessary so that the eggs are always immersed.

Preserved eggs do not boil well as the shells are apt to crack. After some time the whites become thin and watery and it is not easy to separate them from the yolks.

Deep Frozen Eggs. Single eggs freeze very satisfactorily if they are broken into individual waxed paper containers and covered with greaseproof paper. Once frozen these can be packaged in suitable freezer bags. Such eggs can be fried or poached—straight from the freezer, though a more satisfactory result is achieved when the eggs are first thawed out.

For scrambled eggs, omelettes, cake-making and so on, eggs may be frozen together in packages of convenient numbers. In order to prevent the eggs from thickening, lightly mix 1 teaspoon of salt or 1 tablespoon of sugar to every 5 or 6 eggs. The eggs should not be beaten, just stirred sufficiently for yolk and white to mix. Needless to say, it is important to label the packages so that you know which contains salt and which sugar.

Yolks and whites can be frozen separately, the latter just as they are, and the former with the addition of the same amount of salt or sugar as you would use for whole eggs. It is useful to know that 1 tablespoon of thawed yolk equals a normal yolk; 2 tablespoons of thawed white an ordinary white and, obviously, 3 tablespoons of mixed yolks and white, approximately one whole egg.

Commercially Preserved Eggs. Large quantities of preserved eggs are used in commerce, for the bakery, ice cream and many other trades. Whole eggs or separate yolks and whites are frozen, salted or spray-dried to make powder, and albumen is also produced separately. In America, frozen eggs, either entire or separated into yolks and whites, are sold in the supermarkets.

Curiously enough, though eggs are also used in cosmetics, paints and many other products, they don't find their way into custard powder—which, like chips, is one of the bases of our national cuisine. (Incidentally, it is always worth reading the labels of cake mixes, etc., to see whether they contain egg or not.)

EQUIPMENT

For egg cookery, more than any other, your source of heat is important. Temperatures are critical, and unless your hot plates will maintain a true simmer you will find difficulty in producing many interesting egg dishes and sauces.

Gas is more flexible and easily controlled than electricity, but there are electric stoves which will simmer impeccably. If yours does not, there is little you can do. An asbestos mat, so useful with a gas cooker, will damage a radiant plate and cause it to wear out sooner. Complaints to the service engineer will usually result in the cheerful assurance that what is clearly a full, rolling boil is just a 'nice simmer'. Tricity is now overcoming this difficulty by fitting a plate which will go from minimum to maximum at either half or full strength, thus providing a very wide range of temperatures. Unfortunately, this plate is too expensive to be fitted on all their cookers.

The notes which follow are in no sense a complete inventory of kitchen equipment but just a list of things you will find useful for cooking eggs.

Personal preference plays a large part in choosing equipment. Often this seems to have no rational basis, but it is useful at least to know what one can expect from the various materials of which cooking pots are made.

Aluminium and iron will discolour food containing yolk of egg or acids such as lemon juice or white wine. Aluminium itself becomes stained in the course of cooking, but it can be cleaned by adding vinegar to water boiling in the pan. Heavy aluminium pans cook evenly and conduct heat well.

Cast-iron is reasonable in price and long lasting, but rather heavy. It heats up slowly and retains heat. A new pan will require seasoning (p. 50). The pan must be kept dry or it will rust, though a thin film of oil will help to prevent this.

Enamelled cast-iron is easy to clean and can go straight to table from the stove, but care must be taken not to chip the enamel finish. The shallow dishes made for *œufs sur le plat* retain their heat, and if started over too fierce a fire can overcook an egg between the stove and the table unless you are prepared to indulge in a sort of egg-and-spoon race to the waiting consumer.

Enamelled steel, which is coming on to the market in quantities, is light and easy to handle, but is not such a good conductor of heat as iron or aluminium.

Stainless steel is expensive but easy to clean. It is a poor conductor of heat. Don't be tempted to buy a thin stainless steel pan with a wash of copper on the underside. Copper must be at least $\frac{1}{8}$ of an inch thick to be effective. Some pans have a layer of copper sandwiched into the stainless steel of the bottom. This will probably be mentioned on the label, but you can be quite sure that no cheap pan will be made in this way.

Copper is expensive, but it cooks beautifully. In order to prevent dangerous toxic reactions with the food it must be lined with tin. When this lining begins to wear it must be re-tinned: you *can* use a worn copper pan if you wash it immediately before and after use, but it is always a potential danger.

Fireproof glass and pottery dishes are reasonable in price, but will not stand abrupt changes of temperature which might be caused by taking them direct from refrigerator to stove, or pouring cold liquid into a hot dish.

Flameproof glass or ceramic dishes are expensive and heat unevenly, but they hold the heat well and are easy to clean. They withstand changes of temperature well and food can be frozen in them, thawed, and then re-heated in the same dish.

Glazed earthenware, if cracked, can harbour stale grease and spoil the flavour of a dish.

Non-stick finishes do not affect the heat-conducting properties of the basic material, but the grey type will discolour with overheating. Care must be taken with these not to scratch the surface or use abrasives when washing up. The newer black non-stick linings are more robust and it is claimed that one can use metal implements when cooking with them.

Whatever you choose, think carefully to see that size, weight and shape are related to your needs. Test out the balance of the pan and the feel in your hand, and see that the lid fits snugly. The handle is important too. Wooden and plastic handles protect your hands from the heat but they come to grief in the oven. The detachable handles supplied with some pans are very convenient.

It is more economical in the long run to buy the best pans you can afford, but see that you are paying for durable quality and a solid finish, not just a pretty pattern which may end by boring you anyway.

If you enjoy entertaining or have an elastic household, then two sizes of beating bowl and whisk, egg saucepan, omelette pan and soufflé dish are a great convenience.

Egg Saucepan. A small, deep pan with a tight-fitting lid. If made of aluminium it will corrode and become unsuitable for use with other food unless very carefully cleaned or boiled up occasionally with a slice of lemon or a spoonful of vinegar, so it is time-saving to use enamel or to keep a special pan for boiling eggs.

Omelette Pan. The question of omelette pans is discussed in detail on pp. 49–50.

Bowl for Beating. Copper is said to be ideal, but it is very expensive. To get the best from a copper bowl you must have a strong wrist and some skill. (Ninette recommends 150 whipping movements a minute.)

Whisk. If you have a copper bowl you will need a wire hand whisk of whatever shape you prefer. The balloon shape is the most popular. With a china bowl you can use a hand or mechanical whisk, or an electric beater if you prefer.

Wooden Spoon or Spatula. One of these is essential for making scrambled eggs. The spatula, being flat, can be scraped clean on the side of the pan, but there is something satisfying about a wooden spoon. The kind with one edge, or the bottom, cut off flat is handy for scraping the pan as you go along.

Perforated Ladle. The flat round ones are best for lifting poached eggs from the pan.

Slice. A slice is useful when frying eggs.

For rather more adventurous cookery you will need:

Egg Pans. These are shallow china, metal or earthenware dishes for making *œufs sur le plat*. They usually have twin ears or handles.

Bain-marie. This is a large pan holding hot water in which pans requiring only gentle heat are stood. This is essential equipment for a restaurant, but in the home, a deep baking tin or a double saucepan makes a good substitute.

Soufflé Dish. Metal soufflé dishes or 'cases' were often used in the past instead of the porcelain ones now considered necessary. These are made of thin ovenproof porcelain with straight sides which are fluted for strength. It is perfectly possible to cook a soufflé in an improvised dish, provided that you bear in mind that the walls must be as thin as possible so that the heat penetrates quickly and is not retained long enough to cause over-cooking.

Ramekins. These are small fireproof bowls like miniature soufflé dishes, used for making *œufs en cocotte*. They are usually placed in a bain-marie on the stove or in the oven, and will break if used directly on the cooker plate.

After this come various things one can perfectly well do without but which, like all gadgets, can be very useful if they happen to suit you.

Egg Holder. This is used to lift eggs safely in and out of boiling water.

Egg Poacher. The metal egg poachers sold in the shops are really egg steamers.

Egg Coddler. A screw-top china container into which you break an egg and bring it direct to table after it has been cooked by plunging into boiling water. The result, properly timed (p. 36), will be soft and creamy.

Egg Timer. If you buy one of these which is worked by falling sand, make sure that it is timed to suit you. Many, especially those coming from abroad, mark a time too short to please normal British taste in boiled eggs. A 'pinger' is far more versatile and can be used for other cookery as well.

Egg Separator. A shallow cup-shaped device with a slit which allows the white of an egg to run through, leaving the yolk.

Nature has provided a very good substitute in the shape of the two halves of a broken egg shell.

Egg Slicer. A mini-guillotine which slices an egg by means of a row of fine wires. Unfortunately, these frequently break.

Egg Wedger. This divides an egg into eight wedges. A sharp stainless steel knife with a serrated edge will do an efficient, though not perhaps so precise a job.

Egg Rack. Formerly of wood, these are now also made in plastics and will hold eggs upright and point-down in the proper storage position.

Finally, if you like to be really kitted up, invest in some double-branched egg cups to take a pair at a time; a scissor-action toothed gadget to decapitate your eggs, and a set of little woollen bobble caps or small felt cock's and hen's heads to muffle your boiled eggs and keep them hot. You might even find in a junk shop one of those splendid Victorian racks with spaces for egg cups and clips to hold the spoons, and maybe space for salt and pepper too.

EGG COOKERY

In spite of its endless appearances boiled, fried or scrambled, the egg is extremely versatile. At the close of the eighteenth century, the Irish poet, Thomas Moore, wrote these lines about eggs and the French:

> Though many, I own, are the evils they've brought us,
> Though Royalty's there on her very last legs,
> Yet who can help loving the land who has taught us
> Six hundred and eighty-five ways to dress eggs.

Certainly France has produced a wealth of instruction on egg cookery though it is doubtful whether, as the poet optimistically suggests, people in this country have learnt very much from it. However, many are willing to have a go and vary their cooking a little, like the troops during the final summer of the last war, who attempted to fry eggs on the pavements of Rome.

Not only are eggs excellent in their own right, but they will thicken, emulsify, bind, coat or glaze other foods and aid them to whip into a foam. It may help to understand a little of how these various processes happen.

Thickening with Egg. The thickening capacity of an egg depends on the fact that when it is heated it coagulates or solidifies—the yolk at about 154°F (68°C) and the white at about 140°F (60°C). Both together coagulate at between 145° and 149°F (63°–65°C). If an egg is heated very gently the coagulation temperature will be a little higher than usual. With the addition of flavouring, milk and so on, the coagulation temperature will rise so that a custard, for instance, will set between 179°–185°F (82°–85°C). As the temperature rises the protein mass shrinks and exudes water, resulting in curdling.

Eggs will not only thicken but enrich a dish. The yolk should not be added direct to the hot liquid, but first blended with a tablespoon of fresh cream or water. Some of the hot liquid is then stirred in, and the egg mixture added to the hot soup or sauce, stirring until it is thick. Boiling will cause the egg to coagulate and the mixture to curdle, so unless you are sure of your heat source it is wiser to use a double boiler with the inner pan over, not *in* the water. At the first sign of curdling you may be able to save a dish by beating it vigorously in a cold bowl, or adding a tablespoon of chilled cream. One egg will thicken about half a pint of clear liquid.

Emulsions of Egg. Yolks of egg will combine with oil or melted butter to form an emulsion. See the sections on mayonnaise and hollandaise sauces on pp. 72–78.

Binding with Egg. Since an egg is viscous it will bind dry ingredients for rissoles, stuffings, etc., as it coagulates during cooking.

Coating with Egg. Food which is brushed with egg and dipped in breadcrumbs before frying is protected from the hot oil or fat, and emerges with a crisp jacket. White of egg alone is sufficient for this purpose as the albumen it contains coagulates to form a protective coating. If the prepared food is left to stand for 15 minutes before frying, the coating will be crisper.

Glazing. An egg whisked with half a teaspoonful of salt will give a shiny finish if it is brushed over pastry, buns or bread before baking.

C

Whipping Whites of Egg. An egg white contains bubbles of air. When the white is beaten these bubbles separate, becoming smaller and more numerous, and causing the white to fluff out and increase in volume.

Equipment for beating is discussed on p. 30.

There is some difference of opinion about whether whites should be chilled before whipping. Some cooks say that eggs at room temperature will yield half as much foam again as cold ones —others that eggs, bowl and beater should be thoroughly chilled in the refrigerator before use. You can best decide your preference by experiment. There is, however, no argument about the fact that your equipment must be scrupulously clean and dry. (Soap, incidentally, contains fat.) To be on the safe side, rub over the bowl and the whisk with lemon, and dry.

To beat whites successfully use a deep bowl which allows freedom of movement. Ideally, this should be of copper as the slight acidity helps to stabilize the foam (as does a pinch of cream of tartar added just as the whites are beginning to become fluffy). A china, glass or stainless steel bowl will give satisfactory results as well. Mechanical hand and electric beaters spare your muscles but they are more difficult to clean than a whisk, and the resulting foam is not so light and airy.

Beat the whites rather more slowly at first and then increase the pace, but don't stop until they are ready. Over-beating will spoil the foam, so stop beating before the whites become grainy. To test whether the whites are ready, hold the whisk upright. If the tip of the foam curls over, they have reached the 'soft peak stage'; if it keeps its point, they are at the 'stiff peak stage'. The recipe will say which is required.

Beating Yolks of Egg. For certain dishes a perfectly smooth cream of egg and sugar is required, described by the French as '*en ruban*' since the mixture should fall from the beating implement in a smooth ribbon.

Put the sugar in a bowl and make a well in the centre. Drop in a yolk and draw in a little sugar, stirring well. Add the rest of the yolks one by one, incorporating each in turn with more of the sugar. If you are making a cream, use a spatula for the mixing. For cakes, a thick wire whisk is preferable.

Beating Whole Eggs. A whole egg will beat to a pale yellow foam if sugar is added (about 2 tablespoons to each egg). If the beating is done over very gentle heat (not more that 175°F, 80°C), the foam will form more quickly and be more voluminous. At a higher temperature, the mixture will spoil. This egg and sugar foam, with marsala added, is the basis of the delicious Italian *zabaione.*

Incidentally, children can be kept amused for long periods with a cup and spoon, an egg and a dollop of castor sugar. Stirred together, the raw egg and sugar makes a good do-it-yourself pudding. In view of the warning on p. 22 see that the egg and sugar are well mixed so that they become white and frothy, even if you have to lend a hand yourself.

Timing. It is obvious that timing is of great importance in egg cookery. An accurate watch or clock is essential and a 'pinger' is very useful for the less split-second operations, provided you remain near enough to hear it.

BOILED EGGS

Boiled eggs should be very fresh but not straight from the nest; in fact it is only after 12 hours that the white of an egg will set properly when boiled. Before this, it will remain milky.

Though boiling an egg appears to be a simple matter it is something of an art, depending on controlling the temperature of the water and on very accurate timing. Results depend too on the freshness of the egg (a very fresh egg will take a little longer to cook), its size—and even on the taste of the eater. Unless you know his preferences your carefully boiled egg may disappointingly be described as 'hard' or 'runny'.

As a matter of fact, a good cook does not boil an egg at all. She simmers it, because bumping around in fast-boiling water may cause the shell to crack and release ectoplasmic veils of white, whilst the inside of the egg becomes sadly soggy. Fast boiling also spoils the flavour and makes the white rubbery.

A good method of boiling eggs is to put them into half their depth of cold water in a pan with a tight-fitting lid. The eggs should lie in a single layer and close enough to remain steady when the water boils. Bring the water to the boil and at once turn down the heat to simmering point. The chart below shows the number of minutes required *after* the water has come to the boil:

	Large	Standard	Medium
Soft-boiled eggs (the white firm but soft, the yolk liquid)	3	$2\frac{3}{4}$	$2\frac{1}{2}$
Medium-boiled (the white quite firm and the yolk soft)	$4\frac{1}{2}$	4	$3\frac{1}{2}$
Hard-boiled	8	7	6

A slightly easier method is to put the eggs into boiling water which, with a tight-fitting lid, need only be about an inch deep. The heat is then immediately reduced to a simmer. For larger numbers of eggs it is wise to use a wire basket or egg-holder so that all the eggs enter the boiling water at once. The following chart shows the approximate number of minutes' simmering required:

	Large	Standard	Medium
Soft-boiled eggs	$4\frac{1}{2}$	4	$3\frac{1}{2}$
Medium-boiled	$6\frac{1}{2}$	6	$5\frac{1}{2}$
Hard-boiled	12	11	10

A brisk tap on the crown of the egg will prevent it from continuing to cook after you have taken it from the pan.

Very cold eggs should not be plunged straight into boiling water or they are liable to crack. If you are obliged to take them from the refrigerator warm them for a few moments under the tap or in a basin of warm water.

Coddled Eggs

Eggs cooked by this method have delicious creamy whites. They are easily digested and so are suitable for babies and invalids. The egg is lowered into a pan of boiling water, removed at once from the fire, covered and stood 9 minutes for a large egg, 8 minutes for a standard and 7 minutes for a medium one.

A similar result can be obtained by simmering the egg for 1 minute and then leaving it another 5 minutes, covered and away from the heat.

Œufs Mollet

There is no satisfactory translation for *œufs mollet*, which have a firm white and a soft yolk like the medium-cooked eggs shown in our charts. The use of the word *'mollet'* however implies that they are to be peeled and used in various dishes, sometimes as a substitute for poached eggs.

If you are cooking a number of eggs in this way use a rack or basket to lower them all at once into the boiling water. Failing this, put the eggs into the pan and pour boiling water over them, waiting until the water returns to the boil before you begin counting. For times, see the charts on p. 36. Plunge the eggs into cold water as soon as they are cooked.

Shelling *œufs mollet* is a delicate operation, made easier by tapping the shell all over until it is completely crazed. A band can then be peeled all round the middle and the ends of the shell slipped off separately. Any scraps of shell still adhering should be removed under water, not picked off dry.

If they are to be used for a hot dish, *œufs mollet* can be left until needed in a bowl of warm water, and preparing them in advance avoids a last-minute-panic clumsiness. They are, incidentally, easier to shell if they are still warm.

Roasted Eggs

In the days when wood fires were the principal means of cooking, eggs were more often roasted than boiled. An old proverb talks of 'roasting an egg with reason', referring to the care which was needed to cook them evenly.

If you wish to roast some eggs—and they are very good eaten cold with mayonnaise or hot with cheese sauce and cauliflower—prick the rounded ends and lay them on a rack in the oven at 325°F (170°C, Gas 3) for 20 minutes. Since they are surrounded by heat the eggs roast evenly without needing attention.

Hard-boiled Eggs

Boil your eggs according to either of the two methods described earlier. If you wish the yolk to be nicely centred in the white, turn the eggs once or twice during the first two minutes of cooking time. As soon as the eggs are done plunge them in cold water. This makes them easier to peel as the skin shrinks and helps the shell to become detached. It also prevents the eggs from continuing to cook.

To avoid chipping the whites, roll the eggs on the table beneath the palm of your hand before shelling. Some people find it easier to begin peeling at the rounded end, holding the egg beneath a trickle of tepid water.

If shelled hard-boiled eggs are being prepared for a cold dish, stand them until wanted in a basin of cold water. Use warm water if the dish is to be a hot one. If left exposed to the air, the eggs will toughen. If stored in the refrigerator, the yolks will take on a greenish tinge.

If hard-boiled eggs are to be sliced, chopped or used for a picnic, they should be cooked for their full time. If they are to be stuffed or served in a sauce then one minute less will be sufficient.

The separately chopped yolks and whites of hard-boiled eggs (or the yolks rubbed through a sieve for a more delicate effect) make a pretty garnish for salads, cocktail savouries and so on. These are known as 'eggs Mimosa'.

Mishaps when Boiling Eggs

Cracked Shells. The eggs may have been too cold; or perhaps they were dropped carelessly into the pan, or bumped in fast-boiling water. Or they may even have been laid by hens debilitated by life in a battery. This makes a good cover story anyhow.

A useful precaution is to prick the blunt end of the shell with a pin, or with one of those special small gadgets which, when pressed, releases a needle point and pierces the shell in the same way that your finger is pricked to produce a drop of blood for a test.

If an egg does crack, put a teaspoonful of vinegar quickly into the water so that the white does not run out. If the white is already escaping, a tablespoon of salt in the water will congeal it and prevent further damage.

Tough flavourless eggs. These have been boiled too fast. Warning: watch carefully to catch the moment of boiling, turn down the heat to a simmer. And try to be less impatient.

Hard-boiled eggs with a blackish-green interlining. The eggs have been over-cooked. Watch your timing and plunge them straight into cold water when they are done.

Serving Boiled Eggs

Boiled eggs should be eaten very hot and some people bring them to table wrapped in a napkin. Others prefer small woolly bobble caps or felt covers. In order to prevent over-cooking, tap the blunt end of the egg lightly with a spoon before muffling it, or dip the eggs rapidly in and out of cold water.

Most people use the tap-and-peel method to open their eggs but some cut off the top with a quick blow. Louis XV is said to have decapitated his eggs with a fork. Gadget fans can buy small spiked rings with a scissor-type action which will behead an egg without accident.

Some people smash the empty eggshell when they have finished. This may be a release of pent-up aggression, or it may be a survival of the belief that the devil or a witch would otherwise take refuge in it.

Those who enjoy dunking may prefer to empty their egg into a glass, salt and pepper it and sprinkle it with minced parsley or tiny croûtons of fried bread; or scoop it up with fingers of buttered bread or toast dipped in chopped fresh herbs.

Variations on a Boiled Egg

Edouard de Pomiane in his *Cooking in Ten Minutes* says, 'lift out the eggs, put them into egg cups, and without waiting a second slice off the tops and eat them with crisp bread, fresh butter and a glass of white wine. This is a feast.' He also advises eating hard-boiled eggs just as they are with salt, butter and mustard—or even better, with grated horse-radish lightly vinegared.

An amusing variation is to boil eggs for 2–3 minutes only, open them and drain out the white, putting in its place: shallots softened in butter; minced fresh herbs; a little fresh cream; grated cheese and butter, or tiny fried croûtons.

Jacques Manière of the Restaurant Pactole, Paris Vème, prepares eggs as above but completes them with black caviare. The eggs are arranged in egg cups on a silver dish, sprinkled with vodka and flambé to warm the yolks. They are eaten with long slivers of hot-buttered toast.

Irish Eggs, one of Ninette's special recipes, make a delicious dish for breakfast or high tea. 'Wash some newly laid eggs in order to remove the outer film. Rub the shells with best quality butter, using the palms of the hands. When the eggs are well coated with butter, sprinkle with salt and let them stand in a cool place for at least 12 hours. The following day boil the eggs in their shells for 3 minutes. Since the shell is porous, the butter will have permeated the eggs, the taste will be delicious and the texture smooth.'

Stuffed Hard-boiled Eggs

To stuff hard-boiled eggs cut them in half, either lengthwise or crosswise, though in the latter case you will have to slice off the ends so that they will stand firm. Remove the yolks carefully, using a small spoon, and put them into a bowl. Mash them while they are still warm and mix them with the ingredients you have chosen.

Stuffed eggs are usually served cold as an hors-d'œuvre or a luncheon dish, but they can also be covered with sauce and heated in the oven. In either case, if they are not to be used immediately, leave the whites in a bowl of water, drying them carefully before stuffing.

Here is a good basic stuffing for hard-boiled eggs:

Mash 8 hard-boiled yolks with 2 raw ones, a handful of white breadcrumbs which you have soaked in milk and squeezed dry, $3\frac{1}{2}$ oz (90 g) of butter and a good seasoning of salt, pepper, herbs or whatever you fancy. When each of the halved hard-boiled eggs has been piled high with the mixture, spread the rest in a fireproof dish, arrange the eggs on it, dot with butter and brown under the grill.

For cold stuffed eggs take one raw yolk for every 6 hard-boiled, and work in 4 tablespoons of oil *or* 3 tablespoons of melted butter *or* 2–3 tablespoons of fresh cream or mayonnaise, and beat in the flavouring of your choice.

The stuffing must be soft but firm and it will look more attractive if it is piped on with a forcing bag. Leave the eggs in the refrigerator for an hour before serving. If they are to be left longer, it is advisable to cover them with foil or a plastic wrap to prevent drying at the edges.

Here are some flavourings which can be added to the stuffing for cold hard-boiled eggs described above:

2 tablespoons Dijon mustard and 1 tablespoon of chopped capers; a bunch of fresh herbs (watercress, chives, parsley, chervil, etc.); 4 fillets of anchovy crushed with $1\frac{1}{2}$ oz (40 g) of butter and a dash of Worcestershire sauce; 3 sardines, skinned

and boned; $1\frac{1}{2}$ oz (40 g) of tunny mashed with 3 tablespoons of white breadcrumbs, mixed with a small teaspoon of vinegar and a tablespoon of oil to make a smooth paste; a slice of ham minced with parsley; 2 tablespoons of anchovy paste and a chopped shallot.

POACHED EGGS

Poaching an egg, apparently such a simple affair, has led to more spectacular failures than most ordinary kitchen operations. It has also led to deception on a national scale, since the egg poachers sold in the shops never bring the eggs into contact with water, and turn out something more like a rather rubbery *œuf en cocotte* than a poached egg. However, for anyone whose spirit has been broken by constant failure, or who is not willing to take the extra trouble needed for real poaching, the egg poacher certainly produces something more acceptable than a soggy bundle leaking into the toast beneath. For anyone interested and optimistic here is how true poaching should be done.

First, it may be useful to define what one is aiming at, since a properly poached egg is almost unknown in many homes. Ideally, the yolk should be liquid and the white set and entirely enveloping it to form a neat oval. This is very difficult to achieve if the eggs are not fresh, as the white of a stale egg streams away in the water. The same thing may happen with a battery egg.

Having recognized that poaching is not a foolproof operation it is best to treat your eggs individually, or at most in pairs. They will be less likely to disintegrate if, before breaking, you first lower them for thirty seconds into boiling water, either counting or using the second-hand of your watch, so that a thin layer of coagulated white forms inside the shell.

Have a shallow pan of boiling water on the stove and break each egg into a saucer, tilting it gently into the pan. (If you are very timid try putting a little boiling water in the saucer, then break the egg into it. As soon as the white is beginning to set sink the saucer and simmer for about 3 minutes.)

In order to achieve a neat and compact shape, stir the boiling water clockwise to form a whirlpool before sliding the egg into it, or using a metal spoon roll the egg over a couple of times, just as the white is beginning to set. Many cookery writers advise adding a tablespoon of vinegar to every pint of water, and some suggest adding salt as well, though this is said to toughen the white. However, the Egg Marketing Board takes a simplified line—no vinegar or salt—no whirlpools either. But everyone agrees that the egg must be slipped into the water with great care; the pan must not be overcrowded and the water must not rise above simmering point.

If you wish to use the eggs cold or to re-heat them later, they should be put straight into a bowl of cold water. To warm them up, add sufficient boiling water to raise the temperature to so-called hand heat (not more than 70°F, 20°C), or lift the eggs into a bowl of warm water. After a few minutes the eggs will be warmed and can be drained and dried on a cloth or kitchen paper towels. This is the moment to trim them, using a sharp knife.

Poached eggs are ideal for slimming or invalid diets as they require no fat in cooking.

Variations

Try for a change poaching eggs in hot broth, or even beer.

A pleasant change can be made by spreading the hot buttered toast beneath the eggs with Marmite, anchovy paste, meat essence or other savoury spreads.

ŒUFS SUR LE PLAT

These eggs are cooked in a shallow dish or *plat*, in the oven or on top of the stove. The traditional dish has two handles, or ears, and may be made of earthenware, china, glass or metal, the latter preferably copper.

For the oven method, pre-heat to 425°F (220°C, Gas 8). Butter the dish and warm it, break in the eggs, pour over some melted butter and cook for 4–5 minutes until the whites are only just set, as cooking will continue for a few seconds after they have left the oven. If you wish to keep the eggs moist, cover the dish with foil. This will leave the eggs with a thin veil of white and they are then described as *œufs miroir*.

Eggs can also be cooked *sur le plat* on top of the stove over a low heat, watching for the moment when the white begins to set. Beware when using the very thick enamelled iron dishes which heat up slowly but retain heat for a long time. The temptation is to speed up the operation by using too fierce a fire, with the result that the egg becomes overcooked whilst lying on the hot dish after it has left the stove.

Œufs sur le plat, which the Americans describe as 'shirred' eggs, bear a close resemblance to shallow-fried eggs, only the latter are basted while frying and are usually cooked in lard or bacon fat. One also expects a fried egg to be partnered by bacon, sausage or chips. Below we suggest how an *œuf sur le plat* can successfully break into the bacon partnership too.

Warm individual egg dishes and lightly grill a rasher of bacon for each person. Lay one in each dish and finish lining it with two very thin slices of Emmenthal cheese. Break 2 eggs into each. Surround the yolks with single cream and bake as above. Serve immediately.

If you are pushed for cooking space or have no suitable flame-proof dishes, eggs can be steamed on a plate over a saucepan containing boiling liquid (perhaps soup or a vegetable) in the same way that invalid's fish is often cooked. Melt some butter on the plate, slip in the eggs, cover them with the saucepan lid and lift them off as soon as they are ready.

ŒUFS EN COCOTTE

Œufs en cocotte are baked or steamed in small earthenware, metal or china ramekins, the latter often resembling miniature soufflé dishes. Before the egg is put in, the cocotte must be warmed and generously buttered, and sprinkled with salt and pepper, or seasoned later, as you prefer.

If the eggs are cooked in the oven, pre-heat this to 350°F (180°C, Gas 4), and stand the cocottes in hot water to half their depth. Bake for 8–10 minutes, being sure to remove them before they are quite set, as the heat of the cocotte will continue the cooking process. (Unless you are quite confident of your oven temperature it is wise to cover the eggs with a sheet of greaseproof paper or foil.)

When cooking on top of the stove, stand the cocottes in about ¾-inch of water in a heavy frying pan, and when this boils and the butter has melted slide an egg into each cocotte. Top with a dab of butter, cover the pan and simmer for 3–4 minutes or until the white is not quite firm. Serve in the cocottes on individual plates.

The moulded eggs produced by the so-called poacher really belong to this group. They can be made more interesting by being served hot on croûtons, vegetables, ham or chicken purée, etc.; or cold on fish or chicken mousse, artichoke hearts, halved tomatoes or avocados; or served with mayonnaise or other sauces.

Variations on Œufs en Cocotte

All sorts of sauces, purées and savoury mixtures can be placed beneath, around or on top of *œufs en cocotte* before or after cooking. One of the simplest and most delicious is a good meat gravy. Here are some of the classic combinations:

Bordelaise. Poach a marrow bone, or steam it for an hour. As soon as the marrow begins to melt scoop it out and cut it in slices, putting one in each of four buttered ramekins. Break an egg into each, and salt and pepper it. Heat some Bordelaise sauce and pour some round each egg when it is cooked.

With Caviare. Put a tablespoon of cream into each buttered cocotte, then a spoonful of caviare. Pour in the egg, salt and pepper it, and top with a dab of butter. At the moment of serving cover the eggs with chilled cream and caviare.

Périgourdine. Put a slice of foie gras in the bottom of each ramekin, then an egg and seasoning. Ring the eggs, before serving, with Périgueux sauce which you have heated separately.

Soubise. Put a good tablespoon of Sauce Soubise into each cocotte, add the egg and a teaspoonful of meat juice. (Soubise is basically béchamel (p. 108) mixed with onion purée.)

Au Madère. Chop finely 4 mushrooms and a shallot, and melt them in butter until they are almost a purée. Add a little chopped parsley, salt and pepper and a tablespoon of Madeira. Divide the mixture into four buttered ramekins, add the eggs and seasoning and a few drops more of Madeira. You can replace the mushrooms by chopped ham.

With Oysters. Warm 8 oysters in their own liquid over a gentle fire, being careful that they do not boil. Lift them out with a skimmer and divide them between 4 buttered cocottes. Work a teaspoon of flour into a tablespoon of butter and add it to the liquor. Season, and stir gently until the sauce thickens. Break an egg into each cocotte, cover it with the sauce and cook for a few minutes.

Au Vert. Melt two handfuls of green stuff (lettuce, spinach, sorrel, etc.) in 2 tablespoonfuls of butter. When tender, drain off any liquid and chop roughly with scissors. Season with salt, pepper and nutmeg, stir in 2 tablespoons of cream and divide between 4 buttered ramekins. Slide in the eggs and top with butter.

Au Rouge. Proceed as before using tomato purée and a little chopped sweet pepper instead of the green mixture, and surrounding the egg with a ring of hot tomato sauce.

Mornay. Put some cheese sauce beneath the egg and finish with more sauce and a sprinkling of grated Parmesan cheese.

FRIED EGGS

Eggs, in England, are usually shallow-fried. Here is how Mrs Beeton describes the method in her *Dictionary of Everyday Cookery*: 'Place a delicately-clean frying pan over a gentle fire; put in the fat and allow it to come to the boiling-point. Break the eggs into cups, slip them into the fat, and let them remain until the whites are delicately set; and whilst they are frying, ladle a little of the fat over them. Take them up with a slice, drain them for a minute from their greasy moisture, trim them neatly, and serve on slices of fried bacon or ham; or the eggs may be placed in the middle of the dish, with the bacon round as a garnish.'

The fat may be lard, bacon fat or butter and should be about an eighth of an inch deep and, whatever Mrs Beeton may say, not quite at sizzling point or the whites will be leathery and crisp at the edges. She does not touch on the danger of the yolks breaking if the eggs are too cold as, in her day, eggs were not taken out of a refrigerator.

This method of frying eggs is described by the Americans as 'sunny side up'. Unless you specially ask for this, American eggs are turned over and fried on both sides.

Deep-fried Eggs

In France, eggs are usually fried in deep fat or oil. Use a small heavy saucepan and a good depth of oil, which can be re-used as long as it is strained and has not been burnt.

Heat the oil until a small cube of bread, dropped in, will turn brown while you count slowly to sixty. Break the egg into a cup and slide it into the oil. Allow it to cook for 2 minutes, then lift it out with a perforated spoon and put it on to a paper towel to drain. The egg should be a pale golden-brown. Repeat the process with all your eggs, keeping them warm in a very low oven, preferably with the heat already turned off.

A similar effect can be achieved by using fat only about an inch deep, but the eggs must be basted or turned after one minute, and there is a considerable risk of breaking them. Also, their shape will not be so good.

Variations

Both shallow and deep-fried eggs are excellent served on a bed of spinach or savoury rice, with or without fried bananas. They are good, too, with sweet corn fritters, or on a raft of potato mashed with butter, beaten egg, hot milk and chopped fresh herbs, seasoned with salt, pepper, grated nutmeg and a pinch of sugar, and fried a sizzling golden-brown. Add mushrooms and crisp slivers of fried bacon and you have something very good indeed.

Shallow-fried eggs can be given a new twist by crushing anchovy fillets, garlic or green herbs into the butter in which they are cooked. Or, when the eggs have been lifted from the pan, allow the remaining butter to turn brown and mix it with a dash of vinegar and a sprinkling of cayenne pepper. This is a poor relation of *œufs au beurre noir* where the eggs, lifted from their pan into a fireproof dish to keep hot, are baptized with butter (1 teaspoonful to each egg) which has been heated in a clean pan until it is foaming and just turning colour. The eggs are then sprinkled with a tablespoon of vinegar which has been brought to the boil in the egg pan.

SCRAMBLED EGGS

There are several ways of cooking scrambled eggs—and as many of spoiling them. In spite of all the arguments, people usually end by following their own method—provided it is successful.

Utensils are a matter of argument too. Some people scramble eggs in a saucepan; others prefer a bain-marie or a frying pan. Some use a wooden spoon; others a wire whisk or silver spoon, but most remain loyal to their preferences, once acquired.

Certain basic rules, however, apply to every method. These are:

Never attempt to scramble less than two eggs
Make sure the heat is gentle to avoid a rubbery result
Use a thick pan to ensure even cooking
Never leave the eggs by themselves
Remove the eggs from the fire just before they are ready, as the
heat of the pan will finish the cooking

Some cooks advocate stirring the eggs all the time. Others hold
that this slows down the coagulation of the egg protein and allow
them to form large curds, stirring only enough to let the liquid egg
run down to the bottom of the pan.

Methods
A reliable way of scrambling is to take two large or standard
eggs for each person and beat them lightly with a fork so that
whites and yolks are broken up. Season the eggs and pour them
into a pan in which you have melted 1 oz (25 g) of butter. Keeping
the heat low, stir continuously until the eggs begin to thicken.
Remove them from the fire and stir in a tablespoon of single cream
or top-of-the-milk. This enriches the flavour and prevents the
eggs from over-cooking.

Ninette's Own Recipe
Break 5 eggs, keeping a yolk on one side, and put them into a
bowl with salt and pepper and a tablespoon of water. Beat them
lightly to distribute the yolks. Melt ½ oz (15 g) of butter in a heavy
pan, enamelled if possible. Cut another ounce (25 g) of butter into
small pieces and add it to the eggs. Pour them into the pan and stir
continuously with a wooden spoon over a moderate fire. See that
the eggs do not stick to the sides or bottom of the pan. When the
eggs are almost done, add the single yolk, stir and pour immediately on to two warmed plates with or without buttered toast.

Invalid Scrambled Eggs
If the eggs must be especially light for an invalid or a small
child, confine the butter to ½ oz (15 g) for 2 eggs and bring this to
the boil with 1½ tablespoons of milk. Let the liquid cool to blood
heat and then pour the lightly beaten eggs straight into the pan,
season delicately and stir over a low heat, raising the temperature
slightly to achieve the consistency you want.

Buttered Eggs

For each pair of eggs you will need 1 oz (25 g) of butter. Beat the eggs with a fork just sufficiently to break up the yolks and the whites. If you wish to mix them thoroughly without making too much froth, strain them. This has the advantage of removing the slippery 'thread'.

After this, the object is to amalgamate the eggs and butter as closely as possible. Mrs Beeton suggests melting the butter in a basin over boiling water, and pouring it with the eggs into a lined saucepan which you hold over a gentle fire. As the mixture begins to warm, pour it two or three times into the basin and back again. Keep stirring in one direction, taking care that the mixture never boils.

Other cooks prefer to smear half the butter round the pan, using their fingers, pour in the eggs and the rest of the butter cut in small pieces, and stir with a silver spoon, scraping the bottom of the pan so that the egg is detached in buttery flakes which should, ideally, resemble gorse blossom.

An excellent result is obtained by melting a generous amount of butter in the pan, and then adding a further knob just as the egg is beginning to thicken.

It is said that an extra yolk will improve the texture and taste of buttered eggs. A well-known American cookery book suggests adding an extra white, but this may be rather to use up an odd white than to improve the flavour of the dish.

From all this it will be seen that provided you use fresh eggs and good butter, watch your temperatures and concentrate on the job, an excellent result can be obtained in a number of different ways.

Variations

Flavourings for scrambled eggs may be:

Lightly cooked in the butter in which the eggs are to be scrambled. Try finely-chopped bacon, remembering to use a little less butter; thinly sliced raw mushrooms; minced spring onions.
Stirred into the raw eggs, being careful to avoid anything which is too liquid. We suggest crisp crumbled bacon; tiny croûtons rubbed, if you wish, with garlic; chopped anchovies; sliced sauté mushrooms; shredded crab sprinkled with curry powder;

asparagus tips; chopped ham; tinned mussels; sauté aubergines; one or two sliced truffles; grated Parmesan or Emmenthal cheese; capers; shrimps; poached brains; flaked tunny or smoked haddock; fried chopped onions; fresh minced herbs mixed with the eggs before cooking, and sprinkled on top when they are ready.

Used as a garnish. All the delicate vegetables make an excellent garnish for scrambled eggs, especially buttered peas, grilled tomatoes, asparagus, sauté courgettes or aubergines. Try also sausages, bacon, ham, chicken livers or sauté kidneys.

Spread on buttered toast beneath the eggs. Anchovy paste, foie gras, devilled ham, Gentleman's Relish and dip mixes made with cream cheese are all excellent for this purpose.

Fried bread or savoury biscuits make a change from the toast on which scrambled eggs are usually heaped. Fill split rolls with scrambled eggs instead of making sandwiches. The eggs may be served on large sauté mushroom caps or on artichoke hearts; also in scooped-out and buttered baked potatoes, hot hollowed tomatoes or vol-au-vent or pastry cases.

OMELETTES

Some people approach the making of an omelette with quite unnecessary awe. The process is simple, but like all egg cookery, it needs care.

The Omelette Pan

There is a belief that an omelette pan should never be washed. This arose in the days when washing an iron pan would lead to rust. Nowadays, with surfaces such as aluminium, stainless steel and the various non-stick finishes, any heavy pan with an absolutely clean smooth surface is suitable for making omelettes provided it is not too large, has sloping sides and a perfectly flat base. This is a great help if you are pushed for kitchen space, but it is certainly easier to keep a pan in perfect condition if it is only used for the brief cooking of omelettes. In any case, you are unlikely to have much success with the ordinary breakfast frying pan.

A 6–7-inch pan will take a 2-egg omelette for one person and a 9–10-inch pan 3–4 eggs for two people. Unless you are very skilled it is unwise to attempt an omelette larger than this.

If you prefer to use an iron pan, wipe it clean with kitchen paper, rubbing with salt if necessary, and keep it in a polythene bag to reduce the chances of rust forming.

All new pans, except those which are non-stick, should be 'proved' or 'seasoned' by being *either*:

heated very slowly until the bottom is too hot to touch, then rubbed with olive oil and left for 12 hours; wipe clean with a sprinkling of fine salt before use
or well rubbed with the fat of unsmoked bacon which should not be wiped away before the first omelette is cooked
or slowly heated for half an hour with a good covering of cooking salt, rubbed hard with kitchen paper, left to cool, and then wiped out with a dry cloth

Old pans which tend to stick can be improved by any of the above methods, but unless their surface is perfectly smooth they will not be suitable for omelette making.

Preparations

Making omelettes demands a little forethought. Assemble everything you need, including your guests, before you begin. Set the plates to warm (but not overheat, otherwise the omelette will continue to cook and become leathery). See that your flavourings are to hand, any fillings ready prepared and kept hot, and any additions to the egg mixture chopped fine enough to avoid the formation of tiny air pockets during cooking.

As with scrambled eggs, there are various ways of making an omelette and each has its dogged supporters. Experiment to find your own style.

If you are cooking for a large number of people, make a succession of small omelettes. It saves time to break, season and beat all the eggs at once, but unless you are a clever judge of quantity the last omelette is apt to be extra large or small. This can be overcome by choosing a cup or other measuring implement which holds the quantity you want. Two large eggs are equivalent to about 6 tablespoonfuls (about $\frac{1}{3}$ of a cup)—or two double whiskies if this seems easier. Flip the mixture four or five times with a fork each time you use a portion.

Cooking an Omelette

As with scrambled eggs, very little beating is necessary, just enough to mix yolk and white. Elizabeth David advises using two forks, while some chefs are said to find a vigorous shaking sufficient. On no account use a mechanical beater.

Set the pan on a low fire so that it becomes hot all through. Meanwhile, season the eggs, remembering to allow for the salt in any additions. A pleasant tang of garlic can be achieved by rubbing the bowl with a cut clove before beating the eggs.

For a 2-egg omelette, melt $\frac{1}{2}$ oz butter (15 g or a knob the size of a large gooseberry), tilting the pan around so that the bottom and sides become filmed with it. Turn up the heat, and when the butter is sizzling and just about to colour pour in the eggs. Wait for 10 seconds so that the underside is just beginning to set. If you are adding a filling, this is the moment. See that it lies neatly within the borders of the omelette. Lift up the edges so that the uncooked egg runs beneath. All this must be done very quickly.

Whilst the surface is still slightly runny, tilt the pan away from you so that the omelette slides down to the far end and folds over. Then tilt the other way and fold once more. Grasping the handle of the pan in your left hand with thumb and fingers uppermost, slide the omelette on to a warmed plate. If all this is too complicated, use a fork or spatula to fold the omelette in three in the pan, and slide it on to the plate as before.

If you have been successful, your omelette will be creamy inside with a faint golden-brown tinge on the outside.

Here are some simple variations:

Bacon Omelette

If the bacon is salt, put it in a small panful of cold water and bring it to the boil. Drain and dry it and cut it into small pieces. Sauté the bacon in the omelette pan, add a little butter, pour in the seasoned eggs and complete the omelette.

Ham Omelette

Heat some ham, minced or cut in fine strips, in butter, keeping the heat very low, otherwise the ham will curl up and become hard. When the omelette is nearly ready, lift the ham with a strainer and sprinkle it on the surface, just before the omelette is folded.

51

Cheese Omelette

It is better to sprinkle grated cheese into an omelette when the egg mixture is already in the pan. Stir the still-runny surface egg lightly. If the cheese is added before cooking, the omelette is liable to stick.

Omelette with Onions

Brown some onion rings in a butterless pan and when they have taken the colour you wish, add the butter. Pour in the beaten, seasoned eggs and proceed as usual.

One can also brown chopped onions separately in butter and use them for stuffing an omelette.

Omelette with Cream Cheese

For slimmers, this omelette should be made with cottage cheese. For the rest, use a large double cream cheese seasoned with herbs.

With 8 eggs make omelettes as described on p. 51 and stuff them with the cheese which you have warmed in a bain-marie, stirring all the time.

The cheese can also be divided into small pieces and mixed with the beaten egg before the omelettes are made. Be sure that they remain runny inside.

Fillings for Omelettes

All the fillings suggested for scrambled eggs can be used for omelettes too, but be sure that the cooked ones are properly heated before being used, and see that the omelette is not over-loaded. About 2 oz (50 g) of filling is sufficient for a 2-egg omelette.

A tablespoon of chopped parsley or mixed fresh herbs, or 1 oz (25 g) of grated Parmesan, Emmenthal or Sbrinz cheese stirred into the beaten eggs makes a delicious omelette. Sprinkle herbs on top of the former, and try brushing the cheese omelette with butter and sprinkling it with grated cheese—browned under the grill if you wish.

A Soufflé (or English) Omelette

These are usually sweet, though salt and pepper can be substituted for the sugar in the basic recipe. This is made by whisking the yolks of 2 eggs with 2 teaspoons of water and 1 dessertspoon of castor sugar until they are pale and creamy, then whipping the whites until they are just stiff, and folding them into the yolk mixture.

Melt ½ oz (15 g) of butter over a moderate heat. When the pan is hot, pour in the egg mixture and smooth the top until level. Cook without turning until the bottom is golden-brown, then put the pan beneath a hot grill for half a minute, or into the oven at 450°F (230°C, Gas 8) for one minute so that the top becomes golden-brown too. Slide the omelette, folded in half, on to a hot plate, dust over with icing sugar and serve immediately.

A slightly richer omelette results if cream or top-of-the-milk is substituted for water.

Variations for Sweet Omelettes

Sweet soufflé omelettes may be filled, before they are folded, with:

2 tablespoons of hot jam; ginger, lemon or orange marmalade; fruit purée warmed with cream or syrup; bananas sliced and fried in butter with a sprinkling of rum and castor sugar; 1 tablespoon of honey warmed with 1 oz (25 g) of chopped walnuts, 1 teaspoon of lemon juice and a little grated rind; chopped pineapple and grated lemon rind.

A simple variation consists of stirring grated orange or lemon rind, and chopped nuts or peeled sliced almonds, into the egg yolks. Strong coffee or liqueur can be substituted for the water in the recipe or 2 oz (50 g) of chocolate may be melted in the water.

Soufflé Omelette with a Savoury Filling

Beat the yolks of 5 eggs with 2 tablespoons of cream, seasoning, and 1 tablespoon of grated cheese. The beaten whites are folded in as above, the mixture turned into an oval ovenproof dish, and a hollow formed down the middle.

After 8–10 minutes in an oven at 375° (190°C, Gas 5) the omelette is ready to receive the heated filling of your choice. Serve at once.

Spanish Omelette

Basically, the Spanish omelette consists of cooked vegetables heated in oil, with the addition of chopped onion which has been gently fried. Any surplus oil is drained off and the eggs, beaten as for an ordinary omelette and well seasoned, are poured into the pan, stirred once or twice and cooked until the underneath is just set. While the top is still runny, put the omelette under the grill to brown slightly, or turn it in the pan. Loosen it with a palette knife and slide it into a hot dish. The Spanish omelette is never folded but cut like a cake.

The classic Spanish omelette is made with potatoes and onions, though other vegetables such as peas, fresh beans, sliced artichoke hearts, peeled and chopped tomatoes and sweet peppers are sometimes added. Pieces of Spanish *chorizo* sausage, ham, crisped bacon, cooked chicken or prawns make interesting variations. The flavour may also be varied by stirring in a level teaspoonful of paprika or a clove or two of garlic creamed with salt.

SOUFFLÉS

A soufflé is really a thick white sauce enriched with yolks of egg and flavouring, and made light by the addition of beaten whites. It is not difficult to make, provided you stick to a few simple rules, but it is doomed to failure unless eaten as soon as it is ready.

Hot savoury soufflés, which appear rather luxurious, make an economical dish and provide an excellent way of using up leftovers such as cold meat, fish or vegetables. Since they contain a large proportion of beaten egg-white which tends to mute the flavour, they must be well seasoned, so taste your base carefully to make sure that it has a really pronounced and agreeable flavour.

Since a soufflé must be cooked without any delay, pre-heat the oven to 400°F (200°C, Gas 6). Arrange a shelf fairly low in the oven with a baking sheet which will be hot by the time the soufflé is ready to stand on it. (With an Aga, stand the dish on the floor of the oven.)

The Basic Recipe

This will make sufficient for a 1½-pint soufflé dish. Quantities can be increased or decreased proportionately.

3 large eggs and 1 white; 1 oz (25 g) butter; 1 oz (25 g) flour; ½ pint (3 dl) milk

Melt the butter and work in the flour, using a wooden spoon. Allow them to foam together without colouring. Remove the pan

54

from the fire and when the mixture is no longer bubbling, pour in the heated milk and whisk until the sauce is smooth. Season and stir over a low heat for 5–10 minutes more. Allow the sauce to cool until it is not too hot for the tip of your finger and then stir in the well-beaten yolks of the eggs.

Any additions, such as those mentioned on pp. 56–7 are put in at this stage. This basic mixture can be made in advance and warmed gently before proceeding with the soufflé.

Folding in the Whites

Though not in the least difficult once you have the knack, this is the stage which requires the most skill. Trouble may arise from the fact that the term 'folding' is often not properly understood.

The whites must be beaten so that they will stand in peaks (p. 34). If you are using not more than 4–5, stir a large spoonful of the beaten white into the soufflé mixture to soften it a little, then scoop out the rest on top of the mixture. With more eggs, fold in half at a time.

Using a wooden or rubber spatula (or a palette knife or metal spoon) cut down from the top centre of the mixture to the bottom of the pan and, following the natural inclination of your hand, draw the spatula towards you, up the side of the pan and out, lifting some of the mixture from the bottom on to the whites. Repeat this rapidly and lightly, rotating the pan with your left hand. In this way you fold the whites into the mixture without spoiling their light fluffy texture. Don't be over-conscientious. It is better to have a slightly uneven mixture than one which is deflated, but see that you reach right to the bottom and sides of the pan.

Now turn the soufflé into a buttered dish which has been sprinkled with flour or grated cheese and turned upside down to remove the surplus, and transfer it at once to the oven.

Some people like a soufflé to rise above the rim and fix round the dish a band of folded, buttered, greaseproof paper overlapping 3–4 inches at the top. This is removed before serving. Otherwise, the dish must be filled to only about three-quarters of its depth.

If, using a palette knife or the tip of a spoon, you make a deep but narrow groove all round the surface about an inch from the rim, the soufflé will rise into a lovely mushroom shape.

Baking

As soon as it is prepared, put the soufflé in the oven as described on p. 54.

Unless you have an inner glass door, beware of opening the oven for the first quarter of an hour. It is really wiser not to attempt a soufflé unless you are familiar with the oven's performance and are prepared to trust it. A soufflé rises as it cooks and too fierce an oven will accelerate rising and result in hardening.

In about 20 minutes the soufflé should have risen 2–4 inches depending on size of dish and be turning golden-brown. At this point it will be creamy at the centre and rather fragile. Five minutes more will make it a little more stable, but beware of overcooking. Beginners may like to test their soufflé by slipping a fine steel knitting needle from the rim of the dish towards the centre to see if it comes out clean—a sign of readiness. On no account use any thick, cold implement. However, if the soufflé is well risen, the crust resistant to a light touch and the colour appetizing there is no need to worry further.

In case of necessity a soufflé can be left for 5 minutes in the oven with the door ajar after it is ready, but it is far safer to take it immediately to table. If the top shows signs of over-browning during baking cover it with a thin piece of greaseproof paper.

Hot Savoury Soufflés

The simplest and most effective flavouring for a savoury soufflé is cheese. Classically, this should be half Emmenthal and half Parmesan, though any cheese which will grate finely and taste good will do. Some people prefer to dice rather than grate the Emmenthal.

The flavour of a cheese soufflé is improved by the addition of plenty of pepper—even some cayenne if you wish—and a grating of nutmeg or a little mustard. Remember to delay adding salt until you have stirred the cheese into the basic sauce, otherwise it will tend to harden.

The following are some of the many other things which can be used. Be careful that there are no large pieces as this will prevent the soufflé from rising:

chopped cooked lobster, crab or prawns or whole tiny shrimps; flaked tunny, cooked smoked haddock or tinned salmon; finely chopped cooked chicken, turkey, ham or chicken livers; carefully drained spinach, cauliflower or asparagus; mushrooms seethed in butter; minced parsley, chives or chervil

Shredded ham, chicken, etc., mixed with various sauces, provided they are not too wet, can be laid carefully between layers of the soufflé mixture, finishing with a soufflé topping sprinkled with grated cheese and fine brown breadcrumbs. Caviare and mushrooms and so on, and even poached eggs can be used to fill a hollow in the middle of the soufflé. None of these additions should exceed 6 oz (150 g) for a 4-egg soufflé or 10 oz (250 g) for one made with 6 eggs.

Vegetable soufflés are made by combining 4 heaped tablespoons of purée with the basic mixture for a 4-egg soufflé.

For fish soufflés, use the milk in which the fish was poached to make the sauce. The juice of clams, celery and tomatoes can be used for the same purpose.

A Cheese Soufflé made with Egg-whites

Make a basic sauce as in the recipe on p. 54, substituting $\frac{1}{4}$ pint ($1\frac{1}{2}$ dl) of near-boiling cream for the $\frac{1}{2}$ pint of hot milk. Stir in one quarter of the whites of 6 eggs, which you have beaten stiffly with a pinch of salt, and 3 oz (75 g) of Emmenthal cheese cut into small dice and the same quantity of grated Emmenthal, all but one tablespoon. Fold in the rest of the egg-whites and pour the mixture into a prepared soufflé dish. Sprinkle on the rest of the cheese and bake as before.

Soufflés made with Breadcrumbs

Americans sometimes replace the basic sauce in a soufflé base with white breadcrumbs soaked in hot milk ($1\frac{1}{2}$ cups to 3 eggs). This type of soufflé is baked for 40 minutes at 350°F (180°C, Gas 4) in an unbuttered dish and no extra whites are added. Any of the additions described above may be used.

Steamed Soufflés

Savoury or sweet soufflés may be steamed instead of baked, using the usual basic recipe. The additions need not be precooked. The soufflé is usually surrounded with a paper collar (see p. 55) and must be covered with a piece of greaseproof paper to protect it from drips.

When the soufflé feels firm to the touch, usually after about 40 minutes of gentle steaming, it is ready. These soufflés are turned out on to a dish for serving, usually with an appropriate sauce, either surrounding them or handed separately.

Hot Sweet Soufflés

Sweet soufflés can be made in the same way as the savoury soufflé described at the beginning of this section, substituting 2 oz (50 g) of castor sugar for the salt and pepper. But there are other methods of making them which vary from almost foolproof to very difficult. Here, starting with the easiest, are some:

1. A near relation of the soufflé omelette. Though made without flour, it has a firm texture and a stable consistency. Make a thick purée of well-sweetened fruit (about 2 cupfuls to 4 egg whites), flavouring it with grated lemon or orange rind, ginger and so on, as you please. Whip the whites to a firm snow, adding a pinch of salt, and fold them into the purée. Bake at 350°F (180°C, Gas 4) for 25–30 minutes.

2. A delicious soufflé can be made, still without using flour, by creaming the yolks of 3 eggs with a tablespoon of castor sugar, adding 2 tablespoons of whipped cream and 2 tablespoons of the juice from some fresh fruit such as strawberries, peaches, pineapples, etc., which you have steeped for an hour with 2 tablespoons of liqueur and sugar to your taste. The firmly whipped whites of the eggs are folded into the mixture which is then divided into three and poured into the soufflé dish alternately with two layers of fruit. This should be baked for 12 minutes in a moderate oven (350°F, 180°C, Gas 4) then dredged with icing sugar, allowed to caramelize for 2–3 minutes and served immediately.

3. This method is based on choux pastry technique. Heat ¼ pint (1½ dl) of milk, flavoured as you choose, with 2 oz (50 g) of butter. When the milk is boiling, shoot in all at once 3 oz (75 g) of sifted plain flour and 4 oz (100 g) of castor sugar. Work together with a wooden spoon until the mixture is thick and smooth and begins to come away from the sides of the pan. Remove the pan from the fire and let it cool a little, then beat in the yolks, one at a time, and go on beating until the mixture is shiny; then fold in the beaten whites and bake at 425°F (220°C, Gas 7) for about 20 minutes. Lower the heat to 350°F (180°C, Gas 4) for 10 minutes or so until the soufflé is nicely browned.

4. A very light and delicate chocolate, lemon, orange or vanilla

soufflé can be made with $\frac{3}{4}$ pint ($4\frac{1}{2}$ dl) of milk. Remove 2–3 tablespoons and mix them with $1\frac{1}{2}$ oz (40 g) of arrowroot to make a smooth cream. Heat the rest of the milk with 2 oz (50 g) of sugar and some flavouring. This may consist of 4 oz (100 g) of smoothly melted cooking chocolate, or the grated rind and a tablespoon of juice of an orange or lemon, or of vanilla sugar, which is substituted for the sugar mentioned in the recipe. Bring the flavoured milk to the boil and pour it on to the arrowroot. Dot with $\frac{1}{2}$ oz (15 g) of butter cut in small pieces and cover until cool. Beat in the yolks of the eggs, one by one, and fold in the stiffly-beaten egg whites. Bake in a moderate oven for 20 minutes, and dust with icing sugar 2–3 minutes before baking time is up.

5. This method is based on the French *crème patissière*. Infuse a piece of vanilla pod (or grated lemon or orange rind) in $\frac{1}{2}$ pint (3 dl) of milk. Cream 2 oz (50 g) castor sugar with an egg plus one yolk until the mixture flows from the spoon in a smooth ribbon, stir in $1\frac{1}{2}$ oz (40 g) of sifted flour and the hot milk, blending until smooth. Allow the mixture to cool and beat in the yolks of 3 eggs, one at a time. Fold in the stiffly-beaten whites of 4 eggs and bake at 400°F (200°C, Gas 6) for 15 minutes, then sprinkle with icing sugar and return to the oven for another 2–3 minutes. If you are using orange or lemon, substitute lump sugar for some of the castor, and rub this on the rind to extract all the fragrant oils, dissolving the lumps in the milk instead of using a vanilla pod.

All sorts of fruit, not forgetting dried apricots, can be used for sweet soufflés with or without the following additions: diced crystallized fruit or ginger; chopped toasted nuts or slivered almonds; crushed nut toffee or praliné; strong coffee or chocolate or both together; rum, Grand Marnier or Curaçao.

Cold Savoury Soufflés

For a cold savoury soufflé make a basic sauce as described on p. 54, using stock instead of milk and stirring in an extra ounce (25 g) of butter together with the yolks of 3 eggs and any flavourings and additions. The latter, which should not weigh more than about 8 oz (200 g) for a 3-egg soufflé, or 4 oz (100 g) if you are using grated cheese, may also consist of cooked chopped or minced chicken, duck, game, veal, ham, salmon, turbot, sole, smoked haddock, crabmeat or well-flavoured vegetable purée.

Meanwhile, melt 1 tablespoon of gelatine in 3 tablespoons of cold water, standing the bowl in hot water and stirring until dissolved. You may care to add 2 tablespoons of sherry to the gelatine.

Now whisk the gelatine into your basic mixture, letting it fall in a thin stream. Fold in ¼ pint (1½ dl) of lightly-whipped cream. Beat the whites of the eggs to soft-peak stage (see p. 34) and, when the mixture is beginning to set at the edge of the bowl, fold in the whites with a light hand. If you wish your soufflé to stand up above the edge of the dish, fix a paper collar (p. 55). Leave it to set. Use a warm knife to detach the collar before serving and garnish the exposed edge of the soufflé with chopped parsley, etc. The top, too, gives scope for attractive decoration.

Cold Sweet Soufflés

For a classic cold sweet soufflé, dissolve the gelatine as above. Whisk the yolks of 3 eggs with any liquid flavouring and 4 oz (100 g) of castor sugar in a bowl over hot water until they thicken and become creamy. Take care that the water does not boil or touch the bowl.

Remove from the heat and whisk until cold. Whip in the dissolved gelatine, then fold in the cream as above, and any addition you may wish. When the mixture is beginning to set at the edge delicately fold in the egg-whites which have been whipped to a soft peak.

If you wish the soufflé to look pretty use a paper collar and cover the exposed edge with chopped nuts, grated chocolate or toasted coconut. The additions described for hot sweet soufflés can be used for cold.

Another type of cold sweet soufflé is made with a flavoured egg custard into which melted gelatine is stirred, and then whipped cream and white of egg as described above.

Milanese Soufflé

Whisk 3 eggs and 2 yolks, flavouring and 1½ oz (40 g) castor sugar over hot water until thick and foaming. Stir in ½ oz (15 g) of gelatine dissolved in juice or water and whisk in 7½ oz (2¼ dl) of juice, diluted if you wish, over a bowl of ice until set.

MOUSSES

Mousses, which are very like cold soufflés, except that they are less airy and more spongy in texture, provide an excellent way of using up leftovers or making expensive fish, game and so on go further, and with a little care in serving and garnishing will make really impressive party dishes.

Nowadays, the term 'mousse' is loosely used to cover a variety of dishes from a soufflé mixture enriched with extra eggs and cream to a flavoured whipped cream blended with gelatine, or even a blend of chocolate, butter and rum containing no cream at all. Whatever type of mousse you choose it should, ideally, have the lightness of congealed froth and contain no starchy thickener.

Here is a useful basic recipe for a savoury mousse which can be increased or diminished to suit your purpose provided the proportions are maintained.

Blend carefully one pound of cold meat, fish, chicken or game which has been pulped in the liquidizer or by twice-mincing, with 3 oz (75 g) of creamed butter. Stir in gradually a generous $\frac{1}{2}$ pint of cold creamy-textured béchamel or velouté sauce (p. 108). Season, add any colouring you may wish and stir in $\frac{1}{4}$ pint ($1\frac{1}{2}$ dl) of aspic jelly in which you have dissolved 2 teaspoons of powdered gelatine. Fold in 3 or 4 tablespoons of lightly-whipped cream.

Mousses may be served in a variety of ways. If you are pushed for time, pour your mousse into a chilled bowl or individual dishes and garnish it with delicate leaves such as dill or Hamburg parsley, or with sliced truffles, capers, strips of tinned red sweet pepper, black olives, cooked carrot, hard-boiled egg.

If you have a little more time, fill a soufflé dish to within an inch of the top with mousse, smooth it with a wooden spoon and, when it is quite cold, run a little cool melted aspic over the top. Allow this to set and arrange your garnish in a pretty pattern. Let this set in the refrigerator for a few moments and then fill up the dish with cool aspic.

The mousse may also be poured into a fancy mould or a ring, preferably of metal, which you have previously rinsed or lightly oiled, and garnished as above.

For a special occasion, line the mould with aspic jelly. Set the mould in a basin of cracked ice and run spoonfuls of aspic jelly all over the inside until you have made a coating about an eighth of an inch thick. Or fill the mould with melted jelly and as soon as an eighth of an inch has set round the edges, pour out the rest into a flat dish. This can be cut criss-cross into cubes which will serve to decorate the mousse. Arrange your decorations in the jelly lining, holding them in place with a further thin layer of aspic and when this is set, pour in the mousse.

To turn out the mousse, dip the mould for a few seconds into hot water, cover it with a chilled serving dish, turn upside down and loosen with a sharp tap. Some people prefer to stand the mould, upside down, on the serving dish and cover it with a cloth wrung out in hot water until the mousse is set free. If the bottom edge is untidy, hide it with a border of the cubed aspic.

Sweet Mousses

We have mentioned that the term 'mousse' covers a wide variety of dishes. The cost of these varies as widely as their ingredients. Here are some simple methods for making sweet mousses. There are others in the recipe section at the back of the book.

Chocolate Mousse

A reliable old recipe uses 4 oz (100 g) of melted bitter chocolate blended with sugar and 4 egg-yolks, the whites whipped and folded into the mixture. No gelatine is required because the chocolate thickens as it cools.

Chocolate mousses gain by being flavoured with rum, orange juice or coffee.

The Basque form of chocolate mousse is made by melting 6 oz (150 g) of cooking chocolate to a thick cream with 5 tablespoons of plain or flavoured water, lifting it from the fire and beating in $\frac{1}{2}$ oz (15 g) of butter and, one at a time, the yolks of 3 eggs. The stiffly-beaten whites are then stirred into the mixture which is poured into small pots and chilled, overnight if possible.

Fruit Mousses

The simplest, though not the cheapest form is to fold 1 pint (6 dl) of thick whipped cream into each pound (400 g) of sweetened fruit purée and chill it for 8 hours or so.

A more economical version uses a mixture of custard and cream flavoured with fruit juice, with a scant tablespoon (one envelope) of gelatine dissolved in it for each pint of the mixture. If you are using an acid juice, take care to stir the cream mixture until it begins to set, as otherwise it may curdle.

A useful lemon mousse is made by beating to a cream the yolks of 4 eggs with 6 oz (150 g) castor sugar and the grated rind and juice of 2 lemons. Stir in 1 tablespoon of gelatine dissolved in 4 tablespoons of warm water. When the mixture is just beginning to thicken, fold in the whites of egg stiffly beaten. Chill.

CUSTARD AND CREAMS

Thin Custard

Custard may be thick or thin, flavoured in various ways, cooked in the oven or on top of the stove, or steamed. To make thin custard, beat 2 eggs (or 4 yolks) with 4 tablespoons of castor sugar until they are pale yellow and creamy. Whole eggs tend to set the custard, whilst yolks alone make a more creamy mixture. If whole eggs are used, the custard should be strained before it cools. If you stir a small teaspoon of cornflour into the egg and sugar mixture it will help to reduce the risk of curdling.

Warm a pint of milk and flavour it, if you wish, with vanilla; lemon or orange rind; almond essence; rum, sherry or liqueur; strong black coffee; grated chocolate; cinnamon or nutmeg. Stir it into the creamed egg and sugar and heat it gently, using a double saucepan or a bowl over a saucepan of hot water. The custard must not boil or it will curdle. A slightly curdled custard can sometimes be rescued by pouring it into a cold bowl and whisking it vigorously.

Thick Custard

For a thick custard use 4 eggs to 4 tablespoons of sugar and proceed as above, straining the mixture into a bowl or individual dishes. Bake the custard, standing in a pan of warm water, in a moderate oven (325°F, 170°C, Gas 3). A large custard will need 1 hour and smaller ones 35 minutes. If you are steaming the custard, allow an extra egg. Be careful not to use too much sugar as this will result in a spongy texture.

Too hot an oven, or over-cooking, will cause the custard to separate.

A thick custard can be flavoured in the same way as above and gains interest if it is sprinkled with chopped toasted nuts, preserved ginger, preserved fruit, and so on.

A thick custard, when salt and pepper are substituted for sugar, forms the basis of a quiche. A thick sweet custard with the addition of cream and flavouring becomes, when frozen, ice cream.

Crème Caramel

Prepare a caramel by heating 6 tablespoons of castor sugar, stirring from the time it melts until it is a good dark brown. Pour it into a warmed mould, or several small ones, twisting the mould so that the bottom and sides are coated.

Beat together 4 eggs, or 2 whole eggs and 2 yolks, and pour slowly on to them a pint of milk, scalded *not* boiled (185°F, 85°C), which you have flavoured with a vanilla pod. Cook covered with greaseproof paper or foil, standing in a dish of hot water in a moderate oven (325°F, 170°C, Gas 3) for 35–40 minutes, until the custard is just setting. Allow to cool and then turn out. The crème caramel will be extra good if you substitute cream for part of the milk.

PANCAKES AND BATTERS

There are many kinds of batters and with them you can make a whole range of dishes. Wheat, maize, buckwheat or rice flour variously combined with milk, water, beer, eggs, butter or oil produce such different results as pancakes, waffles, enchilladas, Yorkshire pudding, blinis and Foo Yong. Unless exotic fillings are used, such dishes are not expensive.

For the basic English pancake recipe you do not need to use self-raising flour. It used to be thought essential to let the batter stand for an hour before cooking, but with present-day flours this is not necessary. Prepare the batter ahead if you wish, just do whatever is most convenient.

The Pancake Pan. The classic pan is shallow with straight sides and made of cast-iron, but a 6-inch omelette pan makes quite a good substitute.

Before use, heat the pan with a thin film of oil or clarified butter. Pancakes are not fried in fat, merely lubricated so that they do not stick.

Basic English Recipe. The following is a basic recipe for pancakes. Some people prefer to use one egg and one yolk, or to use half milk and half water. This makes a lighter pancake. Extra butter and egg will produce a richer mixture, and for some dishes cream is added. If the butter is omitted the pancake will be rather dry, and more fat must be used in the pan. With a 6-inch pan, the following recipe will produce 8–12 pancakes, depending on their thickness:

4 oz (100 g) plain flour, ½ pint milk (3 dl); 1 standard egg; 1 tablespoon oil or melted butter; a good pinch of salt

Method. Sieve the flour and seasoning into a fair-sized bowl, make a well in the centre, and drop in the egg. Add a little milk and stir, gradually drawing in the flour from the sides. When the mixture has become a thick cream, add the oil or butter and beat well, then whisk in the remainder of the milk. If the mixture is strained into a jug it will be easier to measure it out for each pancake and you will be sure that there are no lumps.

When the greased pan is thoroughly hot, test the batter by pouring a generous tablespoon into the pan, tilting it in all directions so that it spreads evenly. This is a knack and requires a little practice but should not be difficult provided the mixture is of the right thickness and the pan properly greased. If the mixture is too thick, stir in a little more liquid. Make sure that the heat is sufficient, otherwise the pancakes will be flabby.

Pour in sufficient mixture to cover the bottom of the pan and when the underside is golden-brown, loosen the edges of the pancake. Traditionally, pancakes are tossed, and this procedure is best learnt by observation and practice. Unless you are adept, work over a sheet of paper to avoid losing your pancake and your time in clearing up. Mrs Beeton, in her *Dictionary of Everyday Cookery*, suggests that a beginner need only cook pancakes on one side, to avoid the difficulty of tossing them. However, you can perfectly well turn the pancake with a slice or a palette knife. One minute over the heat should be sufficient to cook the other side. Grease the pan lightly between each pancake. You may find an old pastry brush convenient for this purpose.

To keep pancakes hot for a short time pile them, covered, on a plate over a saucepan of boiling water. Pancakes can be made ahead and kept, covered with a cloth, for several hours. To reheat, grease a tin or fireproof dish with melted butter and lay the pancakes on it, overlapping closely. Brush them with melted butter and put them in the oven at 400°F (200°C, gas 6) for 5 minutes, covered with foil. If you wish to keep the pancakes for a longer period, put a layer of greaseproof paper between each and stack them in an airtight tin in the refrigerator. They will keep very well for up to three days.

Pancakes, provided they are enriched with butter as above, can be deep-frozen, packed between double layers of cellophane. They must be warmed up at 400°F (200°C, Gas 6) for 10–15 minutes.

Stuffed Savoury Pancakes

Pancakes may be stuffed with all sorts of savoury mixtures and this is an excellent way of using up leftovers. Prepare the filling and keep it hot while you make the pancakes, then lay a tablespoonful on one side of each and roll it up, turning in the ends if you wish to keep the fillings in place. Ninette recommends sticking the roll together with a little white of egg.

Lay the rolled pancakes, side by side and slightly overlapping in a buttered fireproof dish and cover them with sauce, or sprinkle them with butter and finish with grated cheese or fine breadcrumbs. Heat and serve.

Fillings. These are usually based on a thick béchamel (p. 108), cottage cheese or cream. Here are some ideas for additions:

Mushrooms. Make a béchamel with the butter in which you have softened some chopped mushrooms. Flavour with nutmeg and pepper. Add, if you wish, some minced cold chicken, ham or veal.
Haddock. Stir flaked, cooked haddock and chopped hard-boiled eggs into a béchamel sauce made with the milk in which the fish was cooked. Flavour with lemon juice and chopped parsley.
Shrimps or Prawns. Heat in a curry-flavoured béchamel.
Cabbage. Soften shredded cabbage in butter or dripping, and stir in raisins and chopped onion fried golden-brown. Season with pepper and a little vinegar and simmer beneath buttered paper until soft and compact. Cover the stuffed pancakes with cheese sauce.
Pâté. Fish or chicken liver pâté, shaped into small cigars, makes an excellent filling for pancakes.
Leeks and Bacon. Chop cooked leeks and mix them with crumbled fried bacon and a little bacon fat or paprika.

66

Sweetcorn. Flavour cooked sweetcorn with chopped sweet peppers.

Ham. Mix minced ham with an equal quantity of cottage cheese, bind with fresh cream and flavour with paprika.

Roe. Remove all membrane from a cup of cooked herring, cod or salmon roe and work into a paste with double cream and pepper. Stuff the pancakes and sprinkle with lemon juice and melted butter.

Sausage Meat. Stuff pancakes with fried sausage meat and cover with tomato sauce and grated cheese. Brown under the grill.

Tunny Fish. Drain and flake the fish, and flavour with lemon and a trace of red pepper. Mix béchamel sauce and vary the flavouring with tomato juice or grated cheese.

Instead of stuffing pancakes, try mixing the batter with grated cheese, chopped fried onion or chicken livers, or crumbled fried bacon.

These are just a few ideas. Any mixture which is pleasant in itself and firm enough to stay inside a rolled-up pancake will do.

Yorkshire Pudding

Use the basic batter mixture at the beginning of this section but reduce the quantity of milk so that the mixture will only just drop from the spoon. The batter will be crisper if you use half milk and half water, and lighter if the egg white is beaten and added just before the pudding is cooked.

In the days of large family roasts two or three tablespoons of hot dripping from the roasting tin were used to bake the Yorkshire pudding which was eaten as a separate course before the meat. Now, many households are without dripping, and the Yorkshire batter must be poured into a very hot tin which has been greased with some other fat. Either way, the pudding is put straight into an oven heated to 425°F (220°C, Gas 7) and baked for 30–40 minutes until it is puffed up and well browned.

Sweet Pancakes

For simple sweet pancakes use the basic pancake mixture on p. 65, substituting if you wish a teaspoon of sugar for the pinch of salt. As each pancake is cooked, turn it out on to sugared paper and sprinkle lightly with sugar. Roll up and sugar once more. If the pancakes are to be eaten immediately, they may be sprinkled with lemon juice before rolling, but if kept waiting this will make them heavy, and it is better to offer quartered lemons at table.

If you wish to make your pancakes fluffy, whip the whites separately and stir them in just before cooking.

Stuffings and Sauces. Sweet pancakes are very good stuffed with cream cheese, raisins and sugar; marmalade; apricot, raspberry or damson jam; lemon curd and chopped walnuts; mincemeat; fruit purée with liqueur; ice cream; brandy butter; crushed almond toffee and grated chocolate; fresh raspberries, or stewed apricots with whipped cream.

Whipped cream, grated nuts or orange sauce all make excellent accompaniments.

Try using orange juice instead of milk in making batter. Or stir into the batter crushed macaroons or praliné; chopped toasted almonds; or grated bitter chocolate with a hint of powdered coffee, and put the whipped cream inside the pancakes instead of on top. In this case you must serve the pancakes instantly or the cream will turn into a dispiriting trickle.

A dash of rum added to the batter will give a delicious flavour and make a crisper pancake.

French Pancakes

An old recipe describes French pancakes as being baked on buttered plates for 20 minutes in a hot oven. They are then served with castor sugar and lemon or else piled on a dish with jam or marmalade between each.

To make these, beat 2 eggs thoroughly and work them into 2 oz (50 g) of creamed butter and 2 oz each of sifted flour and sugar. When really well mixed, stir in ½ pint of fresh milk and beat for a few minutes.

Dessert Crêpes

Dessert crêpes, which may be stuffed and garnished or flambé in various ways, must be wafer thin and served very hot. They should be made with butter, not margarine, and cooked in butter rather than oil.

Here is a useful basic recipe which may be enriched with additional butter and eggs, or made lighter by using half milk and

68

half water. The recipe will serve for Crêpes Suzette and is prepared in the same way as the pancake batter described on p. 65. The butter, which should be liquid but not hot, is poured in immediately before the addition of the final liquid. Orange or lemon flavouring is best added by rubbing a lump of sugar on the rind of the fruit and then crushing and stirring it in. For vanilla, infuse a piece of a pod in the milk, then remove it.

4 oz (100 g) flour; 1 tablespoon granulated sugar; a pinch of salt; 2 eggs; ¾ pint (4½ dl) cold boiled milk; 1 tablespoon melted butter; 1 tablespoon of rum or brandy

Snow Pancakes

This is an old-fashioned recipe. Stir ½ pint (3 dl) of new milk gradually into 3 tablespoons of flour, add a well-beaten egg and, just before cooking, 3 tablespoons of real snow. Beat briskly and fry immediately.

Batter Pudding

Prepare and bake in the same way as Yorkshire pudding, adding a little melted butter just before stirring in the last of the liquid.

The pudding may be flavoured, and steamed in a basin standing in boiling water, or served with jam or a compôte of well-flavoured fruit. A little melted butter poured over the pudding is a pleasant addition.

Fritter Batter

A simple fritter batter consists of the normal recipe (p. 65) made a little thinner than usual. For extra crispness use beer or water with a tablespoon of oil instead of milk.

French fritter batter in its simplest form is achieved by whisking the egg white separately and stirring it in just before the batter is used.

Pieces of food are dipped in batter and fried in a deep pan of oil which is hot enough to turn a small cube of white bread golden-brown in 40 seconds. The fritters should have room to move freely. As soon as they are nicely coloured lift them out and set them on kitchen paper to drain before serving piping hot.

Suggestions. All sorts of foods are enhanced by a crisp jacket of golden-brown batter and this is an excellent means of making expensive food such as prawns, lobster and so on go further.

Here are some things which make good fritters:

kidney; sweetbreads; savoury meat mixtures; brains; sausage; pieces of white fish or tunny; scampi; whitebait; sprats; filleted anchovy; cooked cauliflower or parsnip; cheese and potato; the flowers of broccoli; raw mushrooms; well-drained cubes of cucumber; sliced aubergines

For sweet fritters use any firm ripe fruit, whole or sliced. It should be sprinkled with sugar half an hour before it is used, and is much the better for a dash of liqueur.

Fritters made with the flowers of marrows or elder make an amusing variation. In some parts of Europe they use acacia flowers.

MERINGUES

The basic recipe for ordinary or Swiss meringues consists of 2 oz (50 g) of sugar for each white. Two egg whites will produce 12 medium-sized meringues and $\frac{1}{4}$ pint ($1\frac{1}{2}$ dl) of cream will whip up to fill them. If possible, add the whipped cream just before serving.

Variations in texture will result from the type of sugar you use. Castor sugar makes a crisper meringue, granulated sugar a rather softer one. You may prefer to use equal quantities of both, starting with the granulated.

Given such a simple recipe, it is surprising how many things can go wrong, but honey-coloured home-made meringues filled with thick cream are such a delight that it is worth taking a little trouble to avoid pitfalls. Be sure to measure your sugar and remember that beating the whites, which is described on p. 34, is the most important part of the operation.

When you have whisked the whites until they reach the soft peak stage, sprinkle in half the sugar and continue beating until the mixture is shiny and the peaks stand firm once more. If the white is not sufficiently beaten or too much sugar is dumped in at once, the meringues will be sticky. If the sugar is not properly incorporated, they will be leathery. (The same condition will arise if the oven is too hot or baking time is too short.) Now, using a metal spoon, fold in the rest of the sugar (see p. 55).

Some cooks recommend rubbing the baking sheet for meringues

with lard and sprinkling it with flour, shaking off the surplus. This is a messy business and it is much simpler to use a sheet of oiled greaseproof paper or, better still, vegetable parchment. Spoon the meringue mixture on to the sheet in regular egg-shaped dollops about 2 inches apart, or use a forcing bag to make fancy shapes. Sprinkle the meringues with sugar and let them stand for 5 minutes, but not more, before going into the oven.

Properly speaking, meringues are not cooked but just dried out and it is maintained that they can simply be put into a hot airing cupboard for 12 hours. The oven must be pre-heated to the lowest setting. If you suspect that it may be too hot, leave the door ajar. After 2–3 hours, or when the meringues have reached the colour which appeals to you and sound hollow when tapped, they are ready.

Some people prefer pure white meringues. As with the colour of an egg, it is a matter of taste. If you like your meringues to look neat and tidy when they are filled with cream, lift them from the baking sheet when they are ready and still warm, gently thumb a hollow in the flat side of each, then return them to the oven on a wire tray to dry out for a further half-hour.

French Meringue

If you wish to make ornamental rosettes or more complicated shapes such as baskets, a French meringue will be easier to pipe, and it will hold its shape better.

Put 4 egg whites and 9 oz (225 g) of sieved icing sugar into a bowl over a saucepan containing a couple of inches of simmering water. Whisk for about 10 minutes until the mixture is very thick. Remove from the heat and whisk until cool. Use a forcing bag to make the shapes you wish and put them in a cool oven for about 1½ hours to set.

Pavlovas

These are round meringue bases edged with piped meringue, filled with a layer of whipped cream, and topped with fresh or frozen fruit and more cream—or ice cream if you prefer.

Some people find that the Pavlova recipe which follows is easier to manage than the classic meringue base:

Whisk 4 egg whites for 1 minute and then beat in 8 oz (200 g) of castor sugar and a few drops of vanilla or almond essence,

continuing to beat until the whites are stiff. Still beating, sprinkle in
1 teaspoon of vinegar and 1 teaspoon of cornflour, and beat on.
When the mixture stands in stiff peaks, smooth half of it over an
8-inch round drawn on a sheet of oiled greaseproof paper or
vegetable parchment, and pipe the rest in rows round the edge to
form a rim. Bake at 300°F (150°C, Gas 2) for about 1½ hours.
The outside should be crisp and faintly golden and the inside still
a little soft.

Meringue Topping for Puddings
Meringue for topping is made in the same way as Swiss meringue,
using the whites of 2 standard eggs to 4 oz (100 g) of castor
sugar. This is folded in when the whites have reached the stiff peak
stage. The mixture is then piled on the pudding or pie, sprinkled
with granulated sugar and baked in the centre of the oven at
325°F (170°C, Gas 3) for about half an hour or until the surface is
a delicate, pale gold.

For a pudding which is to be eaten cold, the meringue must be
baked at a lower temperature (225°F, 110°C, Gas ¼) for 1½–2 hours
or until it is crisp and firm and an attractive colour.

If the meringue is used to cover ice cream, as in a baked Alaska,
it must be put in the top of a very hot oven (450°F, 230°C, Gas 8)
for not more than 3 minutes or until the meringue is just beginning
to colour.

SAUCES MADE WITH EGG

Sauces made with egg belong to two main families—the cold
mayonnaise group and the hot hollandaise clan. These two basic
sauces have innumerable offspring.

Mayonnaise
Mayonnaise is an emulsion of eggs and oil with various flavourings added. Home-made mayonnaise is so much better than the
bought variety and is not difficult, provided you observe certain
basic rules. It can easily be made in ten minutes, but if you feel
this is too long, or are nervous of failure, we recommend the foolproof blender mayonnaise described below.

An ordinary pudding basin and a wooden spoon are all the
equipment you need for making mayonnaise, though some people

prefer various gadgets, or even a beer glass and the handle of a spoon. Experiment with the various methods to find one which suits you.

If you are making mayonnaise by hand it is important to be comfortable. Choose a bowl which allows you to move your spoon or whisk easily and make sure that it will stay put, leaving your two hands free. Achieve this by standing the bowl in a large saucepan or on a damp cloth.

If you are not expert it is easier to measure the oil into a small jug or bottle, and many beginners find it easier to cut two V-shaped grooves, one on each side of the cork, which allow the oil to fall in drops from the lower groove while air enters the bottle from the upper.

Really good olive oil is expensive, though less so if bought in gallon cans. Some people actually prefer the neutral flavour of the other vegetable oils. If you enjoy olive oil but feel you must economize mix the two. Lemon juice can be substituted for some or all of the vinegar.

In any event, both eggs and oil must not be cold but *chambré*. Eggs from the refrigerator can be gently warmed under the tap and cloudy, chilled olive oil made clear once more by standing in a warm place.

The usual basic recipe for mayonnaise, which provides about six helpings, uses 2 yolks of egg to ½ pint of oil. A third yolk will make a thicker sauce.

Beat the yolks for a moment and then add ½ teaspoon of salt, ¼ teaspoon of dry or French mustard, 1 tablespoon of wine vinegar or lemon juice, and a pinch of sugar. Work these well together and then trickle in the oil, a drop at a time, beating continuously until the sauce has thickened. The beating must be fairly fast but not furious. Two strokes a second is adequate, and this is easily gauged by counting 'one and, two and, three and . . .' with one beat to each word. As soon as the sauce has thickened the oil can be poured in a thin stream. If the mayonnaise becomes too stiff before the oil is used up, add a drop or two of vinegar, being careful to watch the flavour so that it does not become too acid. Never pour the vinegar straight from the bottle but use a spoon or dropper. At the last moment, beat in two tablespoons of boiling water. Test the seasoning.

If you add the whites of 2 eggs beaten to a snow, or a few

73

spoonfuls of whipped cream, you have a *mayonnaise mousseline.*
Mayonnaise can be stored for some days in a screw-top jar in the
refrigerator, if you have no cool storage place.

Remedies for a Curdled Mayonnaise

Curdling occurs when the oil is added too rapidly in the initial
stages of a mayonnaise. The usual remedy is to beat the curdled
sauce, a little at a time, into a fresh egg yolk. However, an extra
yolk is not always available.

Another method is to warm a bowl, place in it a teaspoon of
mixed mustard and beat in the rest of the sauce, a teaspoonful at
a time, making sure that the mayonnaise is completely blended as
you go along. This is a somewhat laborious but useful remedy.

Sometimes a dessertspoonful of boiling water, dropped into the
sauce and beaten with tremendous energy (preferably with a
mechanical or electric gadget) will restore the mayonnaise to
smoothness.

A modest device which works very well, though it slightly tones
down the flavour of the sauce, is to pulp a little white bread with
water until you have a teaspoonful of thick cream and gradually
work the curdled sauce into it. This is an Italian invention.

In every case, you will have to complete the sauce with the rest
of the oil. The thought that a curdled mayonnaise can be rescued
in so many different, though slightly tedious, ways may help to
soothe the nerves, whilst making one a little more careful at the
outset.

Hot Water Mayonnaise

Mix well yolks and seasonings as above, and pour in 1 tablespoon of boiling water. Beat immediately with a mechanical or
electric beater. Whilst still beating, pour in $\frac{1}{2}$ pint (3 dl) of oil in a
steady stream. Unless the beater is electric, you will need a helper
to pour in the oil. Add 1–2 tablespoons of vinegar when the oil is
all used up and the mayonnaise is thick.

Blender Mayonnaise

This is absolutely foolproof and quite good for everyday purposes. Put into the blender goblet 1 whole egg (some people use
the shell too, though we have not found this satisfactory), 1 teaspoon of salt, 1 teaspoon of dry mustard, a dash of cayenne pepper

74

or tabasco, 1–2 tablespoons of wine vinegar and one-third of ½ pint (1 dl) of oil, and blend at high speed for 5 seconds. Remove the lid, lower the speed to moderate and, as the mixture thickens, pour in the remaining oil. Stop blending as soon as the sauce has reached the right thickness.

Aioli
This is a delicious but anti-social sauce usually served with cold fish and a mound of cold cooked vegetables. Crush half a dozen decent-sized cloves of garlic and add them to the egg and seasoning mixture with which you start your mayonnaise.

Mayonnaise Collée
This is a useful sauce for masking cold hard-boiled eggs or fish. It has a more interesting flavour and is lighter than a chaudfroid sauce and is also easier to make.

Dissolve 3 teaspoons of powdered gelatine in 1½ cups of hot water or strained fish fumet and whisk it into 1 cup of mayonnaise. Put it into the refrigerator until half set and then pour it carefully over the cold food. It is unwise to do this more than a couple of hours before a meal, unless a coating of aspic jelly is added to preserve the gloss.

Variations on Mayonnaise
Mayonnaise can be varied with all sorts of additions. Here are some suggestions, each applying to ½ pint (3 dl):

+ ½ cup chopped watercress or chervil; 1 tablespoon lemon juice; 2 teaspoons light French mustard
+ 1 tablespoon anchovy paste or 4 pounded anchovy fillets; 2 teaspoons chopped capers; 1 chopped shallot; 1 chopped hard-boiled egg
+ ½ cup grated and drained cucumber; 2 tablespoons lemon juice; 2 teaspoons chopped tarragon and a pinch of cayenne pepper. Add extra salt, if required, at the last moment
+ the flesh of a tomato chopped with 2 tablespoons capers; 2 anchovy fillets; 2 shallots; 1 clove garlic; 1 tablespoon lemon juice
+ 1 grated apple; 2 teaspoons cider vinegar; 2 teaspoons grated horse-radish; a little salt

✦ ½ cup ground walnuts or hazel nut; 1 tablespoon red wine vinegar; a pinch of paprika

✦ half a grated onion; 1 crushed clove of garlic; 1 tablespoon light French mustard

✦ 1 tablespoon lemon juice; 2 tablespoons ketchup; 1 tablespoon cognac; 1 cup fresh double cream

✦ a handful of chopped walnuts; ½ cup fresh cream; large crushed clove garlic; 2 teaspoons wine vinegar

✦ For fish, try substituting dry white vermouth or absinthe for the lemon juice in mayonnaise

Sauce Rémoulade

Mayonnaise flavoured with anchovies, either crushed or in a ready-prepared paste, chopped capers and fresh herbs becomes a Sauce Rémoulade. A creamier and lighter version is made by pounding the yolks of 2 hard-boiled eggs into a paste, using a drop of vinegar, then mixing in a raw yolk, salt, pepper and a teaspoonful of French mustard. Beat in ½ pint (3 dl) of oil in the same way as for ordinary mayonnaise and season as above.

As a change, substitute half a sweet red pepper and a shallot, both finely chopped, for the mustard.

Vinaigrette Sauce with Egg

Make a vinaigrette with 3 tablespoons of oil, vinegar or lemon juice to your taste, freshly-milled pepper and salt, a heaped teaspoonful of finely-chopped onion or shallot and some chives. Stir in the yolk of an egg boiled for 3 minutes, with its chopped white.

A creamy vinaigrette is made by beating a raw egg yolk with 4 tablespoons of fresh or sour cream and then adding a vinaigrette sauce in the same way that you would oil for a mayonnaise.

Hollandaise Sauce

Classic hollandaise sauce consists of melted butter stirred into a mixture of egg yolks and lemon juice. However, the results are a little dull and not really worth the nervous tension caused by knowing that unless the sauce is handled carefully it will curdle.

A more interesting flavour is obtained if 3 tablespoons of white wine or vinegar are flavoured with herbs and reduced by rapid boiling to one tablespoon. (Ninette suggests substituting white vermouth, sherry, or grapefruit, pineapple or tangerine juice as a variation.) The cooled liquid, whatever it may be, is stirred into the yolks of 3 large eggs which have been seasoned with salt and pepper. Between 6 and 8 oz (150–200 g) of butter, cut into pieces, is then beaten into the egg mixture over a gentle heat. Too sudden a rise in temperature will produce scrambled eggs. Ideally, the sauce should be creamy smooth, just thick enough to coat the back of a spoon.

Edouard de Pomiane suggests making a hollandaise not *in* a bain-marie but *beside* a bain-marie, using a small enamel saucepan and a large pan of boiling water. As soon as the egg yolk begins to thicken the saucepan is lifted to one side and the butter whisked in, piece by piece. Each time a piece of butter does not melt, the small pan is lifted over the boiling water once more and removed again as the temperature rises. Pomiane suggests using the tip of one's finger as a thermometer. As long as one can bear the heat, the sauce will not spoil.

As soon as the sauce is thick and smooth, put it into a warm, not hot, sauce-boat and carry it to table.

If hollandaise sauce is not to be used immediately it can be stood in warm water for up to half an hour. In this case, reduce the amount of butter to 6 oz (150 g) and beat in a little soft butter just before serving. The sauce can be kept warm longer if a pinch of cornflour is worked into the yolks of egg at the start, or a table-spoon or so of béchamel sauce is mixed with the hollandaise. As usual, the price of security is a rather less exciting result.

Béarnaise Sauce

Add to the liquid described for hollandaise sauce ¾ cup of white wine, 1 tablespoon of chopped shallots, 2 teaspoons of chopped fresh tarragon. Reduce and strain. Make the sauce as explained above and finish it with 1 tablespoon of chopped parsley.

Sauce Mousseline

Add either ½ cup of whipped cream or the beaten whites of two eggs to hollandaise.

Sauce Choron

Make a béarnaise sauce, but instead of tarragon, add a little tomato purée.

Sauce Maltaise

Use 3 tablespoons of orange juice and 3 tablespoons of water, reduce them to 1 tablespoon by rapid boiling. Proceed as for hollandaise and before serving sprinkle the sauce with a little grated orange rind.

Sauce for Asparagus

Chop hard-boiled eggs while still warm and put them into a sauce-boat with a handful of finely-chopped parsley, salt, pepper and butter which has been heated until it no longer foams. Stir and serve.

If you prefer, arrange the peeled, hard-boiled eggs and little tufts of parsley round the asparagus and serve the butter separately.

Avgolemono

The Greeks have a delightful way of thickening soups and sauces by beating the yolks of 2 or 3 eggs with the juice of a lemon. For a soup, boil a couple of tablespoons of rice in 2 pints (say 1 litre) of broth and then stir a little of the boiling liquid into the egg and lemon mixture, a spoonful at a time. Pour this back into the broth and stir for a few minutes over a very low heat, making sure that it does not boil.

Avgolemono sauce is simply the early stage of the soup, the egg and lemon being stirred with enough broth to make a sauce of the thickness you prefer. This sauce is refreshing and very good poured over stuffed vine leaves, small meat balls, courgettes sliced and poached, steamed potatoes, artichokes, poached fish, roast veal, turkey or chicken, or sliced fried aubergines.

SEPARATED EGGS

There are various ways of separating the yolk of an egg from the white. It is a good thing to decide which suits you and practise a little, since some white clinging to a yolk will do little harm, but a speck of yolk left with a white can be disastrous. Perhaps the simplest method of separation is to break the egg so that the shell forms two cups and gently pour the yolk from one to another until all the white has drained into the bowl beneath. Here are some other suggestions:

Break an egg on to a saucer. Turn an egg cup upside down over the yolk and drain off the white.

Break the egg into a small, wide-stemmed funnel set over a glass. The white will slip through.

Prick a small hole in the round end of the egg, enlarging it gradually until the white slips through. This method is a little more dangerous as you may pierce the yolk.

If you are a sensual type you may prefer to break the egg into the palm of your hand, as Clement Freud suggests, and let the white run between your fingers into a bowl.

Uses for Separated Yolks

Many dishes require either yolks or whites and it is not always easy to think of an immediate use for the separated half. As a general principle, yolks thicken and enrich a dish, while whites increase its volume and make it lighter. Here are some ideas for yolks:

The yolks can be frozen (see p. 27).

An obvious use for separated yolks is mayonnaise, which we have just described.

Whip the yolks with sugar and marsala to make a zabaione (p. 196), or use them for making marzipan.

Scrambled eggs can be made with yolks alone, adding 2 tablespoons of milk to each yolk. Cook them in a buttered bowl set in a pan of hot water. An extra yolk can be added to ordinary scrambled eggs, or custard, or lemon curd.

A yolk can be hard-boiled in an egg cup standing in simmering water (allow 15 minutes) and then sieved or chopped to make a garnish for salads, sandwiches or toasted snacks.

Yolks of egg improve mashed potatoes, soups, stuffings and rissole mixtures. Also pastry and milk puddings.

Use the yolks with breadcrumbs for coating food before frying, or whisk them with a little milk and brush over pastry that is ready for baking.

Make a mousse-based ice cream with the separated yolks.

Some Ideas for Whites

Freeze them for future use (p. 27), or use them for meringues.

Whites can be brushed over pastry, or the top of a fruit cake so that a crisp layer of sugar will adhere to it.

Whites beaten to a froth can be whisked into a jelly which is just beginning to set, or stirred into a cream or a fruit purée.

Steam the whites in the same way as an egg yolk and use as a garnish.

Dip onion rings in white of egg and then flour and fry them.

Brush the white on to grapes and dip them in sugar. They will dry with a wonderful frosty coating.

Dip the rims of glasses in white of egg and then in sugar. This is likely to appeal more to children than to serious grown-up drinkers.

MILK

THE HISTORY OF
MILK PRODUCTION IN BRITAIN

UNTIL about 1850 milk did not play a large part in the national diet and about a third of the milk produced was used for feeding calves. The smaller towns were supplied direct by farms on their outskirts, but the milk was often dirty or sour and considerably adulterated.

In large cities such as London, herds of cows, bought in calf and sold to the butchers when their milk yield fell, were kept in the town. Of the 24,000 cows estimated to be in London in the early eighteen-fifties, most were kept permanently in stalls and fed on hay and brewers' grains, though a few of the more fortunate grazed in open spaces such as Holland Park. Cows were often brought to the door and milked straight into the householder's jug. Many of them were milked three times a day and the evening milk was used to make butter, but their life was no harder than that of the men who looked after them and had to act as roundsmen, dairy workers and cowmen too.

In 1865–6 the city herds were severely hit by cattle plague and hygiene began to be more strictly controlled. In the meantime the railway network was being extended and the quantity of milk arriving in the capital by rail more than doubled between 1866 and 1868. As the standard of living rose and demand increased, special milk trains brought churns of milk to the platform markets used by the wholesalers.

Road transport opened up new areas of the country and by 1933 half of London's milk was arriving in bulk by road and rail.

London receives deliveries of milk from as far away as West Wales and Cornwall, and just as Birmingham draws its water supplies from a reservoir in North Wales, it is also Welsh pasture which provides a great deal of that city's milk.

Although adulteration of milk has been illegal for a great many years, legislation regarding hygiene and quality was introduced only slowly and it was not until 1901 that the Sale of Milk Regulations, which are still in force, were introduced. In Germany and Denmark pasteurized and sterilized milk were on the market during the nineties, but in this country pasteurization was only officially recognized in 1923.

The demand for milk is increasing steadily but production is increasing faster still. The average yield of milk per cow has increased during recent years from 560 to 820 gallons a year, and milk production in 1968 totalled 19,984 million pints, partly owing to efficient dairy advisory services, but also to the fact that artificial insemination has put the semen from the finest bulls within reach of even the small farmer. One good bull can sire up to 50,000 offspring during his lifetime, or even afterwards, now that storage of semen has been so much improved.

The Milk Marketing Board

During the depression of the thirties thousands of dairy farmers were on the verge of ruin. Supplies of milk, though half those of the present day, exceeded demand and prices were completely uneconomic. In order to stabilize prices and give farmers collective bargaining power the Milk Marketing Board was formed. During the war price-fixing was taken over, and has since been retained, by the Government, but the Board is responsible for all financial transactions between producers and buyers; for the collection and distribution of milk supplies; for advice and assistance to farmers concerning all aspects of milk production; and for running creameries and fleets of transport lorries as well as sales campaigns and publicity.

When allocating supplies, the Board gives liquid milk priority, followed by the requirements for cheese and butter making. Surplus milk is condensed, dried or used for various manufacturing purposes. All milk is rigorously tested, either at the first collection point or, in the case of bulk collections, from samples taken on the farms. Milk received at the big collection depots is cooled and then despatched, usually in insulated tanks, either by road or rail, to centres where it is heat-treated and bottled. Supplies from these centres can be switched at need, under the direction of the central Milk Movements Department.

THE NUTRITIONAL VALUE OF MILK

Milk is not really a drink but a food, and contains about 13 per cent solids—a higher percentage than many kinds of fruit and vegetables—besides some of all the substances necessary to promote growth and support life. It is, in fact, one of the best balanced foods we have. The exact composition of milk varies according to the time of year, the age and breed of a cow, its diet and its family situation, but when milk, as is usually now the case, is collected in bulk the differences are ironed out.

Here are some of the most important constituents of milk:

Protein. One pint of milk contains almost a quarter of the protein needed every day by a normally active grown-up. Protein is essential for the growth and maintenance of flesh and muscle.
Calcium. An essential for the formation of bones and teeth, which are renewed right through life. Natural calcium in its cheapest form is provided by milk and cheese.
Fats. Ordinary milk contains about $3\frac{3}{4}$ per cent of fat, whilst Jersey, Guernsey and South Devon may contain as much as 4–5 per cent. The minute fat globules float to the surface of the milk to form cream.
Carbohydrates. These are present in milk in the form of lactose or milk sugar which in comparison with ordinary sugar is hardly sweet. It is very digestible by human beings, but also by bacteria, which cause lactic acid to form and turn the milk sour.
Vitamins. Milk contains many important vitamins, particularly A, which is necessary for healthy eyes and teeth, and the B group, including thiamine, niacin and riboflavin, which help to prevent fatigue, constipation and lack of appetite. Small quantities of vitamin C are also present in milk. Vitamin C and riboflavin are destroyed by sunlight, and a bottle of milk left on a doorstep for an hour on a sunny day will lose half its vitamin content.

Some Misapprehensions Regarding Milk
Milk has suffered from a number of false assumptions. It is

sometimes thought to be fattening, though its fat content is not large, and it will take the edge off one's appetite for sweet and starchy foods. It is also said to be indigestible if taken with sour fruit. It is true that lemon juice will cause milk to curdle, but that is only what happens naturally when milk meets the acid digestive juices in one's stomach.

The suggestion that milk will turn sour when there is thunder in the air comes from the time before pasteurization when there were no domestic refrigerators and milk was apt to turn in the sultry atmosphere before a storm.

CARING FOR MILK

Milk should be stored in a cool dark place—preferably a refrigerator. It will quickly absorb a disagreeable flavour from food with a strong smell and should be kept covered against possible contamination.

Pasteurized milk will keep for about 22 hours in a kitchen at a temperature of 70°F (21°C) or in a refrigerator for about 4–5 days.

The bottle in which the milk is delivered is the simplest form of container in which to store it. Unfortunately, people have found it useful for storing a number of other fluids too, such as disinfectant and paraffin, facing the distributors with a serious cleaning problem, if not the loss of the bottle. The average milk bottle serves for repeated deliveries and so far has proved more economical for this purpose than other forms of container, though experiments with plastic 'disposables' are now going on. These, whilst presenting in fact a serious disposal problem, at least will not serve as weapons!

Never use cracked or chipped jugs for storing milk but those which have an impervious surface and are, preferably, straight sided. Milk jugs should be rinsed in cold water before washing and in very hot water afterwards, and be turned upside down to dry rather than being dried with a cloth.

Powdered milk must be kept in a closed container or it will absorb flavours and odours from other foods and quickly oxidize and become rancid. Any form of damp will cause it to deteriorate, so make sure to use a dry spoon.

Evaporated milk should not be left on the shelf for more than six months and the tins should be turned upside down from time to time. Once opened, treat it as fresh milk.

Sweetened condensed milk will keep indefinitely in its own unopened can which, since it is tinned by a special process to prevent contamination and has been sterilized, forms the safest container for the milk once opened. Sweetened condensed milk needs only to be protected from dust and flies since the sugar in the milk will, if exposed to the air, crystallize and form a protective coating.

If ordinary milk is frozen it is apt to separate on thawing, but homogenized milk can be kept in the freezer. It takes about seven hours to thaw, but can be gently warmed in a saucepan to hasten matters.

Boiling Milk

Boiling milk destroys most of its vitamin content and causes a loss of calcium, and pasteurization makes boiling unnecessary.

If you should be obliged to use unpasteurized milk which is suspect bacteriologically or keeps badly, then it is best to bring the milk quickly to the boil, watching and preferably stirring all the time, and then cool it quickly.

When the milk reaches a temperature of 160°F (about 70°C) the proteins will form a skin on the surface. Although to many people the skin on milk is repulsive, it has a high nutritional value. Under the skin steam bubbles collect and it is these which cause sudden boiling over. Various gadgets are sold to prevent this, and there are also pans with special pierced lids. One can also use a pan which holds twice the quantity of the milk, but far the best method is to watch the pan and cut the heating period as short as possible.

DIFFERENT KINDS OF MILK

The milk of all sorts of animals, including mares, yaks and llamas is drunk in various parts of the world, but almost all of the milk drunk in this country comes from cows. Only about 5 per cent of the milk drunk in England is sold raw. Such milk used to be described as 'Tuberculin Tested', but all the milk in Great Britain now comes from regularly tested herds where any suspect animal is slaughtered, with the result that bovine tuberculosis is considered to have been eradicated and raw milk is now designated as 'Untreated'.

Farms and all places where milk is processed or bottled must be licensed and inspected by the local Food and Drugs Authority and must conform to the regulations regarding production methods, buildings, water supply and so on.

The various grades of milk on sale are identified by coloured caps which, unfortunately, are still not uniform all over the country. It is therefore worth reading the description on the cap, bottle or carton. The Milk Marketing Board has published a table which describes the various grades of milk now on sale. We reproduce it on p. 87 by the Board's kind permission.

Pasteurized Milk

The object of pasteurization is to eliminate any bacteria which could cause milk-borne disease. As the same time, most of the milk-souring organisms are destroyed, and so pasteurized milk keeps better, though it will no longer sour naturally.

With the method most generally used today, the milk is heated to 161°F (71°C), well below boiling point, and held at this temperature for only 15 seconds, after which it is immediately cooled. In this way, the vitamin C content remains intact and the rest of the vitamins are only slightly diminished.

Sterilized Milk

Warm pasteurized milk is sealed into warm bottles and heated to well above boiling point. Provided the bottles remain sealed, the milk will keep for several weeks and does not need to be refrigerated. The vitamin B_{12} content is unaffected but the thiamin and vitamin C content are reduced by 30 per cent and 50 per cent respectively.

Some dairies sell separated sterilized milk which is useful for fat-free diets.

Ultra Heat Treated (U.H.T.) Milk

This is heated to at least 270°F (about 132°C) for about 1 second, which renders the milk virtually sterile. Packed in sterile containers, this milk will last several months without refrigeration. Once open, it must be treated like fresh milk. This milk is very useful for touring, camping, sea voyages and so on, as well as

Grades of Milk	Definition	Process	Description	Keeping Qualities
Untreated	Milk which has not undergone any form of heat treatment	Bottled under licence by farmer or at dairy	Very apparent cream-line. Nutritional value unaffected. Will turn sour naturally	1–2 days in a cool place. 3–4 days in a domestic refrigerator
Pasteurized	Milk which has been subjected to mild heat treatment to destroy disease-causing bacteria	Milk heated to 161°F (71°C) for 15 seconds and then rapidly cooled to not more than 50°F (10°C)	Vitamin content slightly diminished, will not sour naturally	2–3 days in a cool place. 4–5 days in a domestic refrigerator
Sterilized	Homogenized milk which has been heat treated in the bottle and vacuum-sealed	Pre-heating, homogenization, bottling and sealing. The filled bottles are then heated to 220°–230°F (104°–110°C) for 20–30 minutes and allowed to cool	Rich, creamy appearance and a slight caramel flavour. Vitamin content somewhat reduced. Digestible and keeps well	It should keep for a minimum of 7 days if unopened
Ultra Heat Treated and 'Longlife' milk	Homogenized milk which has been subjected to ultra high temperature treatment—generally referred to as long-keeping milk	Heating to 270°F (132°C) for one second, destroying micro-organisms without producing undesirable chemical changes that would affect flavour	Similar flavour and nutritional value to homogenized milk. Cannot be used for junket	Unopened without refrigeration—2–3 weeks—several months in aluminium foil packs.
Homogenized	Pasteurized milk processed to break up the fat globules and distribute them evenly throughout the milk	Warm milk is forced through a fine aperture resulting in the breakup of the fat globules into small particles which do not rise to the surface but remain evenly suspended throughout the milk	No cream-line, a smooth creamy taste, and readily digestible. Nutritional value —similar to pasteurized. Will not make junket	2–3 days in a cool place. 4–5 days in a domestic refrigerator
Channel Islands and South Devon	Milk from Jersey, Guernsey and South Devon breeds of cow with a minimum butter-fat content of 4 per cent	Available untreated or pasteurized	A high cream content and rich taste	2–3 days in a cool place. 4–5 days in a domestic refrigerator

household emergency stores. It is proving invaluable to explorers.

Longlife Enriched Milk

A cup of coffee is often ruined by milk which has been kept hot over a long period in a café or restaurant. A form of Ultra Heat Treated milk known as Longlife Enriched is now being sold. This has been fortified to bring it to two-thirds the strength of single cream, and so little is needed in each cup that it can be added to hot coffee without itself being warmed.

Dried Milk

There are various brands of dried milk on the market which are very convenient in an emergency. From a nutrition point of view, it is almost as good as the fresh.

Some makes of dried milk dissolve instantly: others benefit from whisking, but all are said to taste better if they are re-constituted at least two hours before use. If you are using milk powder for baking or a sauce, it can be mixed dry with the flour, the necessary water being added with the other liquids.

Dried skim milk is cheaper than the full cream variety. In most cases it will have lost the fat-soluble vitamins A and D together with its butterfat content.

Condensed Milk

Sweetened condensed milk, which may be either full cream or skimmed, is partly preserved by the sugar which is added to it and so does not have to be heated to the same degree as evaporated milk. So, apart from some loss of vitamin C, the vitamin content is little less than that of pasteurized milk. The calorie level is, of course, higher.

Evaporated Milk

Unsweetened evaporated milk is more versatile than the sweetened condensed since you can always add sugar, but you can't take it away. As a substitute for cream it must be used with caution since the flavour is decided and, to many people, not very agreeable.

If the tin is boiled for 20 minutes and then chilled very thoroughly, this milk can be whipped and added to soufflés and creams. It will remain rather foamy and cannot be used for decoration.

Buttermilk

True buttermilk is the liquid which drains out when butter is being churned. This does not reach the retail market, but cultured buttermilk is sold in some shops. Unless buttermilk is stabilized by the addition of a little flour, it will curdle when heated.

If you have some cultured buttermilk for a starter you can make more at home by adding 4 tablespoons of it, warmed to 70°F (22°C), to 1 pint (6 dl) of skimmed milk at the same temperature. Stir well, cover and leave at the above temperature until it curdles, then stir until smooth. Keep it in the same way as fresh milk and serve chilled.

Vegetable Milks

In order to satisfy religious taboos or vegetarian principles, or where milch animals are in short supply, vegetable milks are sometimes used. Ground dried soya mixed with water makes a milk which can be used for feeding babies. A fresh coconut contains 'milk' within its jellied lining or the flesh of a ripe coconut can be grated and soaked in water. This is strained to produce a liquid which is an important ingredient in a curry sauce. Grated almonds, treated in the same way, yield a liquid with a subtle flavour. This is sold, iced, in the streets of Spanish towns under the name of *horchata*.

Junket

This is a traditional dish and certainly one of the most labour-saving ever devised. Foaming milk, warm from the cow, was poured into a dish and rennet added. In a few minutes the junket was ready.

Nowadays, milk has to be warmed to blood heat. To judge this, a clean little-finger makes a handy guide. Add sugar, and rum or brandy if you wish, and a teaspoonful of rennet to each pint of milk and pour it into a china bowl or small dishes. Take care not to overheat the milk or the junket is spoilt.

Unlike jelly, junket sets rather better at ordinary room temperature than in the refrigerator. Once set, the junket can be chilled, but care must be taken in moving it, as once the smooth surface is broken the junket becomes a mass of unsightly curds and liquid.

Brandy is the only really traditional flavouring for a junket, but vanilla, rum, coffee or caramel are all excellent, especially if you place on the top, just before serving, dollops of thick cream and a dusting of nutmeg or cinnamon. A little soft brown sugar is good too.

Remember that a junket can only be as good as the milk of which it is made, and a pint of fresh Jersey milk is a worthwhile investment for such a delicious and labour-saving dish.

By-Products from Milk

Casein, which is the main protein constituent of milk, is used in making paints, glues and plastics. It is usually produced by adding acid to the skimmed milk left after cream and butter are made.

Whey, which is the watery part of curdled milk, contains lactose or milk sugar which is used for various pharmaceutical products. The residue of the whey is concentrated and mixed with meal made from oil seeds after the oil has been removed. This makes a valuable food for calves and pigs.

Buttermilk is usually dried and produced in powdered form for the baking industry and for animal feeding. The buttermilk sold to the retail trade is normally cultured, as this is more uniform in character.

SOURED MILK AND YOGHURT

Soured Milk

Fresh milk turns sour when it is kept, owing to the action of organisms which convert the milk sugar into lactic acid. For hundreds of years man has taken advantage of this process to produce from the milk of cows, sheep, goats, buffaloes and mares a number of different foods of a more or less liquid nature. Of these, the best known in this country is yoghurt, which originated in the Balkans and the Near East. Until fairly recently yoghurt was made by the housewife, using a little from the previous batch as a starter. Now, the manufacture of yoghurt has become a very important commercial enterprise. It seems probable that with the spectacular increase in travel and a consequent interest in new foods the public may come to demand other sour milk products.

Yoghurt

Yoghurt can be made from whole, skimmed or partially skimmed milk, or a mixture of any of these. The fat content varies, low-fat yoghurt being popular with slimmers. Yoghurt contains the valuable nutrients of milk but can be enjoyed by many people who are allergic to the former. Regular use of yoghurt has been found beneficial to sufferers from nervous exhaustion, fatigue, colitis and gastric troubles. It is reputed to be the foundation of the excellent health and longevity of people in certain parts of the Balkans and Kashmir.

Besides the plain yoghurts with their varying fat contents and basic formulas, it is possible to buy yoghurt flavoured with strawberry, raspberry, bilberry, blackcurrant, pineapple, apricot, mandarin, orange, prunes, cherry or hazelnut. Some makes contain pieces of the fruit concerned.

With so much ingenuity going into the manufacture of yoghurt it seems a pity that a satisfactory system of date-stamping the cartons cannot be devised. As it is, the date-stamp is in a code which the shopkeeper does not as a rule understand. At a recent inspection it was discovered that out of 36 retailers 20 had several out-of-date cartons of yoghurt on sale; 28 did not understand the dating code and had received no instructions about the length of time which yoghurt could be kept, and 12 were selling cartons of yoghurt over 21 days old, one of which was, in fact, 70 days old.

Natural yoghurt can be eaten with or without sugar, but it is also excellent as a last-minute addition to soups, sauces and casseroles or, thickened with a little cornflour, as a sauce for vegetables. Take care not to heat yoghurt too vigorously as this will spoil the appearance, though not the taste, of the dish.

Some More Ideas for Yoghurt in Cooking

The fresh, slightly acid flavour of yoghurt gives lightness and a new tang to dishes where you might otherwise use cream. Here are a few ideas:

Spoon yoghurt over white fish before baking it in a slow oven. Pour yoghurt, liberally seasoned with paprika, over sauté veal scallops. Heat for a moment or two and serve at once. Try stirring a carton of yoghurt into savoury rice which you have prepared with fried onions, tomatoes, mushroom, shrimps or whatever you fancy.

Mix a salad of sliced apple and tomato, raisins and a carton of yoghurt with a dessertspoonful of clear honey and a teaspoonful of curry powder, and chill.

To make a change from French dressing, beat a yolk of egg with 2 tablespoons of white wine vinegar, 1 dessertspoonful of lemon curd, 2 cartons of yoghurt, 1 tablespoon of finely-chopped spring onions or chives, a little salt and freshly-milled black pepper.

To make dropped scones in a flash, whisk a beaten egg into a carton of yoghurt. Fold in 2 level tablespoons of sieved flour and a pinch of salt. Cook them golden-brown on each side in a well-oiled pan and eat immediately with butter, jam or honey at tea time; or for pudding with lemon juice and sugar.

For a quick pudding, stir one dessertspoonful of lemon curd into each carton of yoghurt, chill and sprinkle with grated chocolate.

Make a jelly and, when cool, but before it is set, whisk in a carton of yoghurt to each ½ pint. Pour into individual bowls and serve with crisp sweet biscuits and cream.

Try yoghurt as a basis for milk shakes.

Home-made Yoghurt

It is not difficult to make yoghurt at home.

Yoghurt can be made in an open-mouthed thermos flask, but it is usually more convenient to have individual portions. Collect the number of pots, jars or impervious cartons you will require. (Four 5-oz or five 4-oz containers will hold a pint.) It is not absolutely necessary to have lids on the jars while the yoghurt is being made, as a layer of foil will do instead, but once made, the yoghurt must be covered unless it is to be eaten at once.

Find a cake tin into which the jars will fit, leaving room for a lining of insulating material. Expanded polystyrene is excellent for this purpose. Cut two rounds to fit the inside top and bottom of the tin and an overlapping band to line the sides. Cover the lining with plastic or a clean napkin so that it keeps fresh.

You will need a little yoghurt as a starter. The best milk for the purpose is either skimmed or ordinary, not full cream. Heat the milk to 180°F (82°C) and pour it into clean jars which have been placed ready in the insulated tin. Allow the milk to cool to between 106°–109°F (41°–43°C). Take one teaspoonful of milk from each jar and, for 1 pint, mix the total with ½ teaspoonful of yoghurt starter. Re-distribute this between the jars, stirring well. You must work very fast. Place the insulating pad on top of the jars, with foil beneath if they are lidless, and close the lid of the tin. Room temperature should not drop below 60°F (15°C). If your kitchen becomes cold at night, the yoghurt can be made in the airing cupboard. At the end of 8 hours the yoghurt should have set.

If not, the starter may have been added when the milk was too hot, thus killing the bacteria, or you may have used yoghurt which was too old, or jolted the yoghurt during the incubation period.

Sometimes the batch can be rescued by going through the whole process again, using a fresh starter of yoghurt.

It is important to keep a little of each batch as a starter for the next.

Yalacta Products of Otley, Yorkshire, produce kits of various capacities which are very convenient for making yoghurt at home.

Kéfir

This is a pleasant fizzy, slightly alcoholic drink which is made by adding yeast and a culture of certain lactic bacilli to milk. The culture, which becomes gelatinous on contact with milk, collects on the side of the vessel and resembles small yellow cauliflowers. It can be scraped off, washed and drained for re-use.

To make kéfir, soak the dried grains of the culture in tepid water for 2 hours and then put them into milk which has been boiled and cooled to 71°F (22°C) using a dessertspoonful of grains to each pint. Add an equal quantity of sugar to make the drink pleasantly fizzy. Cover the vessel with a cloth and let it stand for 24 hours, stirring from time to time. Strain it into screw-top bottles which should not be quite full. Put the bottles, lying down, in a cool place and shake them after a few hours. In 2–3 days the kéfir will be ready. Wash the culture, which can be re-used at once. If not used immediately, it must be re-washed every two days to keep it alive.

Kéfir grains can be obtained from Chas. Hansen's Laboratories Ltd, Manfield House, Strand, London W.C.2.

CREAM

REAM has always been something special. For thousands of years farmers' wives skimmed by hand the cream which had risen to the top of their milk, like the housewife nowadays who removes the 'topper' from the milk bottle to pour it over the children's pudding. Now, even the farms which produce cream for local sale have mechanical separators, but the greater part of the cream produced commercially in this country comes from vast centrifugal plants at the dairy centres, which can be regulated to produce the exact percentage of butterfat required.

Cream consists of the same components as milk, though in different proportions. The higher the butterfat content, the greater the quantity of fat-soluble vitamins A, D, E and K it contains. With a lower butterfat content, the proportion of protein, lactose, calcium, riboflavin and niacin will be higher.

Some kinds of cow, such as the Friesian, yield very white milk and cream with especially fine and digestible fat globules, though the fat content may be as high as in the darker creams.

HOW TO KEEP CREAM

The table on p. 95 gives an idea of the keeping qualities of the various forms of cream, though the periods shown are minimum. For example, fresh double cream which has been kept cool and unopened will last up to 10 days in a refrigerator, though it is always best to buy little and often. Any type of cream, once opened, must be kept covered and cool and used reasonably quickly.

Double cream can be frozen in special freezer waxed cartons,

94

Types	Standards	Processing	Description	Keeping Quality
Single	Legal minimum of 18 per cent butterfat	Homogenized and pasteurized by heating to about 79.5°C (175°F) for 15 seconds then cooled to 4.5°C (40°F)	Sold in sealed bottles and cartons. Will not whip	2–3 days in summer 3–4 days in winter—in a refrigerator
Double	Legal minimum of 48 per cent butterfat	As for single cream except that most double cream is not homogenized	Sold in sealed bottles and cartons. Can be slightly thinned (1 tablespoon top of milk to ¼ pint cream) before whipping	2–3 days in summer 3–4 days in winter—in a refrigerator
'Extra Thick'	As above	Homogenized and pasteurized	Sold in cartons. Will not whip but is thick and useful for spooning	As above
Whipping	Between 35 per cent and 42 per cent butterfat, usally about 40 per cent	As for double cream	Formerly sold only to trade. Sale to public, in sealed cartons, is now on the increase	2–3 days in summer 3–4 days in winter—in a refrigerator
Clotted	Legal minimum of 48 per cent butterfat, usually about 55 per cent	Heated to a temperature of about 82°C (180°F) and after cooling for about 12 hours, the crust is skimmed off giving the cream a crumbly texture	Usually packed in cartons by hand	2–3 days in summer 3–4 days in winter—in a refrigerator
Long-Keeping	48 per cent butterfat	Pasteurized in bottles at 65.5°C (150°F) for 30 minutes and heat sealed before cooling to 4.5°C (40°F)	Sold in sealed bottles. Will not whip	2–3 weeks under refrigeration
U.H.T.	Usually about 18 per cent butterfat	Homogenized and heated to 132°C (270°F) for 1 second and cooled immediately	Packed in foil-lined containers. Appears thick, but will not whip	2–3 months if unopened. Needs no refrigeration
Sterilized	Legal minimum of 23 per cent butterfat	Homogenized and heated to 104°–110°C (220°–230°F) for 20 minutes and cooled slowly. The very high temperatures account for the slightly caramel flavour	Sold in tins. Butterfat content is low, but sterilization causes thickening	If unopened should keep indefinitely

taking care to leave a little room for expansion. The cartons in which cream is sold are not suitable for freezing unless they are given an outer wrapping of aluminium foil.

Frozen double cream will whip, but it is not good with coffee as the globules of fat tend to separate. If you intend to freeze a dish containing cream, it is better to choose a recipe which entails heating the cream.

DIFFERENT KINDS OF CREAM

By law, cream must be pure and contain no additives. The table on p. 95 describes the different kinds of unsoured cream on sale in this country.

Single Cream
This is homogenized to keep the fat evenly distributed, and it will not whip.

Double Cream
People are often puzzled to find that although the minimum butterfat content of double cream is fixed by law, the cream from two equally reliable firms differs very much in thickness. This may be due to two factors.

Cream becomes thicker as it ages, so very fresh cream may appear thin. Double cream is not usually homogenized as this would prevent it from whipping, but it does normally undergo heat treatment at very low pressure. The degree of heat treatment influences the thickness of the cream.

A heavily homogenized double cream which is very thick, but which will not whip, is now on sale. This is usually labelled 'extra thick'.

Whipping Cream
As will be seen from the table on p. 95 cream with a butterfat content of between 35 per cent and 42 per cent, which is more suitable for whipping, is now being produced.

Clotted Cream
Not so many years ago, the milk for clotted cream was scalded over a wood fire in the farmhouse kitchen, giving a wonderfully subtle flavour to the golden, wrinkled crust.

96

Now, steam has largely replaced the wood fire and a great deal of clotted cream is mass-produced, but it still has to be packed by hand, layer upon layer, into its cartons.

French Cream

With French *crème fraiche* or *crème double*, the ferments and lactic acids have been allowed to work naturally so that the cream thickens without souring, though it has a faintly sour flavour. This cream can be boiled without curdling and will keep for at least 10 days in the refrigerator. Before whipping, it must be thinned by the addition of 1 part of cold milk or iced water to 3 parts of cream.

If a recipe requires French cream, stir a teaspoon of sour cream into ¼ pint (1½ dl) of double cream and leave it to stand at room temperature until thickened.

Home-made Cream

There are small emulsifying machines on the market which will make just under 1 cup of cream if you melt 4 oz (just over 100 g) of unsalted butter or margarine in ¾ pint (4½ dl) of milk. Keep the mixture at an even blood heat, stirring and testing with your finger as you go.

Fill only half the bowl of the machine at a time and pump hard and evenly. When you have turned all the butter and milk mixture into cream, stir it with a fork and chill. Before using, stir once more. This cream is not easy to whip, but a teaspoonful of powdered gelatine dissolved in a tablespoon of water and added to the milk before you start will help.

COOKING WITH CREAM

Cream enhances most dishes, but it has to be used with a certain care. If you are using single cream, bear in mind that it has been homogenized and will not whip. If your recipe calls for double cream remember that single cream is only half as rich. Doubling the quantity will not help, as you will have too much liquid. The addition of a teaspoon of flour, mixed with a little cold water, to every ¼ pint (1½ dl) of single cream before it is cooked, will make up the body which it lacks though not, of course, the flavour.

When adding cream to an already cooked dish it is always

G   97

advisable to boil the cream beforehand for a few moments. It will be less likely to curdle.

Sometimes a sauce made with double cream refuses mysteriously to thicken. This may be due to a change in the diet of the cows at the time of the equinox. It does not affect the flavour of the cream and can be remedied by stirring in a yolk of egg if the thickness of the sauce is important.

If cream is very thick, gently stir in a little milk. This will make the cream blend more evenly and lessen the danger of separation.

How to Whip Cream

To whip successfully, both cream and basin should be chilled. Go gently at first until the cream is frothy, and then faster as it becomes thicker. Stop whipping as soon as the cream has reached the right stage. Over-beating will make it buttery. If this happens, it may sometimes be rescued by whipping in 1–2 tablespoons of 'topper' or evaporated milk.

Note that a blender will *beat* cream, not whip it. This must be done with a mixer or by hand. A little icing sugar, added to the cream after whipping, will help it to keep its shape. Too much sugar makes the cream watery.

Other flavourings such as grated chocolate, instant coffee, toasted nuts, liqueurs, nutmeg, crushed nut brittle or peppermint rock, either singly or in combination, can be folded in with the sugar.

When an especially light and fluffy cream is needed, fold in one white of egg, beaten to soft peak stage (p. 34), to each $\frac{1}{4}$ pint ($1\frac{1}{2}$ dl).

Whipped cream will keep for several hours in the refrigerator. If you turn it into a fine sieve over a bowl any liquid which drains out will be run off.

If you are folding whipped cream into other ingredients, be sure that they are cold, otherwise the cream will lose its fluffiness and turn thin.

Whipped cream can be piped (using a rose tube) in separate rosettes on to a sheet of waxed paper on a tray and frozen. Store the frozen cream 'flowers' in a container in the freezer, ready to decorate sweet dishes.

If you badly need a substitute for whipped cream, try using evaporated milk as described on p. 88, remembering though that it cannot be used for decoration.

SOUR CREAM

Now that most milk and cream undergo some form of heat treatment they will not turn sour, merely putrid. Soured or cultured cream (the names are virtually interchangeable) is produced by the addition of suitable cultures to the pasteurized product. Soured cream has a pleasant smooth texture and a fresh, slightly sharp taste. It can often be substituted for ordinary cream, giving a refreshingly different flavour, and making a dish lighter and more digestible.

Home-made Sour Cream

It is possible to make sour cream at home if you can lay your hands on some cultured buttermilk. (The acid content of the natural sort is too variable to be sure of success.) Assuming that you can do this, and it may sound a little like Marie Antoinette's recommendation to eat cake if you haven't got bread, pour 1 cup of single cream into a jar, add 5 teaspoons of cultured buttermilk and shake vigorously. Stir in another cup of single cream, cover and leave the mixture to stand at a temperature of 75°–80°F (24°–27°C) for 24 hours. You can use the sour cream at this stage or, better still, put it in the refrigerator for 24 hours before using. An easier way is to add 2 tablespoons of lemon juice to $\frac{1}{2}$ pint (3 dl) of cream and let it stand in a warm place until thickened.

Some Sauces made with Sour Cream

One carton of cultured sour cream can quickly be used to produce any of the following sauces:

To serve with grilled mackerel or herring, or with cold salt beef: blend in 1 tablespoon of English, or Dijon mustard; a dash of sugar; 1 teaspoon of vinegar; salt and pepper

To make cucumber sauce for hot or cold fish: blend with the sour cream $\frac{1}{2}$ teaspoon of made mustard; 1 tablespoon wine vinegar; 1 teaspoon castor sugar; salt and pepper. Stir and add some chopped, drained cucumber

A useful sauce for shellfish, tunny or cooked trout can be made from 1 tablespoon of tomato ketchup, salt and pepper and a dash of Worcestershire sauce blended with soured cream

To make Stroganoff sauce: blend 2 oz (50 g) sliced button

99

mushrooms and a small chopped onion, both softened in butter, with ½ teaspoon tomato purée. Stir in the sour cream, heat and season. Serve with strips of steak or chicken, fried in butter

To vary grilled sausages, sauté kidneys or liver, make a sauce by simmering 3 tablespoons of vinegar, 4 tablespoons tomato ketchup, 2 oz (50 g) soft brown sugar, 4 tablespoons of water, with a small chopped onion until they are reduced to half a cupful. Cool a little and stir in the cream

A lemon sauce for pancakes, baked apples, fluffy rice and so on, is made by stirring 1 tablespoon of lemon juice blended with 2 oz (50 g) icing sugar into the cream

Blend the cream with 1 oz (25 g) of chopped walnuts, 1 oz (25 g) castor sugar and 1–2 tablespoons of rum to make a wonderful sauce for ice cream

For game, blend 1 tablespoon flour with a large chopped onion which you have completely softened in butter. Stir in ¼ pint (1½ dl) of bouillon. Let the sauce thicken but not boil. Add a carton of sour cream.

ICE CREAM

Mrs Beeton observed that to make ice cream you would require ice tubs, freezing-pots, spaddles and a cellaret. Nowadays, most people make do with a refrigerator. But churn-made ices are still far the best. Sadly, we have neither the time to make them nor the space to describe them.

Cream for ices should never be whipped beyond the soft peak stage (p. 34), otherwise they will be unpleasantly buttery. Freezing deadens flavours, so an ice cream should have a decided taste and be well sweetened, but take care to keep close to the proportion of sugar recommended in the recipe. If the mixture is under-sweetened it will have an unpleasant rocky texture, while with too much sugar the ice will not be firm enough.

Choose a dish for serving ice cream which suits its shape, and chill it well. Chill the serving spoon too.

Refrigerator Ice Cream

Refrigerators vary in their performance, so if you are making ice cream be sure to read the instructions for your own make. The classic mixtures for ice cream are based on custard, egg mousse or thick fruit pulp, all with added cream. For the sake of economy, or to make things easier, various modifications have been invented. For instance, a teaspoonful of gelatine dissolved in a little cold water and stirred into each pint of the mixture will help to prevent the formation of ice crystals.

Always set the dial of your refrigerator to 'Coldest' at least half an hour before you begin, and chill all the implements and ingredients you use.

Any metal container of a suitable size and shape can be used to make ice cream. When filled nearly to the top, cover the container with a layer of foil, as this helps to stop the formation of ice crystals.

Once the mixture begins to freeze firm round the edges, usually after half an hour or so, it should be beaten, either in the container or a chilled bowl. This will make it freeze more quickly and evenly. Any additions or flavourings which you could not dissolve in the mixture should be stirred in at this stage. About 40 minutes later, beat again. The time taken to freeze the ice cream will depend on the make of the refrigerator and the thoroughness with which your implements have been chilled.

Custard-based Ice Cream

Beat 2 whole eggs, 2 yolks and 2 oz (50 g) of sugar together until they are thoroughly blended. Strain ½ pint (3 dl) of milk, in which you have infused a vanilla pod, on to the egg mixture. Mix well and warm over a slow fire, stirring until the custard is thick and creamy. Strain once more and whisk as it cools. Add ½ pint of lightly-whipped cream when the custard is cool. As soon as it is cold, put it in the refrigerator freezing tray.

The ingredients can be blended in the liquidizer and then stirred over a low heat until the custard thickens.

Custard powder, mixed with sugar and an egg yolk before the addition of milk, will provide an acceptable ice cream for a hungry family, especially if you are a little imaginative with the flavouring and accompaniments.

French Custard Ice Cream

Put ½ pint (3 dl) of single cream, 3 tablespoons of vanilla sugar and 2 large beaten eggs into a double saucepan and cook, stirring all the time, until the custard makes a thin coating over the back of the spoon. Finish as before.

Mousse-based Ice Cream

Dissolve 2½ oz (65 g) of sugar in 6–7 tablespoons of water over a low heat, then boil rapidly until the syrup has reached a temperature of 215°–220°F (102°–105°C). Stir together the yolks of 3 eggs. Pour the syrup, which has been removed from the heat for half a minute, on to the eggs and whip until thick. Add ¾ pint (4½ dl) of thick cream, partially whipped.

Dairy Ice Cream

Beat ½ pint (3 dl) of double cream with 2 tablespoons of milk in a chilled bowl until they are fluffy. Stir in 4 level tablespoons of sifted icing sugar and vanilla or other flavouring. Add, if you wish, the stiffly-beaten white of an egg and a pinch of salt.

Ice Cream made with Apricots and Evaporated Milk

To be enjoyable, an ice cream made with evaporated milk must have a fairly strong flavour to disguise the taste of the milk. Coffee produces a good result, but best of all are dried, not tinned, apricots.

Put through a Mouli or blender ¾ cup of cooked, sweetened apricots which you have drained of their juice. Soak 1 teaspoon of gelatine in 2 tablespoons of cold apricot juice and then dilute it with 2 more tablespoons of juice. Add this to the apricot purée and freeze until just setting round the edges. Whip 1¼ cups of evaporated milk as described on p. 88, adding ½ teaspoon of vanilla essence and ⅛ teaspoon of salt. Fold this into the apricot mixture and freeze.

Blender Fruit Ice

Fruit purée sweetened with icing sugar can be whisked in the blender with double cream to make an easy and very pleasant ice cream. It is better to avoid very acid fruits for this purpose, as there is a danger of curdling.

Ices made from Home-made Cream

Prepare some cream as described on p. 97. Flavour it and put it into the freezing tray until it is setting round the edges. At this point you can stir in one of the additions mentioned below. Beat the mixture well and freeze.

Snow Ice Cream

If you are lucky enough to live in a clean place and are not too fussy about germs, you can delight the children by arranging in a dish mounds of snow, light and not compacted, and pouring over it sweetened fruit juice, or cream with jam or some other flavouring.

Additions to Ice Cream

The recipes given above can be flavoured in all sorts of ways, though it is a pity to mask the flavour of real cream ices. Each suggestion below is for 1 pint of ice cream, and is added at the first beating (p. 101).

$\frac{1}{2}$ cup toasted nuts; $\frac{1}{4}$ cup preserved ginger, finely chopped, with a tablespoon of the syrup; $\frac{1}{2}$ cup grated chocolate; 1 tablespoon liqueur, rum or sherry; $\frac{1}{2}$ cup crushed macaroons; $\frac{1}{2}$ cup crushed praliné or brittle nut toffee; $\frac{1}{2}$ cup chopped candied fruits; 1 heaped teaspoonful instant coffee mixed with 1 dessertspoonful of hot water and then chilled; a handful finely-chopped pistachio nuts; 2–3 tablespoons chopped maraschino cherries with 1 tablespoon of their syrup; 1 teaspoon finely-grated orange peel and 1 tablespoon Cointreau; 2 level teaspoons finely-grated lemon peel; $\frac{1}{4}$ lb (about 100 g) freshly-sliced strawberries or whole raspberries

All kinds of sweet sauces, hot or cold, can be poured over ice cream or served with it. These are useful, especially for adding interest to economical recipes or bought ice cream.

BUTTER

THE exact chemical composition of butter is one of the most successfully guarded secrets of the cut-throat commercial world—perhaps because the cow can't talk—and attempts to synthesize it have so far been unsuccessful. Every pound of the butter made in this country contains the cream from about 18 pints of milk. The cream may be 'sweet' or 'ripened'. Most of our butter and that from New Zealand and Australia is made of 'sweet' pasteurized cream, but European butter is usually made of 'ripened' cream which has been slightly soured by the addition of special cultures. Sweet cream butter keeps very well, but has a rather less rich flavour than that made from ripened cream.

THE NUTRITIONAL VALUE OF BUTTER

Not surprisingly, butter contains the same fat-soluble vitamins, A, D, E and K as cream and the energy-producing properties of butterfat. The vitamin content may vary a little according to the time of year it is produced.

THE PRODUCTION OF BUTTER

Only about one-tenth of the butter eaten in Great Britain is produced here. The rest is imported, mainly from New Zealand, Denmark, the Netherlands and Australia.

In these countries, as here, the farmhouse churn has almost disappeared and cream, after testing and usually pasteurization, is separated into vast centrifugal churns which can hold up to seven tons. The buttermilk is drained off and used for manufacturing and animal feeding while the butterfat, after washing and working into butter, is packed into the familiar half and quarter pound blocks or rolls, and into 56-lb boxes for the wholesale market or cold storage. The proportion of salt, which is added after the butter is washed, varies according to regional preferences. The yellow colour, considered so typical of butter, is given by the addition of carotene.

A large proportion of our home-produced butter is made during the spring when milk production is at its peak.

HOW TO KEEP BUTTER

Different types of butter have different keeping qualities. Manufactured butter will keep longer than butter made on the farm, and salt butter will keep longer than fresh. Most of the butter we buy in this country will keep, refrigerated, up to six weeks.

Butter should be stored in as cool a place as possible, preferably in the refrigerator, and well wrapped. It is handy to keep sufficient for the day's use in a cool part of the kitchen so that it will be soft enough to spread, but again this should be covered and never exposed to heat or sunlight. Remember that butter, like other dairy products, absorbs smells.

Certain types of plastic gradually become rancid in contact with butter and it is safer to use containers of glass, china, or earthenware with a glazed lining. The old-fashioned earthenware butter coolers with a water-jacket were ideal, but are no longer easy to find. A useful substitute can be made by standing the butter dish in a shallow pan of water and covering it with an up-turned flower pot which you have previously soaked.

COOKING WITH BUTTER

When butter is heated it melts, and as its water content evaporates, the butter begins to foam. At this stage, it is not hot enough to brown anything. If you continue heating, the butter foams freely, but it has still only reached about 212°F (100°C). As the last of the liquid evaporates the foam vanishes, and the butter will turn light and then dark brown, and finally burn. If you mix oil with the butter the same pattern is repeated, but at a higher temperature and so the risk of burning is lessened.

When frying meat or making an omelette, watch the foam. As it subsides, the butter will be at the right temperature.

Clarified Butter

Clarified butter is required for some recipes and it is also used to seal potted shrimps, duxelles and so on. During clarification the salt is removed, as well as the casein and lactose, and the resulting butter will burn less easily.

Heat the butter gently until it is frothing but not coloured. Skim off the foam from the top and pour the clear yellow liquid through a strainer lined with muslin, leaving the milky residue in the bottom of the pan. Fresh unsalted butter need not be clarified. (Margarine is clarified to remove its water content which evaporates during heating. The resulting clear oil is strained and poured into a jar when cool.)

Brown Butter *(Beurre Noisette)*

Cook the butter over a moderate heat until it is a pale nut-brown. Add the juice of a quarter lemon to each 2 oz (50 g) of butter and flavour it if you wish. Brown butter is excellent with vegetables such as broccoli and asparagus, or poured over brains.

Black Butter *(Beurre Noir)*

Beurre noir, which is a deep mahogany-brown, not black, is classically served with skate, but it is good with other things too. It is easier to make both this and *beurre noisette* with clarified butter as there is no sediment to burn or turn bitter.

Cook 2 oz (50 g) butter until it turns deep mahogany-brown, then allow it to cool. Reduce 1 tablespoonful of vinegar, seasoned with salt and pepper, to half. Add 1 tablespoon of minced parsley. Strain the butter into the vinegar pan and re-heat without boiling. For skate, add 1 dessertspoonful of capers.

Beurre Manié

This is used for thickening soups and sauces, the liquid in stews and casseroles and so on. Work butter and flour to a smooth paste, using rather more of the former, and add it in small pieces to the dish you want to thicken. *Beurre manié* can be whisked into a soup or sauce, but where there are pieces of meat or fish which would break if stirred, gently shake the pan until the butter mixture is

blended in, bringing the liquid slowly to the boil as you do so. It
must not boil fast.

How to Finish with Butter or *Monter au Beurre*
Wait until the soup or sauce is quite ready, then remove it from
the stove, add the butter in small pieces, letting each one in turn
blend in. If the dish is allowed to boil after this the butter will
turn oily and lose its flavour. If necessary, the dish should be kept
warm in a pan of hot water, but it is far better to serve it at once.

Softening Butter
Butter spreads much better if it is soft. To soften it, put the
butter, cut in pieces, into a bowl which you have warmed with
boiling water and then dried. Beat the butter until it is a smooth
cream, free from lumps. When making savoury butters, add
flavourings such as those described on pp. 110–113 at this stage.

Expanded Butter
As an economy measure, or for reasons of diet, butter can be
'stretched' considerably. Soak 1 tablespoon of gelatine in ½ pint
(3 dl) of water until it has dissolved and then warm it carefully.
Cut ½ lb (200 g) of butter into pieces and put it in a bowl over hot
water. Whip the gelatine mixture gradually into the butter, beating
until all the bubbles have disappeared. The butter can then be
poured into pots and served well chilled.

A simpler method is to beat in 2–3 tablespoons of warm milk
or water for every 4 oz (100 g) of butter.

To Remove the Salt from Butter
Cover the butter with boiling water and wait until it becomes
cold. The butter will rise to the top, leaving the salt in the water.

To Remove Taint from Butter
If butter should have an unpleasant taint, cut it in pieces and
soak it for an hour in fresh, cold milk. Wash the butter in cold
salted water.

SAUCES BASED ON BUTTER AND FLOUR
Sauces, like many other pleasant experiences, are the result of

liaisons which bind and enrich them. One of the most frequently used is butter and flour.

Sauce Béchamel

If you take 2 level tablespoons of sifted white flour and work it into $1\frac{1}{2}$ oz (40 g) of butter over moderate heat until the mixture is foaming but not turning colour, you will have a white roux. Heat $\frac{1}{2}$ pint (3 dl) of milk and stir a little of it into the roux, taking care to mix well and prevent any lumps from forming. Over a low heat, add the rest of the milk, stirring all the time. If you wish to improve the flavour of the sauce, infuse an onion and some herbs or a clove of garlic in the milk with which you make the sauce, and add extra butter at the end. A grating of nutmeg, some lemon juice or a drop or two of Worcestershire sauce adds interest. Using this method you will avoid the main pitfalls—an over-thick or lumpy texture, and the disagreeable flavour of insufficiently cooked flour, and you will have achieved what passes nowadays for a sauce béchamel. The original version is more elaborate.

Béchamel is one of the *sauces mères* or basic types which can be developed into many other sauces. It can be made in advance and kept hot over simmering water, or put in the refrigerator for a while. In order to prevent a skin forming, cover the surface with a thin film of milk or melted butter. Always re-heat over a pan of hot water.

Sauce Velouté

Simple velouté sauce is made in the same way as a béchamel, using white stock from chicken, meat or fish, with the addition of some cream and a little lemon juice.

Velouté is the basis of such sauces as *poulette*, with the addition of egg yolk, lemon, chopped herbs, and a little mushroom juice; *chivry*, with tarragon, chives, chervil and spinach; *duxelles*, with the addition of shallots, white wine and mushrooms, and of many others. An interesting curry sauce is made with velouté, chopped hard-boiled eggs and parsley. The curry powder is mixed in with the flour.

Sauce Bâtarde

This sauce is sometimes described as mock hollandaise. To make it, blend 1 oz (25 g) each of butter and flour over a moderate

heat and whisk in all at once ¾ pint (4½ dl) of boiling white stock or
the water from well-flavoured vegetables. Blend an egg yolk with
2 tablespoons of cream and beat into this, very little at a time,
¼ pint (1½ dl) of the hot sauce. Beat in the rest in a thin stream and
return the mixture to the pan. Bring fairly slowly to boiling point
and boil for 5 seconds. Add seasoning and 1-2 tablespoons of
lemon juice off the heat. Finish with butter.

Butter and Cream Sauce

Elizabeth David in her *French Country Cooking* describes a
delicious sauce made by heating in a large frying pan 3 oz (75 g)
of unsalted butter until it is foaming but not coloured and then
stirring in ½ pint (3 dl) of thick cream which amalgamates with the
butter in a few seconds to a thickness which will coat a spoon.
This is excellent with cold chicken.

Some Suggestions for Transforming Béchamel Sauce

A simple béchamel sauce, unless you improve it in ways such
as those suggested above, is not very interesting, but it is an excellent base for other flavours. Try adding, to each cupful of sauce,
some of the following:

+ a tablespoonful of anchovy paste and a teaspoon of lemon juice
+ 4 oz (100 g) of sliced mushrooms which have been sizzled in
  butter and, at the last moment, a little minced parsley
+ 3 tablespoons of capers and parsley, coarsely chopped
+ 2-3 tablespoons grated horse-radish with 2 teaspoons of lemon
  juice and ¼ cup of fresh cream
+ about 1½ oz (40 g) grated cheese and, if you wish, a yolk of egg
  and ¼ cup of fresh cream. This is sauce mornay
+ 2 tablespoons tomato purée or ¼ cup of tomato pulp

A very good sauce for pouring over cold chicken or veal; pâté
de foie gras rolled in ham; moulded eggs and so on, is made by
mixing béchamel sauce and a jelly made with bouillon flavoured
with sherry or marsala. Decorate the dish with strips of truffle or
smoked tongue.

Mishaps

In order to avoid burning, use a thick-based pan and keep
stirring. Better still, keep your saucepan inside another filled with
hot water. Once the sauce is scorched, nothing can be done.

If a sauce is too thick, bring it to simmering point and beat in, a tablespoonful at a time, cream, milk or stock.

Too thin a sauce can be thickened by stirring over moderate heat until it has reduced. Or else, whisk in *beurre manié* (p. 106) off the heat.

If a sauce becomes lumpy, work it through a fine sieve and warm it gently for 5 minutes. Or whizz it in the blender.

SAVOURY BUTTERS

Savoury butters are useful for sandwiches and cocktail spreads and they give a finish to grills and portions of fish. A layer of savoury butter on the toast beneath scrambled or poached eggs changes their character completely.

There are a number of classic butters, more or less elaborate, some of which we will describe. Other very simple combinations are quickly made by beating herbs and flavourings into butter as suggested on p. 113.

It is a good idea to make a double quantity of savoury butter and store half of it in a small pot, or in the form of a roll, well wrapped, either in the refrigerator or the freezer. The roll shape is convenient as it can be sliced and used, still hard and chilled, on top of a sizzling steak or a poached egg.

If you are making savoury butter in a blender, don't soften it as much as when you are working by hand.

Montpellier Butter

Plunge a handful of tarragon leaves mixed with chives, chervil and a few leaves of spinach, into boiling salted water for 1 minute. Drain them and pat dry in a cloth. Chop the herbs finely and add 2 tablespoons of capers, 6 fillets of anchovy (soaked to remove the salt, or use the kind which are packed in oil), a clove of garlic, pepper, 6 hard-boiled yolks of egg, 8 oz (200 g) of slightly salted butter, $\frac{1}{2}$ glass of olive oil and 2 tablespoons of wine vinegar.

Pound the solid ingredients in a mortar, or use a blender, adding the ingredients a little at a time.

Beurre Blanc

This is a speciality of Western France and is often thought to be difficult to make. Judge for yourself. It is traditionally served with pike or shad which has been poached in court bouillon, but would be good with other fish.

It is said that to make a perfect *beurre blanc* one should use slightly salted butter which has not been over-churned, mixed with vinegar made from muscadet wine. Apart from this, there do not seem to be any special complications.

Simmer 2 tablespoons of chopped shallots over a low fire with ½ glass wine vinegar (or if you prefer, vinegar mixed with some of your court bouillon). When you have about a tablespoon of liquid left, whisk in ½ cup of butter a little at a time. The sauce must be creamy.

Garlic Butter

This can be made by poaching 6 cloves of garlic in boiling water for 5 minutes and beating the result into ½ cup of butter, with the addition of salt to taste.

For a rather more robust version, chop roughly 2–3 cloves of skinned raw garlic, sprinkle them with salt and then crush them to a cream beneath the blade of a kitchen knife held flat, and using a sideways movement. Work the garlic into the butter.

Maître d'Hôtel Butter

Beat a teaspoon of finely-chopped parsley and a tablespoon of lemon juice into 2½ oz (65 g) of butter. Season with salt and pepper.

Pats of *maître d'hôtel* butter are served, chilled, on top of grilled steak, kidneys *vert près*, fish and so on.

Beurre Colbert

This is *maître d'hôtel* butter with the addition of chopped tarragon and a dash of meat glaze.

Marchand de Vin Butter

Reduce about a tablespoon of finely chopped shallots in ¼ pint (1½ dl) of red wine to about a tablespoon, and beat the cooled result into 2½ oz (65 g) of butter, adding salt and pepper and a little meat glaze.

Beurre Bercy

The method is the same as for *marchand de vin* butter, but using white wine instead of red, and lemon juice instead of meat glaze.

Butter for Snails

The following butter is sufficient to prepare 2 dozen large snails. It is also excellent with mussels, on steamed potatoes or with entrecôte steak.

Mix 6 oz (150 g) of butter with a good tablespoon of chopped shallots, 1 clove crushed garlic, 1 scant teaspoon each of chopped parsley and chervil, salt and pepper.

Add, if you wish, other herbs such as the tender leaves of celery, minced, and a sprinkling of nutmeg.

Lemon, Orange or Grapefruit Butter

Blend 2½ oz (65 g) of softened butter with 2 tablespoons of lemon, orange or grapefruit juice and 1 teaspoonful of the grated rind. Season with salt and pepper. This butter goes with canapés made with fresh or smoked fish.

Mustard Butter

Mustard butter is excellent with grilled meat, cucumber canapés or sandwiches, cold meat or tomatoes.

Mix a tablespoon of Dijon mustard with a teaspoon of lemon juice, salt and, if you like, a teaspoon of finely-chopped herbs or shallots and blend them into 2½ oz (65 g) of softened butter.

Paprika Butter

Paprika butter, which is made by blending 2½ oz (65 g) of butter with 1 tablespoon of paprika, salt, pepper and a tablespoon of minced onion, can be used, with tiny cubes of crisp-fried bacon, to stuff mussels.

Beurre Ravigote

Take a handful of mixed fresh herbs (watercress, spinach, chervil, chives, tarragon, etc.). Blanch them for a minute or two in boiling water, drain and pass them through a Mouli or blender. Work the herbs into 2½ oz (65 g) of butter. Season, and serve the butter with poached fish, or spread beneath thin slices of Emmenthal cheese or prawns for canapés.

Anchovy Butter

Work 4 pounded fillets of anchovy and a few drops of anchovy essence to give a nice pink colour into 2 oz (50 g) of softened butter. Add pepper and a sprinkling of lemon juice and either a crushed clove of garlic *or* ¼ teaspoon of onion juice.

This butter can be used alone, as a spread, or in making open sandwiches and canapés with other materials. It is also excellent slipped at the last minute into the body of a grilled fish.

Some Additions to Softened Butter

All sorts of flavours can be blended into softened butter and here are some suggestions. The quantities shown are sufficient for 2 oz (50 g) of butter:

> 2 tablespoons ketchup; 1 tablespoon horse-radish sauce; 1 tablespoon chopped dill; 2 tablespoons minced parsley with ½ teaspoon onion juice; ¼ cup grated Parmesan or blue cheese; 2 tablespoons chopped watercress or chives; 1 tablespoon chutney; ¼ teaspoon curry powder; a sprinkling of Worcestershire sauce

BUTTER CREAMS

There are various ways of making butter creams for icing and filling cakes, and we suggest four different types. All of them can be given various flavourings such as 2 tablespoons of liqueur or strong coffee, or the grated rind and 2 tablespoons of the juice of an orange or lemon.

Butter creams can be stored in the refrigerator for several days, or the freezer for several weeks. Allow them to return to a workable consistency at room temperature. A tablespoon or so of lukewarm unsalted butter will restore them if they begin to separate.

Simple Butter Cream

This cream can be made by hand, but it is hard work. It is better to rinse out the bowl of the blender with hot water and dry it; then beat, all together, 2 yolks of egg, 2 oz (50 g) of sifted icing sugar and 6 oz (150 g) of softened unsalted butter. Add any flavouring you wish and run at moderate speed for 5 minutes or until the cream is smooth. Chill the cream, keeping it soft enough to work. As the sugar does not dissolve completely, this cream is slightly grainy.

Custard-based Butter Cream

This type of butter cream is light in texture and better in cold weather.

Boil ¼ pint (1½ dl) of milk with 2 oz (50 g) sugar and pour it on to the creamed yolks of 2 eggs. Stir well together and thicken on the stove without letting the custard boil. Strain and cool. Cream 6–8 oz (150–200 g) of unsalted butter and whisk it, little by little, into the custard. Add flavouring.

Meringue-based Butter Cream

Whisk the whites of 2 eggs with 4 oz (100 g) of sifted icing sugar over gentle heat until a meringue forms which will keep its shape. Whisk for a few minutes more, off the heat. Beat 6 oz thoroughly creamed butter into the meringue by degrees. Flavour to your taste.

Mousseline Butter Cream

This is rather a firm cream which will keep its shape even in hot weather or a very warm room.

Dissolve 2 oz (50 g) of sugar in a bare 5 tablespoons of water, then boil it until it reaches a temperature of 215°–220°F (102°–105°C). Pour the syrup on to the yolks of 2 eggs and whisk until thick. Cream 4 oz (100 g) of unsalted butter and beat in the mousse mixture little by little. Flavour the cream as you wish.

CHEESE

A S SOON as the first hungry nomad found himself with a little milk to spare, the invention of cheese became a necessity. The problem was no doubt solved spontaneously when it was discovered that, at the end of a hard day's riding, the milk remaining in the pouch made from an animal's stomach, which had dangled all day from the saddle, had turned solid due to the rennet in the lining of the stomach. This same process of renneting is used in cheese-making today.

Man has recorded facts about cheese since he first made his wedge mark in the wet clay of Sumeria, and there are frequent references to it in Greek and Roman literature and the Bible.

The ancient Greeks were devoted to cheese, using it instead of sweets as a treat for their children. The Romans took over many Greek recipes and built special kitchens for cheese-making—a refinement which was not introduced into British houses until the end of the eighteenth century.

It is not surprising that after the long occupation the British, including the Welsh and Irish, should have adopted the Latin root, *caseus*, for their word cheese, but it is curious that the Latin nations in Europe should have split on this matter, the French and Italians deriving their *fromage* and *formaggio* from the Roman *formia*, which described the little rush baskets in which cheese was made, whilst the Spanish and Portuguese took their *queso* and *queijo* from the same root as ourselves.

By the end of the seventeenth century the value of cheese was beginning to be generally recognized. It formed the main source of protein in the diet of the workers, but while the country labourers could enjoy home-made cheese, these in the towns could only afford the cheaper skim milk kinds such as Suffolk Thump, which has now happily disappeared. For the gentry there were excellent cheeses, some made from recipes preserved by the monks.

In early Victorian times cheese fell a victim to snobbishness, the simpler varieties being regarded as rather plebeian. The French, on the other hand, remained keenly interested in all forms of cheese, though their leading cookery writers made rather patronizing comments on our own, remarking that there were one or two English cheeses not without merit. Cheshire cheese, how-ever, under its French description, 'Chester', was much appre-ciated.

In 1870, the first English cheese factory was set up near Derby. The manufacture of cheese became centralized, and many varieties disappeared, some of them unmourned, though many of them must have been excellent. The remaining local cheeses owe their sur-vival to the fact that while milk supplies in their areas were suffi-cient to meet the demand for cheese-making, local transport was insufficiently organized to remove the milk for mass production.

The greater the amount of milk drunk, the fewer the varieties of cheese a country will develop, as there will not be a large surplus of milk which must be used up. So we, in Great Britain, have only nine or ten really important cheeses whereas Winston Churchill once remarked of the French that a country which made two hun-dred cheeses couldn't go wrong. In fact, it is reckoned that there are over three hundred and sixty branded cheeses on sale in France and more than six hundred varieties if you count the farmhouse cheeses made from family recipes.

Cheese-making is the process of precipitating the solids in milk. This basic process may be varied to produce great families of cheeses with innumerable offspring. Even the identical process, carried out in a different area, may give rise to a new cheese, since so much depends on the breed of the animal from whose milk it is made, the pasture on which it is fed and the water that flows there. Time, too, plays its part since cheeses, like people, may suffer a complete transformation as they age.

Cheeses fall into broad groups according to the method of pro-duction. There are fresh unfermented cheeses (p. 120) and the group of soft cheeses like Brie and Camembert which owe their flavour to bacterial action. The hard-pressed 'uncooked' cheeses are of the Cheddar type and the hard-pressed cooked cheeses include Gruyère and Parmesan. Blue cheeses owe their veining to moulds present in the ripening rooms or injected into the cheeses. The packaged cheeses owe a great deal to artifice.

Cheeses derive their names from all sorts of connections. Some are named after the place where they were first made (Cheddar, Leicester), or marketed (Stilton, Parmesan); or their makers (Gervais), or inventors (Petit Suisse, Bleu de Laquille); or ingredients with which they are made (Sage Derby, Grappe) or which they accompany (Bierkäse); or the animal whose milk forms their base (Chèvre, Pecorino). The many cheeses with saints' names or ecclesiastical echoes remind one of the monks who first made them.

THE NUTRITIONAL VALUE OF CHEESE

The nutritional value of cheese varies according to the composition of the milk or cream from which it is made, and from which it will take most of the fat content and the bulk of the protein.

Hard-pressed cheeses such as Cheddar, Cheshire, Lancashire and Derby, are excellent sources of fat and protein, containing weight for weight nearly twice as much of the latter as prime beef. They are rich in phosphorus, and a good source of vitamins A, D, E and B_2. Two ounces of any of these cheeses contain more calcium than the same amount of cod, beef, bread, or half a pint of milk or one egg.

Wholemeal bread and butter, a hunk of cheese and a tomato make a perfectly balanced meal and, packed into a sandwich, a very mobile one. Make the sandwich butter-side out and let it turn golden-brown on a hot griddle, and the result is even better than the sum of its parts.

Cottage cheese is high in protein but its calorie count is only about a quarter that of the hard-pressed cheeses, hence its value in slimming.

Though easily digested, cheese has been accused of causing indigestion and bad dreams. When cheese is over-cooked it becomes leathery and the trouble may have been caused by bad cooking, or over-indulgence.

BUYING CHEESE

Unless you know and trust your supplier it is wise to be cautious when buying cheese. In France, it is not too difficult to find a knowledgeable cheese merchant who takes a delight in his job, appreciates your interest, allows you to taste his cheese and is happy to advise you. In England this is not so easy.

The next best thing to tasting a cheese is to look at it carefully. This, at least, is possible in a supermarket and if you choose a store with a keen buyer and a large turnover the chances are that you will find excellent cheese in a fairly limited range.

Cheddars and their close relations should be firm without deep cracks or any mould in their interior, and on no account sweating greasily.

Blue-veined cheeses should look soft and not dry. The veins should contrast cleanly with the body colour and any dark blotches are suspect.

Soft firm cheeses like Port-Salut or Gouda keep well, and it is unusual to find a really bad one. Look out for any signs of dryness.

When buying cream cheese it must be remembered that the fat content of French cheeses, always carefully stated on the package, is calculated as a percentage of the dry solids only, and water can be used *ad lib.* to make up the bulk, whereas the English fat content is taken as a percentage of the *whole* so that the 50 per cent fat content of an ordinary English cream cheese is higher than the 60 per cent shown on the wrapper of a Petit-Suisse triple-cream, to take an example.

Cottage cheese is made of cooked skimmed milk curd which is drained and washed in cold water and then given the thinnest coating of cream. It contains only 4 per cent fat. Curd cheese is made from whole milk and contains 12 per cent fat, while in cream cheese, as we have said, the fat content is half of the total cheese.

If you are buying Brie by weight, so that you are able to see the cut surface, try to find one without a white chalky layer in the centre. This is a sign of immaturity and connoisseurs say that it is not easy to ripen a Brie once it has been cut. Once a Brie is over-ripe, it flows right out of its crust. This is not the same as the gentle oozing of a Brie which is *à point*. In order to satisfy the demand for smaller quantities of cheese, some of the French manufacturers are producing Brie ready-cut in wedges and then wrapped. André Simon maintains that while these are good enough for the uncritical, it is better to buy the small whole cheeses, complete with their natural rind, which are now on the market.

When buying a whole Brie or Camembert, insist on opening
the box. The cheese should be plump and resilient with no sign of
sinking at the centre. The wrapper should look clean, but as
French producers have been known to issue clean wrappers and
instructions for making a jaded Camembert appear freshly-boxed,
have an exploratory sniff too.

Rather than accept a Brie or Camembert which is not in good
condition, switch to a substitute brand of cheese. Both Brie and
Camembert should be good from October until April, and at their
best during the latter half of this period.

If you are buying Parmesan in the piece, try to make sure that
it was made in Italy and is not a foreign copy. The best of the
Italian Parmesan should be stamped 'Parmigiano-Reggiano' and
the less uniformly reliable kind, 'Grana Padano' (see p. 148).
With ready-cut pieces of Parmesan these identifications are usually
lost, so try to taste it, if you can, and make sure that you are not
buying one with an inferior flavour. Parmesan is a very expensive
cheese.

Mature Parmesan is yellow and a younger cheese will look
whitish. White 'bruise' marks left by the cheese cutter are not
important, but white speckles are a sign that the cheese is too
dry.

If you are going to use Parmesan as a table cheese, then choose
a younger and rather softer one. For cooking, a well-matured
Parmesan has more flavour. Grated Parmesan is a convenience,
but it can be a disappointment. It is more expensive, and the
flavour is not so good, since when grated it gradually dissipates. It
is really worth the trouble of grating it yourself. Try to buy a
rather chunky piece. Thin wedges of Parmesan break on the grater
and although you can have the pleasure of eating the broken pieces
as you cook, it is rather an extravagant procedure.

STORING CHEESE

Ideally, one should store cheese as little as possible, buying it in
quantities which can be consumed quickly. In the days of cellars
and vast cool larders with slate shelves, storage presented less
difficulty. Nowadays, many people can only choose between a
refrigerator and a warm heated kitchen.

If cheese is kept in too warm a place it will ferment. If the temperature is too low it dries rapidly. In too moist an atmosphere it mildews, and when the air is too dry it hardens at the edges.

Cheeses are usually sold in a proper condition for eating. The problem is to maintain this state at home. A cheese needs whatever moisture it has. Air will dry a cheese through evaporation, but the cold coil in the refrigerator will draw off the moisture faster still. So cheese must be closely wrapped. Ordinary paper is not suitable; greaseproof paper does not adhere closely enough and even foil, if re-used, tends to crumple and leave air spaces. Self-clinging wrap may be used several times, being careful to leave the clean side outermost, or it will be greasy to the touch. It is worth remembering that mould spores tend to form on the wrapping and contaminate the cheese, so be generous with fresh wrappings.

As storage space with a consistent cool temperature is rare in the modern home, it is generally agreed that cheeses are best kept in the lower part of the refrigerator, but since cold mutes all flavours, it is important to take them out at least half an hour before eating.

Soft Curd Cheeses (cottage cheese, mozzarella, Boursin . . .). Those sold in cartons are best stored in them. The packaged cheeses, once opened, can be kept in cartons or pots, or their own wrappings, as most convenient.

Cream Cheeses (Petit-Suisse, Fromage de Monsieur. . .). Though essentially short-lived, these cheeses are fairly stable and can be eaten and put back in the refrigerator several times without suffering harm. This is probably due to their high cream content.

Free-flowing Soft-ripening Cheeses (Camembert, Brie . . .). Whilst still uncut, keep in the refrigerator so that they do not become over-ripe too quickly. Once cut, wrap them in aluminium foil and place them inside a polythene bag or plastic box and keep at room temperature, finishing them as soon as possible.

If you wish to ripen a Brie or a Camembert, keep it in its own wrapping, beneath an upturned basin or deep lid, at room temperature (60°–65°F, 15–18°C), or wrap it in plenty of newspaper. (If the temperature is too high, the cheese will ripen outside while the inside lags behind.) Turn the cheese over every 12 hours or so, and test it with your finger tips to see if it is ready.

If you wish to hold back a cheese, put it in the lowest part of the refrigerator, again wrapped in newspaper.

Firmer Soft-ripening Cheeses (Reblochon, Pont l'Evêque . . .). These cheeses are less delicate than the previous group but need care, as they will continue to mature in the refrigerator and can deteriorate suddenly. Treat any leftovers in the same way as Brie.

Blue-veined Cheeses (Stilton, Roquefort, Gorgonzola . . .). Such cheeses should be wrapped in the usual way. Some people prefer to put the package into a plastic box before it goes into the refrigerator.

The Firm Cheeses (Cheddar, Cheshire, Derby . . .). Storing half a pound of cheese between one meal and the next is a simple matter, explained above. If you should have a really large piece of cheese to deal with, cut off and use a piece at a time and store the rest at a cool, even temperature. Constant trips to table will spoil it. To help preserve the cut surfaces, rub them lightly with butter, or seal the pores by smoothing the cheese with the blade of a knife. If it *should* get too warm and begin to sweat, wipe it with a cool damp cloth and put it for a little while in the refrigerator.

Vacuum-packed Cheese. This cheese will keep indefinitely unopened, though if it becomes too warm it may sweat. If so, remove the wrapper and let the cheese dry in the air. It can then be re-wrapped but will not keep long.

Freezing Cheese. Contrary to many people's belief, cheese can be deep-frozen, provided you observe certain precautions. The flavour of the cheese will be unaffected, though the texture may become a little crumbly, but it will at worst be useful for cooking. All cheeses must be wrapped in some material which is impervious to the escape of moisture.

The soft-cheeses and the blue-veined varieties should only be frozen when they have reached maturity. They will not become over-ripe, but leave the freezer as they entered it.

If cottage cheese becomes grainy, it will be improved by stirring in a little cream. Frozen cheeses should be thawed in the refrigerator for an hour or two.

If you merely want to be sure of having some cheese in the house for cooking purposes, then it is probably simpler and saves freezer space if you buy a packet of vacuum-packed cheese.

Some Hints

Small pieces of blue cheese make an excellent spread if they are beaten with an equal quantity of butter and a dash of brandy. This will keep in a small closed jar for a long time.

Hard cheese scraps, grated and stored in a screw-top jar in the refrigerator, are useful for sauces and sprinkling.

If you should find a mite—which is only a miniature member of the spider family—in your cheese, don't make a scene. It is perfectly harmless, and there must be something nice about a creature who is as fond of cheese as you are.

HOW TO SERVE CHEESE

The first time a piece of cheese is served it will look neat but not gaudy, as the Victorian sales plug went, but its reappearances are apt to be increasingly depressing. To avoid this, be careful not to buy too much at a time. Always see that the cheese goes to table looking appetizing. Trim off any mould and use sound but unattractive pieces, where possible, for cooking. A buffet is enlivened by fantasy, but a cheese board should be more sober. However, day-to-day cheese, especially if it is to be the mainstay of a meal, gains enormously if it is presented on an attractive dish or a wooden board with a few herbs, or lying in a basket on a bed of fresh leaves.

Wherever possible, offer with cheese a choice of bread and biscuits: rye bread, a long French loaf, Pumpernickel, Bath Olivers, water biscuits and so on. The choice is endless. It is easy to keep a store of many of these in the house, and with a freezer all of them are available at any time. Hot garlic bread sizzling with butter or a crisp green salad changes ordinary cheese into something splendid.

For a dinner party, look for a cheese which is out of the ordinary. Unfortunately, by the end of a good dinner people often have no appetite left for cheese, but something unexpected may tempt them.

COOKING WITH CHEESE

In general, cheese for cooking is chosen to suit the kind of heat it will be subjected to. The recipe usually indicates which cheese is suitable, but it may be useful to remember that a well-matured cheese with a high fat content will blend with other ingredients better than one which has only been matured for a short time.

Parmesan and Sbrinz, grated, are ideal for sprinkling over hot soups or pasta. Parmesan mixed with Emmenthal makes a well-flavoured fluffy soufflé, the former providing the flavour and the latter a rich creamy texture. Cheddar bakes well, and Lancashire and Leicester are generally agreed to be best for toasting. The blue cheeses add an unexpected tang to stuffings for pancakes, fish, ravioli, vol-au-vents, sauces and even salad dressings.

But whatever you are using, remember that cheese should be melted rather than cooked. Too high a temperature will cause the cheese to curdle (although the addition of a little flour will help to prevent this). Too rapid heating will make cheese stringy. So if you are making a sauce, add the cheese at the last and be sure that it does not boil.

EQUIPMENT FOR CHEESE COOKERY

The most important implement used especially for cheese cookery is a really good grater and there are a large number to choose from, starting with the ordinary metal kind, either flat or made with four sides so that it will stand up by itself. The latter is less tiring to use.

Mouli make an excellent small drum-shaped cheese mill which you turn by hand. An Italian plastic grater in the shape of a small mug with a flat domed top is now on sale. Beneath the lid is a grater on which pieces of cheese are laid. The lid is replaced and the cheese grated by a backwards and forwards screwing motion without damage to your nails or finger tips.

After the hand graters come the electrical devices starting with the liquidizer and on to the useful small Bamix mill which attaches to the hand-held beater. It is worth remembering that however good your grater, it will not work unless the cheese is firm and dry —otherwise it will produce a soapy mass.

It is easier to make sandwiches and savouries of the semi-hard cheeses if you use a slicer. Originally from Scandinavia, these have a wide blade with a transverse slit which you draw across the face of the cheese, cutting slices effortlessly.

If you have fallen for Swiss fondue (see p. 175), it is worth buying a special set with a bowl on a stand and a flame beneath, and long forks for spearing pieces of bread. This is almost indispensable if you wish to make the fondue at table, though it *can* be made in the kitchen and kept going over a candle or spirit flame warmer.

SAUCES MADE WITH CHEESE

Cheese and Tunny Sauce for Pasta

Take 8 oz (200 g) of well-drained cottage cheese. Mix this with a small tin of tunny flakes in oil, 2 anchovy fillets, a handful of chopped parsley, $\frac{1}{2}$ clove of garlic creamed with salt beneath the blade of a knife, a teaspoon of lemon juice and a dash of cayenne pepper.

Mix everything well, adding enough olive oil to make a smooth, creamy sauce. When the pasta is ready, pour the cold sauce into a heated salad bowl and tip the well-drained pasta on to it. Stir quickly and serve at once.

Blue Cheese Sauce

This sauce is excellent with grilled meat, poached fish or sliced potatoes, carrots, peas and other vegetables.

Make a béchamel sauce as described on p. 108. Lift it from the fire and stir in 2 oz (50 g) of crumbled blue cheese. Roquefort, Danish Blue, Mycella or Gorgonzola are all suitable. It depends on the strength of the flavour you prefer. Warm the sauce for a moment or two without letting it boil, and stir in $\frac{1}{2}$ cup of cream.

Cottage Cheese Sauce

This is a quickly-made sauce which goes well with grills, poached fish, *fondue Bourguignonne* and so on. It can be made with herbed cream cheese instead of cottage. In this case, omit the tarragon.

Break up 6 oz (150 g) of cottage cheese with a fork and stir in 1 tablespoon of finely-chopped tarragon and a tablespoon of Dijon mustard. Season with salt and pepper, and a teaspoon of lemon juice. Heat the sauce without allowing it to boil, stirring all the time.

A cold version of this sauce is made by adding a handful of chopped fresh herbs, 1 tablespoon of capers, 2 tablespoons of

CHEESE

tomato ketchup, and the same quantity of Dijon mustard and lemon juice mentioned in the above to the cottage cheese. The sauce should be well stirred.

RINDLESS CHEESE

The traditional cylinders and wheels of cheese, even when mass-produced, have to be turned and cared for during ripening. Their rounded shapes are awkward to lift mechanically and need extra storage space, so the factories hit on the idea of making large blocks of cheese weighing between 9 and 40 lb. These are film-wrapped and heat-sealed.

There is no denying that a cheese made with a natural rind and matured in the traditional manner can have a finer flavour and a great deal more charm than its rindless counterpart, but one is apt to forget that in the old days much of the traditional cheese which found its way on to the market was of poor quality. Now, regional cheeses are being made which are of a uniform high quality, and the small shopkeeper who could not afford to buy a whole cheese and would have been obliged to confine himself to selling processed cheese and spreads, is able to cope with block cheese and extend the range of his stock.

Very much to be deplored, however, is the tendency with cheese, as well as wine, to prepare a basic 'mix', and with the help of colouring and flavouring, produce imitations of regional products. Some large firms such as Sainsbury's, who have a very high standard of quality control for their dairy products, are holding out in this matter and insisting that the cheese they sell shall be the genuine article, even though in rindless form.

PROCESSED CHEESE

Unfortunately progress cannot be halted and there are always new corners to be cut. Processed cheese is the great convenience food —handy for the manufacturer because any cheese which is not quite perfect, or which would tie up too much capital if it were left to ripen, can be ground up, emulsified and turned into a uniform product; and grand for the shopkeeper since it has a very long shelf life and there is no waste.

Cheddar, or any of the natural cheeses, usually of the hard-

125

pressed variety, may be treated in this way. Actually, the fore-runners of all the processed cheeses were the small silver-paper-wrapped triangles of 'Gruyère' first made by the Swiss. These contain both Emmenthal and Gruyère but the two together, in this form, have acquired a character of their own.

Cheese emulsions may be transformed with the help of flavourings such as garlic, bacon, shrimp, paprika, pineapple, kirsch, nuts, olives, onions, celery, tomato or just smoke into a variety of cheese spreads. They may not taste of cheese, but you can choose some other flavour instead. So why grumble—as long as there is still real cheese for those who like it?

Unless their wrappings have been undone, processed cheeses and spreads need not be kept at a cool temperature and are just as at home on the Amazon as in the Arctic, since they are practically sterile—brave new cheeses, sealed off from the outside world in the plastic which they increasingly resemble.

ENGLISH AND WELSH CHEESES

In England and Wales nine important cheeses have survived the pressures of modern life and the last war and are reaching a wide market, though owing to labour problems and the economics of the dairy industry the farmhouse cheeses seem doomed to disappear.

However, there are still cheeses made in the traditional manner, some wonderful farmhouse Cheddars and Leicesters, the incomparable Stilton and the rare Dorset Blue Vinny. The more people appreciate and buy these, the better their chances of survival.

It takes about 8 pints of milk to make one pound of Cheddar or other hard-pressed cheese, and of every 100 pints of milk produced in this country over twelve go to cheese-making, and most of this cheese is eaten at home—over 100,000 tons of it in 1969 alone.

Regional preferences play a large part in the colouring of cheese. Red Cheddar is popular in East Anglia and parts of Kent and Scotland. Most of the red Cheddar is made in New Zealand and coloured for these markets. Cheshire cheese, which is produced in Cheshire, Derby, Nottingham and Shropshire as well as parts of Wales and the West Country, is preferred white in the region of its origin, whilst the rest of the country has come to expect

CHEESE

Cheshire to be 'red'. (Incidentally, people will insist with real conviction that a cheese tastes different when in fact it has only been treated with a tasteless colouring matter.) The table which follows gives a brief description of the most important English and Welsh cheeses. The weights shown are approximate since, for instance, a Cheddar cheese can lose up to 10 per cent of its weight if it is matured for a long period. All but the Stilton, Blue Wensleydale and the Dorset Blue Vinny are also made in 10 and 40 lb rindless blocks. The Blue Vinnys and Blue Wensleydales are not easy to come by.

	DESCRIPTION	RIPENING TIME
Caerphilly	Close-textured, moist white cheese with a mild, slightly salty flavour. 8–9 lb cylinders	minimum 2 weeks
Cheddar	Varies with age from firm texture and mild taste to a pungent, golden, slightly crumbly cheese. 10–50 lb cylinders	3–24 months
Cheshire	A savoury, crumbly-textured faintly salt cheese, off-white, apricot or sometimes blue-veined. 10–50 lb cylinders	minimum 6 weeks
Derby	White to honey-coloured with a buttery open texture and clean, tangy taste. Sage Derby is mottled with green. Cylindrical, 9–30 lb	minimum 4–6 weeks, best at 6 months
Dorset Blue Vinny	Straw-coloured with light blue horizontal veins. Dry crumbly texture becoming very hard. Pungent flavour. 10–12 lb wheels	minimum 4–6 months
Double Gloucester	Golden crumbly cheese with delicate, creamy flavour. 9–30 lb cylinders	minimum 3–4 months, best at 1 year
Lancashire	Soft, crumbly cheese which can be spread. Mild and slightly acid when young. Stronger than Cheshire or Cheddar when matured. Cylindrical 9–40 lb	4 weeks–3 months
Leicester	Bright orange cheese with loose texture. Tastes creamy with very faint lemon tang. 9–45 lb cylinders	best between 3 and 9 months
Stilton, Blue	A blue-veined, pale yellow cheese shading to amber near the crust. Has a superb rich and mellow flavour	3–6 months
Stilton, White	An open-textured cheese with a clean, mild flavour	minimum 3 weeks
Wensleydale Blue	Texture is soft and close. Leaves a lingering creamy flavour. 10–12 lb wheels	6 months
Wensleydale White	Mild white, firm cheese, slightly salty with a hint of honey. Wheels, 10–12 lb	3 weeks

Caerphilly

Caerphilly has been for generations a miners' cheese. It is digestible enough to be eaten in large quantities while at work, and its moist texture and mild but salty flavour make it ideal for the hot, thirsty conditions below ground.

The yield of Caerphilly is large in proportion to the milk used, and as it matures quickly the financial return is rapid as well as good. Many farmers who still make the slow-maturing farmhouse cheeses would have been obliged to give them up but for their profitable sideline in Caerphilly.

Cheddar Cheese

By the beginning of the nineteenth century the making of Cheddar, which had been described as early as 1650 as 'an excellent, prodigious cheese', was reduced to a standard system which could be used by any country with sufficient enterprise and a suitable milk supply. Factories making Cheddar cheese sprang up all over the place, some good and some not so good. The first shipment of dairy produce, including Cheddar, reached Britain from New Zealand in 1867.

Cheddar cheese seems to have aroused the competitive spirit, and one is constantly told of monsters, the most famous in this part of the world being the 1000 lb giant made to celebrate the wedding of Queen Victoria. The makers, a group of farmers from East and West Pennard in Somerset, asked if they might borrow the cheese for publicity purposes and were surprised when the Queen subsequently refused to take it back. Perhaps such a large cheese posed storage problems even in a palace.

Of the types of Cheddar on sale here, Australian and New Zealand are the mildest, the English usually the mellowest, and certain types of Canadian have the strongest flavour.

To make Cheddar cheese, tested milk is pasteurized and then poured into vast steam-jacketed vats. A 'starter' of milk-souring bacteria is added, and then rennet to coagulate the milk. Up to this point, the process is common to a large number of cheeses, but now the cheddarizing begins. When the curd has hardened to a moderate firmness, it is cut into $\frac{1}{2}$-inch cubes by the alternate action of two grids of knives, one set vertically and the other horizontal. As the whey separates, the curd is gently heated to about 100°F and stirred for about an hour, so that the particles shrink and harden under the increasing acidity of the whey, and finally settle into a solid mass at the bottom of the vat. This mass, cut in blocks, turned at intervals and later cut into strips, is piled into high stacks so that its own weight helps to press out the whey.

When ready, the curd is put through a mill and broken into small pieces which are salted and cooled. The curd is then weighed into cylindrical moulds, traditionally about 11 inches high and 12 inches in diameter. These are lined with a cloth or 'bandage' which stays on the cheese to the end of the maturing process, and the cheese is pressed for from thirty-six to forty-eight hours. The 'green' cheese is then set to ripen. After from three to six months, the action of the bacteria turns the flavourless, rubbery curd into a cheese with its own characteristic flavour and texture.

Young Cheddar is good eaten with sweet butter, crisp biscuits and celery, or as a ploughman's lunch with bread, pickled onions and a tankard of beer. Mature Cheddar is better still. Both will melt smoothly for cooking, or grate when dry.

Mature Cheddar is aged for from eighteen months to two years.

Farmhouse Cheddar

The supply of good Farmhouse Cheddar cheese was never plentiful and even in the eighteenth century it was wise to bespeak a cheese in order to be sure of getting it.

The number of farmers who still make their own Cheddar cheese is dwindling rapidly, though eighty-five registered farmhouse cheese-makers still work under contract to the Milk Marketing Board.

Farmhouse Cheddar is made with whole, unpasteurized summer milk from a single herd of cows, occasionally augmented by milk from neighbouring herds which have enjoyed similar grazing. Basically, the process is the same as with factory-made cheese, but the batches are smaller and they are matured longer, and the whole process is carried out, and not merely supervised, by experts. So the price is higher, but it is well worth it.

Cheshire Cheese

Cheshire cheese is believed to be several hundred years older than Cheddar and may even have been in existence before the Roman occupation of Britain. It is certainly mentioned in the Domesday Book.

This cheese, which is known to the French as 'Chester', is more difficult to imitate than Cheddar, perhaps because it owes some of its special flavour and subtle tang to the milk which comes from the salty pastures of the great Cheshire Plain.

There is a saying that Cheshire is like the Union Jack—red, white and blue. In reality, the 'white' is almost cream, the 'red' is a warm apricot and the 'blue' is enlivened by the veining caused when spores of *Penicillium glaucum* blow into the unripened cheese. Because blue cheeses were produced by chance and in limited numbers, they were more expensive. Now, these cheeses are produced at will by injections of mould, but there is still a marked price difference.

Red Cheshire cheese is coloured artificially with *annatto*, a harmless vegetable dye made from a plant which grows in the Amazon Basin, where it is popular as a face and body paint amongst local Indian tribes. Before *annatto* came to this country, marigold and carrot juice and other not so innocuous dyes were used to colour cheese.

Farmhouse Cheshire cheese is becoming rare. Unlike the factory-made Cheshire, it is well ripened. Cheshire is excellent for toasting and for Welsh Rarebits, and was the favourite cheese of Dr Johnson.

Cheshire-Stilton

This is a type of Stilton whose flavour has something of the Cheshire quality. These cheeses are not widely sold.

Cotherstone

Sometimes called 'Yorkshire Stilton', Cotherstone cheese is now very rare. It is made in the Valley of the Tees. It is a rich cheese, becoming unctuous as it matures.

Derby

People disagree in their descriptions of Derby cheese, various authorities claiming that it resembles Lancashire or Dunlop or mild Cheddar, and even that it is identical in flavour with Double Gloucester.

Derby is at its best when it is six months old. After this, the cheese may 'disimprove' as the Irish say, due to its high moisture content. Owing to its unpredictable behaviour Derby tends to be sold too young, before it has had a chance to develop a real flavour of its own.

Sage Derby is made by putting layers of chopped sage leaves into the cheese, giving it an attractive tang and a speckled appearance. Nowadays, an essence is used which lends a blotchy and rather synthetic appearance. Some manufacturers are returning to the sage leaves, which are actually cheaper than essence, but the cheese must then be eaten fresh or it becomes too biting. This gives rise to turnover problems, and it is to be feared that convenience, as usual, may win.

Derby goes well with all but very acid fruits.

Dorset Blue Vinny

This cheese is sometimes called 'Blue Vinny' and sometimes 'Dorset Blue'. To make things simpler, the names are often combined. There is also some variation in the spelling and, as is the way with whisky, an 'e' is sometimes inserted before the final 'y'. The word 'vinny' is derived from an old Saxon name for mould. For this is one of the oldest cheeses in the country and might have been one of the finest had it not been made with skimmed milk. This gives it a dry texture which becomes so hard with age that an old story tells that a train once ran on Blue Vinnys instead of wheels. Before the hard stage is reached, the cheese is rather crumbly.

There was, at one time, a factory in Sherborne making Blue Vinnys. Now they are all made on Dorset farms and as the production is small, they are difficult to find. The cheeses are a pale straw colour with blue veins running horizontally through the centre. The flavour is pungent and may have been praised rather more than it deserves, as the rarity of this cheese makes it rather a find.

Double Gloucester

Double Gloucester, when it was made from the milk of the dark brown Gloucester cattle, was a superb cheese, but though the Gloucester milk was rich, the yield was comparatively low, and the breed has been replaced by others more productive. So, following the usual pattern, Gloucester cheese is not what it was, though it can be very good at about a year old when it has acquired a flavour somewhere between a Cheshire and a Cheddar.

During the eighteenth century the cheeses were coloured with carrot juice in order to give them a rich glow, but other cheeses followed suit and the cheesemakers of Gloucester and Berkeley had to find a different way of drawing attention to their product. The rind of the Double Gloucesters was cured to a blue-black with vegetable juices, which also protected them from mites. The process was very laborious, however, and it was decided to paint the cheeses red instead—a practice which still continues.

For the London market Double Gloucester, like Cheshire, is tinted with *annatto*. Locally, it is left in its natural, creamy colour.

Single Gloucesters are the same shape as the Double, but half as thick, and are eaten young, at about six weeks. They do not travel well and are seldom seen outside their own area where their mild, fresh flavour is much appreciated.

Lancashire

This cheese used to be a staple food of the Lancashire mill workers in the cotton towns and it is still sometimes crumbled over Lancashire hot pot to give it extra flavour. The farmhouse manufacture of Lancashire cheese is dying out.

Lancashire can be spread with a knife, and melts to make an excellent Welsh Rarebit. If it is not too young, it is also good for Mornay sauce. The cheese does not travel too well and will not keep long. In spite of this, it is appearing in shops over a wide area.

Leicester

Leicester cheese, like some famous heads of hair, is dyed a flaming red, in both cases a come-on gimmick which has no influence on the flavour of the product. The cheese, which melts in a highly desirable way, must be cut gently or it will crumble. It can develop faults in flavour which, luckily for the purchaser, are betrayed by the presence of light patches in the cheese.

Stilton

Stilton is the most august of the British cheeses and has made frequent appearances in literature. It received its first publicity, and its name, when it was sold at the Bell Inn at Stilton to travellers on the Great North Road. Which of the ladies to whom it is attributed actually invented the cheese is a matter for argument, but she must have had the devotion of a good nanny, as Stiltons need constant care and attention, requiring to be turned during ripening more frequently than other cheeses and brushed to keep them free of mites. As demand increased, the farmers' wives became slaves to their cheeses, working from 4 a.m. until dark. In 1910, the farmers of Melton Mowbray, the Dove Valley and the Vale of Belvoir founded a co-operative for the manufacture of Stilton cheese.

Where farmhouse Stiltons took eighteen months to mature, an adequately ripe Stilton of uniform quality can now be produced in four months, though the cheese will benefit greatly by longer maturing. It takes seventeen gallons of milk to make a 14-lb Stilton.

It is sad that such a magnificent, honest cheese should have become the object of so much chi-chi, being soused with port and messily spooned out of its rind. As André Simon remarked, 'A drenching with port will mask the faults of an imperfect cheese, but there is not a vintage in the world which will improve a good one.' It is true that a glass of port goes perfectly with a Stilton, but so does Chablis with oysters and you would not dream of pouring the wine into the shells. The drenching technique may have started when a landlord set an off-colour Stilton cheese to catch the drips beneath a leaky port barrel, found that the result was acceptable and the idea caught on.

Unless a Stilton is to be eaten rapidly, so that it can all be spooned out before it has time to dry, it is better to cut it in the way recommended by the Stilton Manufacturers Association. The cheese is first divided in half horizontally and the upper half stored away. Slices are then cut, a layer at a time, by drawing a knife, level, through the cheese at about half an inch below the surface. This layer can then be cut in wedges.

White Stilton

This is a pleasant, undistinguished cheese, not in the least like the blue-veined beauty it would have become if tended long enough for the moulds floating in the air of the maturing room to set to work.

White Wensleydale

Wensleydale cheeses come from the Valley of the Ure in Yorkshire, where they were first made by the monks. The original cheeses were all marbled. When white Wensleydale is just old enough to come on the market it has a fresh flavour not unlike Caerphilly. After maturing a little more it acquires a creamy Cheddar-like taste with a hint of honey.

This kind of Wensleydale, which is usually sold in small 1-lb cylinders, can be spread to make cocktail savouries and so on.

Blue Wensleydale

It is not known whether the monks who originated Wensleydale cheese were aware of the saleability of the trouble-free, immature

133

white version. Probably they would not have been interested in the quick return, which plays no part in a life of dedication.

The shape of a blue Wensleydale resembles a Stilton, though the rind is corrugated instead of crinkly, owing to the different way in which the cheese is wrapped. The flavour resembles a delicate, creamy Stilton. Like other cheeses which require considerable time and care in the making, this is becoming more and more scarce.

THE SCOTTISH CHEESES

Dunlop

When a Dunlop cheese is mature, from about four months old, it bears a strong family resemblance to a young Cheddar. It has a rather more resilient texture with a clean, sweet flavour and a mildly acid bite. It has the same useful properties too, being excellent for melting, and is at its best eaten with fresh butter and bread or biscuits. In accordance with its honest qualities, the cheese is undyed and keeps its natural creamy colour and suggestion of fresh milk.

In Scotland, Dunlop is often eaten at two months old and at this age is extremely mild and a trifle characterless.

Dunlop has been made in Ayrshire since the recipe was brought over from Ireland during the reign of Charles II.

Ayrshire Soft Cheese

This wonderfully soft, rich creamy cheese of almost a pouring consistency comes from Ayrshire cattle feeding on lush pastures in the Lowlands of Scotland. Its salty, delicate flavour blends perfectly with oatcake or crispbread. We find it excellent stirred into soups or sauces, or poured over vegetables with a dusting of chopped parsley.

Islay

Islay is a mini Dunlop.

Caithness

This is a full-fat soft cheese from the extreme North of Scotland which is aged for at least sixty days. The flavour is pleasant and medium-strong and the cheese, which is in the form of a small, plump square sealed in a wax coating inside a tartan wrapper, is a soft maize yellow.

Morven
Another North of Scotland cheese presented in the same manner and aged for the same period as the Caithness. It has a few tiny holes and a flavour and texture which somewhat recall a Dutch Gouda.

Morven is also made with a flavouring of caraway seeds.

The Highland Fine Cheeses
Until the last war it was usual for Highland housewives to bake their own bread and make their own cheese, but with the disappearance of the family milch cow a number of traditional cheeses vanished and they have only been revived owing to the enterprise of the Stone family of Blarliath Farm in Ross-shire. In 1962, following the extraordinary local demand for Highland Crowdie cheese which Mrs Stone had made from a family recipe, it was decided to turn some buildings on the farm, which were part of an old brewery of the Dukes of Sutherland, into an extension of the existing creamery. A company, Highland Fine Cheese Ltd, was formed to make cheese according to traditional recipes, using the best of the original Highland methods. In 1965 they started, through Crowson & Son, distribution on a national scale. The following are the cheeses which they are producing—over 50,000 a week at present:

Highland Crowdie
This is a slimmers' cheese, being high in protein and low in fat, but its delicate freshness is far more appetizing than our rather lumpy cottage cheese. The curd of Crowdie is finely ground so that the texture has a grain reminiscent of semolina or the flesh of certain ripe pears.

Crowdie with Cream
When there was cream to spare a Highland family would stir it into the Crowdie. Crowdie with Cream is one-third fresh double cream mixed with two-thirds of Highland Crowdie. Not quite so slimming, but absolutely delicious eaten with oatcake or crisp biscuits, and both the Crowdies go well with light red wines such

as the younger clarets—and even with a dry white wine or champagne.

Double Cream Cheese
Made from fresh double cream, this is the counterpart of the famous Continental *crème double*.

Caboc
This is an ancient cheese, originally from the Western Highlands. The recipe, which is believed to have come from Mariota de Ile, daughter of the Macdonald of the Isles in the fifteenth century, has been handed down from mother to daughter in the family of Mrs Stone.

Caboc is an unusual, firmly soft double-cream cheese rolled in toasted pinhead oatmeal. It needs no butter and is rich enough to harmonize with full-bodied red wines.

Hramsa
This traditional cheese (the name is pronounced 'Ramsa'), is made with double cream and the leaves of wild garlic gathered in the hills by the local children. The garlic leaves, which give their fresh flavour to the cheese, have always been esteemed by the Celts for their healing properties, and have even been credited with magical powers.

IRISH CHEESES

Of the cheeses made in Ireland, all but two are acknowledged copies of established brands. Let us hope that they stick to this honest approach and don't stage a re-christening party like the Danes.

Blarney
This cheese reminds one of the intriguing animal formerly in the London Zoo, the tigon—half lion and half tiger. It is a pale, mild-flavoured semi-soft cheese with the small holes of the Gruyère and the red skin of an Edam. 'It is wholly Irish in origin', says the official hand-out. 'There are no English or French Blarneys.' Indisputable.

Wexford

Wexford is also described as of wholly Irish origin. It is an orange-coloured cheese with a distinctive sharp flavour and a texture similar to Cheshire.

FOREIGN CHEESES

To describe all the interesting cheeses which are produced in France alone would fill a book, so as our space is limited we have concentrated on the foreign cheeses which are at present on sale in the United Kingdom. These are bound to increase, so we have left some blank pages at the end of the book where you can note down new arrivals as you hear of them. Friends may suggest cheeses to sample when you are on a trip abroad, or there may be discoveries which you make when travelling and which you wish to record.

The spelling of cheese names varies considerably. We have put an alternative spelling only where there might be confusion.

When writing about cheese it is difficult to describe flavour and texture. Even one's own impressions vary according to the condition of the cheese and the context in which it is eaten. All honest appraisals are subjective, and there is no accurate way of conveying them in words. So we have tried to give a guide to what may be expected of a cheese, and hope you will enjoy comparing this with what you, personally, discover.

Appenzell

This is a full-fat Swiss cheese similar in appearance to Gruyère. At an early stage in its making the cheese is steeped in a vat of white wine or cider, with added spices, which gives it a piquant though mellow flavour.

A sharp version of Appenzell called Raess is made with skim milk. Appenzell cheese was known over a thousand years ago and was recorded during the reign of Charlemagne.

Banon

Banon was originally made from goat's milk by peasants in the Dauphiné and Haute Provence. Now that Banon is in commercial production the goat's milk is often mixed with cow's. If the label does not specify the origin of the milk it will be from cows only.

These cheeses are dipped in a mixture of brandy and *marc* and then in the leaves of rosemary and winter savoury, or wrapped in chestnut leaves which have also been dipped in the brandy mixture. Traditionally they were dipped in brandy and left to ripen in stone jars.

Beaumont

This, like Reblochon, is a mountain cheese from Haute Savoie. When young, this cheese is mild and pale but it acquires a rather strong flavour and deepens in colour with age. Beaumont, which is large with an orange rind, is usually sold under the brand name of Girod.

Bel Paese

A member of the Italico group, this cheese only came on the market about fifty years ago. It is popular in many countries because of its delicate flavour, good keeping qualities and exceptional uniformity of texture. Bel Paese is an uncooked fast-ripening cheese, mature in five weeks, which is made from cow's milk by the methods originally used by the peasants in Lecco near Lake Como.

Apart from being an excellent dessert cheese, Bel Paese melts beautifully and can be used for cooking instead of ricotta, which is less widely distributed abroad.

Bleu de Bresse

In its ideal state, Bleu de Bresse, which is somewhat reminiscent of a Gorgonzola, is wonderfully soft and thickly creamy, with a rich subtle flavour in its dark blue veins. Being sold foil-wrapped and boxed it is difficult to tell whether it is in good condition, and once over-ripe it has a strong, salt taste and becomes disagreeably dry, so it is important to buy this cheese from a merchant you can trust.

Bleu des Causses

A Roquefort type of cheese but made with cow's instead of ewe's milk in the Massif Central area, and matured in limestone caves. This cheese has a high fat content and a less piquant flavour than Roquefort. A number of other blue cheeses more or less resembling Roquefort are made in central France.

Boursin and Boursault

These are two versions, made by rival companies, of the same triple cream cheese. These soft, thick creamy cheeses may be flavoured with garlic, herbs or pepper. Although wrapped and not boxed, they travel well.

Brie

For those who have never encountered a Brie in perfect condition it may be difficult to understand the ecstasy which this cheese arouses. It is really worth going to an experienced merchant and asking him to choose a cheese which is *à point*—or even travelling to the Seine-et-Marne department of France to discover the perfection of which Brie is capable.

Though Brie is made in various districts, the best is the Brie de Meaux and best of all, the farmhouse kind. This is marked 'Brie fermier' whereas the factory-made kind is marked 'Brie laitier'. It is a large round cheese and very thin.

Vivienne Marquis and Patricia Haskell in *The Cheese Book* give a very good description of the flavour of Brie, 'part mushrooms, part cream, part cognac, part earth—as earth smells upon the roots of leeks, with a shade of truffle and with something of the scent of ripe Anjou pears . . .' The texture is smooth and heavy, with a satin gloss.

Brillat-Savarin

This is also a triple cream which, unless it is well *chambré*, tends to be a little grainy. It is a fairly recent production and has an attractive appearance.

Cacciocavallo

This is a hard uncooked cheese originally made in the Province of Sorrento in Southern Italy, but it is now produced in various other regions, including England. This seems strange, as the cheese keeps and travels well, but importation has proved both difficult and expensive.

Traditionally, the curd of Cacciocavallo is shaped by hand into a distorted figure of eight, the upper part forming a small knob so that the cheeses can be linked in pairs by plaits of straw. They are then hung astride a pole to dry after passing through a salt bath. This gave rise to the name Cacciocavallo.

The body of the cheese is smooth and firm and almost white, with a flavour rather like a mild, buttery Cheddar, and the rind is yellow and shiny. Table cheeses ripen for 2–4 months, and those for grating from six months to a year.

Caciotta

There are many local varieties of Caciotta, which is made from cow's, ewe's or goat's milk in different parts of Italy, and the flavour varies accordingly. All have in common a smallish, flat cylindrical shape.

Camembert

Since Camembert was allegedly invented by Marie Hamel (whose statue, unfortunately, lost its head in the War) it has been copied all over the place and has cropped up in many strange forms. It is a widely travelled cheese and sometimes arrives in such a tired condition that a local copy may actually prove more acceptable than the original.

Before Monsieur Ridel invented the chip box, Camemberts were sold half a dozen at a time, wrapped in straw, in the markets.

Camembert once cut will continue to ripen normally. The symptoms of immaturity are similar to those for Brie and the period when a Camembert is perfect lasts only for a few days. Once over-ripe, the cheese has a bitter taste and a horrible taint of ammonia. The rind looks blotchy with a rusty deposit.

Canned Camemberts are not satisfactory and range from positively nasty to just different. Even the best have a faint taste of tinned milk.

Canadian Cheddar

The Canadians make the best Cheddar outside the British Isles and the matured wheels resemble our own Farmhouse. It is very sad that the average age of the cheese-makers of Ontario is sixty-two, and young men are not training for the craft. So it seems that this splendid cheese will disappear.

Carré de l'Est

This is a square cheese somewhat resembling a Camembert in flavour and texture. It is soft and slightly salted with a high fat content. One type has a washed crust and the other, reddish-brown and slightly mouldy on the outside, is described as '*fleuri*'.

Chèvre

Chèvre is a generic term for cheeses made with goat's milk. A large variety of these are made in France but few are exported and many never even reach Paris. The young ones have an agreeable bite and the mature tend to be extremely strong. A number of chèvre cheeses are imported into this country.

Coulommiers

Less mature and mellow than Brie, though of the same family, Coulommiers is in season from November to March. It is, in fact, a poor relation, being smaller, thicker and less elegant. It carries a hint of Camembert.

Danish Blue, or Danablu

Danish Blue was produced just before the First World War by Marius Boel, who grew the special mould on home-baked barley bread. The cheese is strongly veined and has a buttery consistency resulting from the creamy homogenized milk of which it is made. The export version has a higher cream content, lighter veining, and lacks the special minty tang of that produced for the home market, and it tends to pall after a time. It is excellent, however, when combined with other ingredients in spreads, sauces and salad dressings.

Demi-Sel

Demi-Sel is a fresh cream cheese containing 2 per cent of salt, not enough to give a salt taste. These small square cheeses, which mostly come from Normandy, are wrapped in square packages. They are sold under various brand names such as Pommel and Gervais.

Dolcelatte

This is a factory-made member of the Gorgonzola family, very mild, and with a delicate pale greenish complexion.

Edam

The Dutch have been exporting cheese for hundreds of years, since the thirteenth century in fact, and it is not surprising that they should have specialized in Edam and Gouda, two trouble-free cheeses with unsurpassed keeping qualities, robust enough to be bundled into the hold of a ship and able to resist extremes of temperature.

Edam, the football cheese with the crimson rind, is made from partially skimmed milk and quickly becomes firm enough to hold its characteristic shape. Like Gouda, it has when young a mild, clean flavour and smooth texture, excellent for slicing, though not suitable for grating or cooking. It is best eaten with bread or biscuits and butter.

As it ages, Edam darkens and hardens and takes on a surprisingly rich and unusual flavour.

Emmenthal

It is gradually coming to be accepted in this country that the cheese with the large holes which used to be known as Gruyère is, in fact, Emmenthal. It would be interesting to discover how it was that this cheese went so long under a false name. Now that the name is being straightened out it looks as though the Swiss were determined to look after the pronunciation too, as their publicity material omits the usual 'h' in the name which should not be pronounced anyway.

Emmenthal, which is a firm pale cheese with a wonderful, hazelnut flavour and a hint of the rich mountain milk from which it is made, has been copied, and even faked, all over the world. The characteristic large holes have been gouged out of other cheeses or stamped from cheese slices in a clumsy attempt to pass them off as genuine emmenthal. This cheese is excellent, grated, for cooking and is sometimes mixed with grated Parmesan.

To make genuine Emmenthal requires consummate skill and even a finely tuned ear and touch, since the moment when the holes have reached the right size and the cheese must be moved from the warm fermentation chambers to cool ripening rooms is judged by the sounds given off when the cheese is tapped. At this point the cheese is aged from four to ten months.

Emmenthal cheeses have gradually grown from their original size of about 10 lb to a legal export minimum of 145 lb, and some even reach 220 lb. These huge cheeses are protected by a thick natural rind which, being porous, allows the cheese to mature with the help of the salt which is rubbed in after washing.

It is sad that the Swiss cheese-makers have yielded to the temptation to make a rindless Emmenthal which, as might be expected, loses most of its character once it is stripped of its plastic overcoat.

Epoisses
This is a smooth cheese from the Côte d'Or made in the form of a small cylinder and sometimes flavoured with black pepper, fennel seeds or cloves, or soaked in white wine or *marc*.

Esrom
Esrom is a close relation of Port-Salut, made in Denmark. It has more character than the French original and is sometimes inclined to be a little strong. It has the advantage, though, of being much cheaper than the French cheese.

If Esrom is chilled when you buy it, be sure that it has no trace of pungent smell, and taste it, if you can.

Excelsior
A rich cream cheese with the texture, though not the fat content, of a triple cream. It belongs to the same family as Brillat-Savarin.

Fontina
Fontina is a wonderful cheese made, traditionally, from ewe's milk in the Val d'Aosta on the Swiss border of Italy. It is a splendid, stable cheese having something of the tang of a Gruyère on a sweet, nutty foundation of the best Emmenthal. At room temperature, the creamy texture is satin-smooth.

There are many imitations such as Fontal and Fontinella, but the true Fontina d'Aosta is wheel-shaped, creamy in colour, punctured here and there by very small holes, and encased in a light brown, waxed rind with an interesting, uneven colour pattern.

Fontina melts beautifully and is the basis of the Piedmontese *fonduta*, when it is soaked in milk, melted and served with white truffles.

Fourme d'Ambert
This is a drum-shaped, sharp blue cheese made in the Cantal district of the Auvergne. It is slightly salt, and crumbly in texture.

Fromage de Monsieur

A double-cream cheese first made in Normandy about seventy-five years ago. It is now produced industrially and exported in small round chip boxes. Having a high fat content, it will pass muster before it is really ripe, and it is unusual to find a Monsieur that is not intolerable condition, though occasionally one may be a little over-salted. When mature, this is an excellent cheese.

Gaperon

A buttermilk cheese from the Auvergne which can be eaten either fresh, or ripened on a bed of rye straw. Slightly acid when young, it finally becomes dry and piquant.

Gjetost

Described as the 'Norwegian national cheese' and pronounced 'Yet-ost', this strange blend of cow's and goat's milk is making a name for itself in Europe. It has the same café-au-lait colour and appearance as a light fudge, and even a sweet taste. The consistency is firm enough to allow it to be sliced with one of the special slotted cheese-cutting gadgets.

Though it can be melted and used to make sauces for game and so on, Gjetost is best eaten with soft breads, including baps, thin crisp flatbread or biscuits and butter.

Gorgonzola

Originally made in a small village of this name near Milan, Gorgonzola is now produced over a wide area in the plains of Northern Italy. It is a splendid creamy cheese with a special rich flavour and pale, greenish veining.

Gorgonzola, which is exported in large quantities, is at its best after five or six months.

Gouda

Gouda, which is made from whole milk, is not initially firm enough to hold the cannon ball form of Edam and is produced in the conventional wheel shape.

Gouda is rather similar in flavour and texture to Edam and has the same long history. Like Edam, it changes with age from a dependable rather uninspiring cheese to something really memorable, especially if it bears the mark 'Boerenkaas' which shows that it is a farmhouse cheese. Without tasting a Gouda, it is still possible to have some idea of its age by seeing if the sides have swelled out from the clean vertical of a young cheese to the rounded contours of one that has matured.

Gruyère
This is not the smooth, nutty cheese with the large eyes which has been known under the name of Gruyère for so long, but a smaller cheese with smaller holes and a rind not smooth, but crinkled and a little greasy. The texture is creamier and the flavour a little more acid than Emmenthal.

The two cheeses come from nearby areas, Gruyère from the French side of the Jura and Emmenthal from the eastward slopes. The former is more popular in Switzerland and the latter abroad. Both are excellent for cooking and combine with one another, melted in white wine, to make a Swiss fondue.

The French make a good Gruyère, both in the country bordering on Switzerland and in the Haute Savoie.

Jarlsberg
Once more, the feeling that any cheese with large eyes is bound to be a 'Swiss' is apt to lead to misunderstanding. Whilst a very pleasant cheese, Jarlsberg lacks the rich subtleties of an Emmenthal and, to be fair, the Norwegian official hand-outs describe it as a 'Norwegian speciality' and the flavour as 'a cross between Gouda and Emmenthal'.

Kernhem
About ten years ago the Dutch developed this new cheese of a smooth, full-bodied type similar to many of those formerly made by the monks. It is worth trying.

Kümmel
Cheeses from various countries are flavoured with caraway seeds or *kümmel*, which give a distinctive aromatic taste and make a pleasant contrast with the smooth texture of such cheeses.

Langres
Langres is an ancient cheese going back nearly fourteen hundred years to the time of the Merovingian kings, though its production

is now rapidly declining. Fine and creamy and not unlike a Livarot, this cheese is best at about four months.

Leyden
The university town of Leyden in Holland has produced a cheese branded with the crossed keys of the university arms, and flavoured with caraway seeds. It is sold either young, or matured as 'old Leyden'. The cheese is firm and pale yellow with green markings. In the older version the caraway seeds themselves seem to have matured to add an especial punch to the flavour.

Le Roi
This triple-cream cheese is a recent arrival here. When the cheese is *chambré*, its bright yellow body is traversed by tiny glistening rivulets. The crust is a crinkled pale fawn with fine etchings of white mould.

Limburger
Though often believed to have originated in Germany, this cheese was first made in Liège and sold in Belgium. Now, it is copied all over the place. It is a soft-textured cheese with a strong, rather coarse flavour which is not to everybody's taste.

Livarot
Livarot, which is named after a small town near Caen in Normandy, is one of the very strong cheeses, but subtler than Limburger. The ripening process, which is carried out in closed rooms after salting, turning and salting again, is all-important. The process takes place without any injection or spraying and the rind slowly turns to a dark red-brown (assisted by a final touch of colouring matter) surrounding a soft yellow body. The cheese goes well with cold, dry white wine or Calvados, and crisp bread or biscuits. The rind is removed before the cheese is eaten.

Livarots are not easy to export, as the soft ripe body tends to escape from the crust and has to be supported by bands of split reeds or a wrapping of sedge, but some reach this country in good condition. They are in season during autumn and winter.

Maroilles
Maroilles cheese was first made a thousand years ago by the

monks of the Abbey of Thierache near Lille and it is an important member of the group of strong cheeses. Nicknamed *Vieux Puant* or Old Stinker, the soft golden body of the cheese is less alarming than the powerful odour of its rind would suggest.

After four months Maroilles is like a stronger Pont l'Evêque with a similar basic taste and texture, and the same square shape. Maroilles Gris, which is twice salted, takes twice as long to mature and is really powerful.

Mozzarella

Originally from the Province of Naples and made of buffalo's milk, Mozzarella is now made in other parts of Italy as well, using cow's milk which is quite a satisfactory substitute.

Fresh Mozzarella, which is white and tender and oozing with whey, is used in many regional dishes and is the mainstay of pizza.

Cacciocavallo is really a matured Mozzarella.

Since every scrap of food was precious in the hungry South, the whey which ran out when mozzarella was made would be turned into butter. To store this safely in the heat, the peasants contrived to fit it into the centre of a cheese—a far greater miracle than the lump of iced butter inside a *Côtelette à la Kiev*. The cheese protected the butter, and the butter kept the cheese moist, and when the cheese was cut, the two complemented one another perfectly. This wonderful invention was called Manteca. Now, smaller versions called Burrini are being imported.

Munster

This cheese, which is semi-soft and powerful in flavour, belongs to the same group as Maroilles and Pont l'Evêque. It is made in the Vosges and in various districts of Alsace. Sometimes it is flavoured with cumin seeds.

Mycella

Formerly called Danish Gorgonzola, this cheese was re-christened some time ago. The name comes from the mycelium mould which produces the green veins running through the yellowish body. It is a pleasant full-fat cheese, not so well known as Danish Blue, but far more subtle.

Neufchâtel

Made from exceptionally rich milk in the department of Seine-Inférieure, this cheese changes as it matures from a creamy softness to a firm texture and a fairly strong flavour. The small heart-shaped or cylindrical cheeses are produced in many local varieties under different names.

Parmesan

Parmesan cheese was already famous in the thirteenth century, when it was mentioned by Boccaccio. It is a cheese whose life span is measured in years rather than months.

At first, Parmesan was made in the neighbourhood of Parma, but its production gradually spread to Reggio Emilia and a large area north of the Po. In order to settle disputes, the Italian Government decreed that cheese from the original area should have the right to be called Parmigiano-Reggiano, whilst that produced north of the Po would be known as Grana Padano, *grana* being a generic term for such grainy cheeses.

The production of Parmigiano-Reggiano is governed by very strict regulations. The milk of which it is made must be absolutely uniform in quality and the cheese-making season, which opens in mid-April, closes on November 11th. During the final ripening period, the cheese is rubbed with a mixture of oil and *terra umbra*, which is a mineral-rich, blackish earth. This completes the dark, gleaming rind which protects the cheese from the damaging effects of light. The older a Parmesan cheese, the more valuable, and the gradings Vecchio, Stravecchio and Stravecchione show whether they have matured for two, three, or four years.

Grana Padano, on the other hand, is variable in character, due to the uneven quality of the milk from which it is made and the fact that winter cheeses are not so good as those made from summer milking.

Grated Parmesan is excellent in sauces and soufflés and for sprinkling, but it is also wonderful as an after-dinner cheese. The only difficulty is that one is inclined to eat too much, and a good Parmesan is very expensive.

Shopkeepers in Italy used to advise one to wrap a precious piece of Parmesan in an oily rag and put it in a cool place. Now, they are inclined to murmur 'Frigidaire' and look uncomfortable when pressed.

Pecorino

This generic term covers all the cheeses made in Italy from ewe's milk. The two best-known kinds are Pecorino Romano, which is very sharp, and Pecorino Sardo from Sardinia.

The rind of the Pecorino is rubbed with oil and a yellow earth, and the body is white or pale yellow, and compact. The table version is matured for only 5–8 months and is milder and less hard than the fully-ripened kind.

Pecorino is used in the South as a substitute for Parmesan, but there are certain dishes, such as the Genoese *pesto* sauce made with oil, basil and garlic, which call for Pecorino.

Petit-Suisse

These cheeses are not, as might be supposed, Swiss, but are named after a young Swiss cowherd who suggested to his employer on a Seine-et-Oise farm that she should add fresh cream to the curd used for cheese-making. This resulted in a delicate, faintly sour cheese which is excellent with castor sugar and fresh fruit. These cheeses are now sold in small cylinders in a paper casing.

Pipo Crem'

This is the export name for the French cheese Grièges. It is, perhaps, the most delicate and moist of the blue-veined cheeses owing to the extra cream it contains. Since it is sold by weight and one can inspect the cut surfaces, it is easier to choose than many of the other blues.

Pont l'Evêque

Most of this cheese is now produced industrially in Normandy, though some is still made on the farms in the Pays d'Auge. It is one of the great monastic cheeses with a long history, already considered venerable when it was re-christened in the thirteenth century. The flavour bears a similarity to Camembert, but where this cheese becomes runny with age, Pont l'Evêque dries up and sticks to its paper wrapping, losing its plump contours and yielding texture.

A perfect Pont l'Evêque has a pale yellow body with small shining holes which gradually fill up at room temperature. The flavour is rich and distinctive and the texture clinging to the point where it will draw out in soft strings. Pont l'Evêque, like its companions from Normandy, goes well with cider and Calvados. It is best in winter and autumn.

Port-Salut or Port-du-Salut

This cheese was originally made by the Trappist monks of Entrammes. When a group of Trappists returned from exile in Switzerland after the French Revolution they re-named the priory the Abbey of Notre Dame de Port-du-Salut and proceeded to make cheeses, using the knowledge they had acquired during their enforced sojourn in the Swiss Alps. Some of these cheeses were sent for sale to Paris and became so popular that the monks registered the name, and later sold the right of manufacture to a commercial cheese-maker. In 1936 the monks were awarded the sole legal right to both the name and its contraction, Port-Salut, but in spite of this it is still pirated.

Young Port-Salut is bland and resembles the buttery cheeses, but as it mellows it acquires a subtle flavour which goes well with full-bodied red wines and with puddings or fruit. The texture is similar to a Bel Paese and with maturity it takes on something of the flavour of a Camembert.

Provolone

Whilst the word 'provo', meaning ovoid, has been extended with a number of charming Italian terminations to indicate a range of sizes from the tiny Provoloncino to the large Provolone, the shape may resemble anything from a pear or a sausage to a gourd. The firm pale cheese fills out the curves of its glistening amber skin, which is grooved by the twine which has bound it. The flavour of the cheese is similar to Cacciocavallo, but with a more interesting softly smoky tang, in the case of Provolone Dolce. Provolone Piccante is more strongly flavoured and sometimes almost too sharp.

Reblochon

Reblochon is a sort of Alpine Port-Salut made in the mountains of the Haute Savoie from the rich milk of the fawn Tarentais cows. Similar in shape to a Camembert, it is at its best from May to September. The pale cream body is firmer than a Camembert and the crust varies from orange to a ruddy chestnut colour. Once past its prime, Reblochon turns bitter.

Ricotta

Like other peasants in the poorer regions of Southern and Central Europe, the frugal Italians discovered that an excellent creamy cheese could be made from the albumen in the whey left when other cheeses were made.

Ricotta is like a very delicate, smoother and creamier cottage cheese. The flavour is so adaptable that it makes the ideal base for *canelloni* stuffing or *lasagne* and is wonderful whipped into tiny dumplings with egg, spinach and nutmeg. It is also very good just eaten with sugar and cinnamon or ground black coffee, or layered into fruit tarts and puddings.

Ricotta is sometimes aged until it is dry and then used for grating.

Rigottes

Small round cheeses made from cow's milk, sometimes mixed with goat's. Those from the Lyons area have a fairly firm texture and a pale yellow crust; the Rigottes de Condrieux are softer with a reddish crust.

Robbiola

This cheese comes from the northern part of Lombardy. It is a rich cheese which may be either a mild *dolce* or a *piccante*. The latter is sold, wrapped, in portions of about ¼ lb.

Roquefort

The discovery of Roquefort was one of the famous legendary accidents and its happy result was known to the Romans and praised by Pliny. (I refer to the shepherd's abandoned bread and curd cheese found days later covered with the now famous blue mould.)

Roquefort, the greatest of all the blues, is made by injecting curd from sheep's milk with *penicillium roqueforti* and ripening it in the cool, draughty caves of the Causses district south of the Massif Central. The name Roquefort was already protected by Charles VI of France in the fifteenth century but the district of Roquefort itself was too small to supply increasing demand for the cheese and, despite repeated edicts, the area where Roquefort cheese could legally be produced was gradually extended to cover almost the whole of the Causses district.

The ripening of Roquefort is more important than the quality of the milk used, and as the production of local ewe's milk is inadequate, supplies are drawn from places as far distant as Corsica, in the shape of curd already inoculated with the special blue mould. This is sent to Roquefort for ripening.

St Florentin

St Florentin is a triple-cream cheese which has been made in the Auxerre for nearly a thousand years, but it was not until recently that sufficient was produced to allow of export. This mild, creamy cheese is packed in foil and may be either round or crescent-shaped.

St Nectaire

St Nectaire is a monastery cheese which has been made in the mountains of Auvergne since the Middle Ages from the milk of the same Tarentais cows as Reblochon. This cheese ripens on mats of rye straw in deep cellars formerly used for wine, and develops a crust of blended yellow, red and white. It combines the characteristic Port-Salut flavour with the light mountain-cheese taste of Emmenthal and goes very well with full-bodied red wines as well as rosés and dry white wine.

St Paulin

This cheese is almost indistinguishable from Port-Salut and might even have masqueraded as such were it not for the question of infringement of copyright. It has the same pale, smooth body and a thin beige crust.

Samsoe

Samsoe, which is named after an island in the Kattegat, used to be called Danish Swiss, but except for the small holes it more nearly resembles Edam, with a faint nutty undertone. More Samsoe is produced than any other cheese in Denmark. At six months old, it is at its best.

The Danes make a number of cheeses similar to Samsoe, some of which are imported into this country. In 1956, the Danish

Government re-christened eleven of their cheeses with names such as Fynbo, Maribo and Tybo. But in spite of their different names and the variety of their shapes, sizes and colours, there is very little to distinguish the flavour of one from another. Danbo, a member of the group, used to be called Danish Steppe.

Sbrinz

This is the forerunner of all the typical Swiss cheeses and was already famous in the time of the Romans. When young, it is similar to Emmenthal and Gruyère but with age it becomes granular and very hard, and takes on increasingly the quality of Parmesan. It is excellent as a table cheese and for grating; and at half the price of Parmesan one can enjoy it with an easy conscience.

Sbrinz takes a minimum of one year to mature for ordinary use. At this point, the rind is rubbed with linseed oil to hinder further evaporation and the cheese can then continue to mature and improve almost indefinitely. It is even said to be good after a hundred years. The older cheeses do not, as a rule, leave Switzerland.

Schabzieger or Sapsago

This is a hard cheese for grating, light green in colour and made in the shape of a truncated cone. Like Sbrinz, it has a long history, four or five hundred years at least. Schabzieger, which is also known as Sapsago and by various other names, is made in Germany as well as Switzerland. Basically a rather dull sour skimmed milk cheese, it gains a distinctive sharp flavour from the leaves of blue melilot, a kind of clover which is said to have been first used by itinerant Irish monks, either because they liked the taste or were perhaps homesick.

Smoked Cheese

Smoked cheeses travel well and it seems inevitable that the number imported to this country will increase. German and Austrian smoked cheeses in large or small sausage shapes with the same firm texture and thin gleaming skin as Provolone are on sale now. They are very convenient for picnics or for eating a little at a time.

Stracchino

For centuries the cows driven down from the Alpine pastures

through the Plain of Lombardy to over-winter in the South were *stracca* or tired after their long journey, so the cheese made from their milk was called Stracchino. This rich, beautifully creamy cheese has only recently been imported, as it does not stand up to travel as well as its near relative, Taleggio.

Taleggio

This is the only matured member of a group of soft white Italian cheeses, none of which are good travellers. It is a post-World War I product of the town of the same name in Lombardy. After ripening for at least forty days, Taleggio has a rough pinkish crust and a smooth creamy body. The bland flavour, which becomes stronger with age, has a faint tang. Be careful to see that this cheese is plump and resilient without any unpleasant smell, and that its wrappings are clean and loose, otherwise it is over-ripe.

Tête de Moine

A full-fat semi-hard cheese from the Bernese Jura which is rather different from the usual type of monastery cheese, being milder in flavour.

Tilsit

This was originally an East German cheese. Tilsit made in Norway is now being exported to Britain. The flavour, which somewhat resembles a Danish Port-Salut, is full and a little sharp, and the body is pierced with tiny holes.

Tome

This is a Savoyard dialect word for cheese and covers a whole group of varying character. Tome au Raisin is easily recognized by its crust of purplish-black dried grape skins and pips. Without this intriguing coating it seems rather doubtful whether people would be interested in this white, slightly stodgy cheese.

It is surprising to see in some shops Tome au Raisin labelled 'Spread'. This, we understand, is to conform with designations laid down by our food authorities.

Tome de Savoie, with its light body and ruddy rind, resembles a mild Danish Port-Salut.

Vacherin

There are various kinds of Vacherin, both Swiss and French. The Vacherin Fribourgeois, which is sometimes used to make Swiss fondue, is tender beneath the rind and firmer in the centre. It is milder than Gruyère and paler. The softer version of this cheese is eaten with a spoon.

Vacherin Mont d'Or is made in the Canton of Vaud during the autumn and sold, after two or three months' ripening, between mid-October and January. It is a soft white, creamy cheese with an excellent flavour. The rind is sometimes bound with strips of birch bark.

The French Vacherin des Beauges is becoming rare. What is still available is made from the especially rich milk of cattle which come down from the high pastures to graze on second-crop hay. This cheese, too, is eaten with a spoon.

RECIPES

COLD SAVOURIES

Hors-d'œuvre in Aspic

1¾ pints (1 litre) aspic made with white wine or stock and some sherry ✦ ½ cucumber ✦ salt and pepper ✦ 3 tablespoons cream ✦ ½ teaspoon chopped tarragon ✦ lettuce leaves ✦ 4 small tomatoes ✦ 5 hard-boiled eggs ✦ 4 anchovy fillets

Pour a ½-inch layer of aspic into a glass dish and let it set in the refrigerator. Sprinkle the sliced cucumber with salt, drain well and arrange it, seasoned and mixed with cream and chopped tarragon, on the aspic. Surround this with shredded lettuce and rings of peeled tomato. Chop one egg and sprinkle it over the tomato rings. Halve the others, garnish them with strips of anchovy and arrange them on the dish. Cover with the rest of the aspic and chill.

Pear Hors-d'œuvre

4 cooking pears ✦ 5 lumps sugar ✦ ⅓ pint (2 dl) water ✦ 3 teaspoons lemon juice ✦ ½ cucumber ✦ salt and pepper ✦ 1 carton yoghurt ✦ 2 tomatoes ✦ 3 tablespoons oil ✦ 1 tablespoon wine vinegar ✦ lettuce leaves ✦ 12 spring onions

Make a syrup with the sugar, water and lemon juice. Halve the peeled pears lengthwise, scoop out the cores and cook them in the syrup until soft but still firm. Drain and cool, reserving the syrup for a pudding. Dice the sliced cucumber, sprinkle with salt, and let stand for 20 minutes. Rinse, drain and pat dry. Season and add yoghurt. Peel and pip the tomatoes, chop them roughly and sprinkle with a dressing made by mixing oil, vinegar and seasoning. Garnish with spring onions trimmed to leave a little of the green stalk.

Parsley Balls

8 oz (200 g) cheese ✦ 2 tablespoons beer or dry white
wine ✦ 1 tablespoon Dijon
mustard ✦ butter ✦ salt and
pepper ✦ a large handful
parsley

Grate the cheese, add the beer or
wine, mustard and enough butter to
make a smooth firm paste. Season, and
make balls the size of a walnut, and
roll them in chopped parsley. Chill in
the refrigerator until ready to serve.

Paprika Balls

8 oz (200 g) cream cheese ✦
1 teaspoon softened butter ✦
1 egg yolk ✦ 1 teaspoon
kirsch ✦ salt and pepper ✦
paprika

Work all the ingredients but the paprika together and make into balls the
size of a small walnut. Sprinkle with
paprika and chill for half an hour.

Russian Stuffed Peppers

4 plump green peppers ✦
5 oz (125 g) cottage or cream
cheese ✦ 2 shallots ✦ 1 tablespoon paprika ✦ salt and
pepper

Plunge the peppers into boiling salt
water. When they are tender, drain
them without breaking, peel them and
carefully remove the seeds and stems.
Mix thoroughly the cheese, chopped
shallots and seasoning. The mixture
must be firm with a definite pink
tinge. Stuff the peppers and put them
in the refrigerator. When they are very
cold, cut them in slices.

Pickled Eggs

1¾ pints (1 litre) cider vinegar or white wine vinegar ✦
a walnut-sized piece of
peeled root ginger ✦ 8 pep-
per-corns or a small chilli
pepper ✦ a small piece of
cinnamon stick ✦ 4 cloves ✦
2 tablespoons brown sugar
✦ 1 clove garlic ✦ 14 hard-
boiled eggs

Simmer the vinegar, sugar and spices
for 15 minutes in an enamelled saucepan, then cool and strain. Arrange 14
hard-boiled eggs in jars, cover them
with spiced vinegar and cover securely.
They will be ready for use in 3 weeks.

Stuffed Brussels Sprouts

1 lb (400 g) brussels sprouts ✦ 4 oz (100 g) cottage or cream cheese ✦ 1 tablespoon grated horse-radish ✦ salt and pepper ✦ about 1 tablespoon fresh cream

Choose medium-sized sprouts. Trim off wilted leaves and cut the bases so that they stand upright. Plunge them into an uncovered saucepan of boiling salted water for 4 minutes. Drain. Mix the cheese, horse-radish and seasoning with enough cream to make a smooth paste. Arrange the sprouts in a dish, separate the leaves and stuff delicately. Chill for half an hour.

SOUPS

Stracciatella

This is one version of a soup which is very popular in Italy. Since the egg is poured into the boiling broth it curdles and floats in the soup like scraps of rag or *stracci.*

3 eggs ✦ 2 tablespoons grated Parmesan ✦ 1 tablespoon white breadcrumbs ✦ ½ teaspoon grated lemon rind ✦ salt and pepper ✦ flour ✦ 1¾ pints (1 litre) chicken broth

Beat the eggs with the cheese, breadcrumbs, lemon rind, salt and pepper and enough flour to turn the mixture into a thin cream. Heat the broth and when it is boiling, gently pour in the egg mixture, whisking as you do so. Remove from the fire after 2 minutes and sprinkle with parsley.

Garlic Soup with Egg

4 trimmed slices white bread ✦ 2 tablespoons wine vinegar ✦ 5 oz (125 g) skinned almonds ✦ 4 cloves garlic ✦ 2 tablespoons olive oil ✦ 1¾ pints (1 litre) chicken broth ✦ salt and pepper ✦ 4 eggs

Soak the bread in vinegar, squeeze dry, and crumble. Pound the almonds, garlic and oil. This can be done in a blender. Add the hot seasoned broth little by little. Return it to the fire, removing the pan as soon as it boils. Break an egg into each bowl, pour in the soup and serve.

Cheese Soup

2 oz (50 g) butter ✦ 2 table-spoons flour ✦ 1¾ pints (1 litre) milk ✦ 8 oz (200 g) grated Emmenthal or Par-mesan cheese ✦ 7 table-spoons fresh cream ✦ salt, pepper and paprika

Make an extremely thin béchamel sauce (p. 108) and stir in the cheese. When this has melted, remove the pan from the fire, add cream, salt and pep-per and pour the soup into 4 plates. Sprinkle with paprika and serve.

Emergency Soup

This is Marion Smith's Scottish recipe.

3 tablespoons oats ✦ 1 pint hot water ✦ 1 onion ✦ 1 pint (6 dl) milk ✦ 6 medium-sized potatoes ✦ 1 oz (25 g) butter ✦ salt and pepper ✦ chopped parsley

Put the porridge oats into a bowl with hot water and let them stand, covered. Chop the onion finely and infuse in the milk without boiling. Meanwhile cook potatoes in their skins, peel and mash. Beat in the milk, onion and butter. Season, and add the strained liquid from the oats. Bring to the boil and sprinkle with chopped parsley.

Chestnut Soup

1 lb (400 g) chestnuts ✦ 1 onion ✦ 1 oz (25 g) butter ✦ 1 pint (6 dl) milk ✦ chicken broth ✦ salt and pepper ✦ ½ teaspoon sugar ✦ 6–7 table-spoons fresh cream ✦ croûtons

Cut a cross in each chestnut. Heat in a moderate oven until they peel easily. Soften chestnuts and chopped onion in butter for 10 minutes. Add milk and broth and cook for an hour, then put through the food mill and return to the fire. Season, add the sugar and cream and heat without boiling. Serve with fried croûtons.

Toasted Flour Soup

This is a Swiss recipe.

1 oz (25 g) butter ✦ 2 table-spoons flour ✦ 1 small onion ✦ 2 pints (12 dl) milk ✦ salt and pepper ✦ 2 eggs

Lightly brown the flour and butter to-gether, stirring with a wooden spoon. Add the chopped onion and the milk, little by little, being careful to avoid lumps. Season, and simmer for 5 minutes. Beat the eggs with 2 table-spoons of milk, in the tureen, and add the strained soup, beating constantly.

Sour Milk Soup (from Austria)

4 potatoes ✦ 2 hard-boiled eggs ✦ 2 tablespoons flour ✦ 1 pint (6 dl) sour milk or buttermilk ✦ a bunch fennel leaves ✦ ½ oz (15 g) butter ✦ 1 teaspoon caraway seeds ✦ 1 pint (6 dl) water ✦ salt and pepper ✦ 6–7 teaspoons sour cream

Boil the potatoes in their jackets, then peel and cube them. Coarsely chop the still-warm hard-boiled eggs. Mix the sour milk, flour and chopped fennel. Stir the butter and caraway seeds together in a saucepan and cook for 10 minutes. Add the sour milk little by little but do not boil. Add the sliced potatoes and chopped hard-boiled eggs, season and finish with the cream. If the soup boils the milk will curdle.

Haddock Soup

Marion Smith's recipe from Scotland.

smoked haddock weighing about 12 oz (300 g) ✦ 2 medium-sized onions ✦ 4 tablespoons flour ✦ 1 pint (6 dl) milk ✦ 5 tablespoons dry white wine ✦ salt and pepper ✦ nutmeg ✦ 1 tablespoon chopped parsley ✦ 1 hard-boiled egg

Put the haddock and the whole onions into a frying pan and cover with cold water. Bring slowly to the boil and simmer for 10 minutes. Lift out the fish and remove the skin and bones and put it with the chopped onions into a saucepan. Sprinkle with flour and mix smoothly, adding the cold milk, little by little, and the strained liquid from the haddock. Add the wine, pepper, nutmeg and salt if required. Bring to the boil and pour into a soup tureen which contains the cream. Sprinkle with chopped parsley and hard-boiled egg.

This soup can also be made with cod, but in this case, make a final sprinkling of paprika.

Consommé with Tomato Flan

2 eggs ✦ ¼ pint (1½ dl) milk ✦ 7 tablespoons thin tomato purée ✦ ½ cup grated cheese ✦ ½ teaspoon wine vinegar ✦ salt and pepper ✦ a pinch sugar ✦ 2 pints (12 dl) chicken or beef bouillon ✦ chives

Beat together the eggs, tomato purée, cheese, hot milk, vinegar, salt, pepper and sugar. Pour the mixture into a rectangular shallow ovenproof dish and cook surrounded by hot water in a moderate oven (350°F, 180°C, Gas 4) for 45 minutes.
Heat the bouillon and pour it into four plates. Cut the hot flan into squares and divide them between the plates. Sprinkle with chopped chives and serve.

Cream of Carrots

1 oz (25 g) butter ✦ 1 chopped onion ✦ 1 lb (400 g) carrots ✦ 1¾ pints (1 litre) milk ✦ a pinch sugar, salt ✦ ½ teaspoon paprika ✦ 1–2 tablespoons fresh cream ✦ parsley

Heat the butter in a saucepan and sweat the onion until tender, but not brown. Add the carrots, sliced in rounds, cover and cook gently for 10 minutes. Add sugar, seasoning and milk. Cook until the carrots are tender. Put through a Mouli or blender and re-heat. Just before serving stir in the cream and sprinkle with chopped parsley.

Cold Soup with Yoghurt

4 tomatoes ✦ 1 small cucumber ✦ 2 cloves garlic ✦ 4 tablespoons wine (or cider) vinegar ✦ salt and cayenne pepper ✦ ½ teaspoon paprika ✦ 3 cartons yoghurt

Peel the vegetables, slice them finely and put them in a salad bowl with the salt and vinegar. Mix well and let stand for several hours. Put through a Mouli or mixer and then a hair sieve. Add cayenne pepper, paprika and yoghurt. Mix well and chill for 2 hours. Serve very cold.

Buttermilk and Cucumber Soup

2 small cucumbers ✦ 2 cloves garlic ✦ 3 tablespoons wine (or cider) vinegar ✦ salt and pepper ✦ 1¾ pints (1 litre) buttermilk ✦ 1 family-sized carton yoghurt or ½ pint (3 dl) fresh cream ✦ mint or fennel

Grate the unpeeled cucumbers fairly finely. Add crushed garlic, vinegar, salt and pepper and steep for an hour. Stir in the buttermilk and chill for 2 hours. Just before serving add the yoghurt or cream and a little chopped mint or fennel.

A few shelled shrimps or prawns make an excellent addition.

Portuguese Soup

1¾ pints (1 litre) chicken broth ✦ 2 eggs ✦ ¾ cup white breadcrumbs ✦ ¼ cup chopped parsley ✦ 1 tablespoon lemon juice

Bring the broth to the boil and stir in, a spoonful at a time, the eggs, breadcrumbs, parsley and lemon juice which have been well mixed. Take care to avoid lumps.

LUNCHEON AND SUPPER DISHES

Tomato Eggs on Croûtons

4 tomatoes ✦ olive oil ✦ 2 cloves garlic ✦ salt and pepper ✦ 4 basil leaves ✦ 8 rounds of white bread, trimmed ✦ 4 slices ham ✦ 1 oz (25 g) butter ✦ 8 eggs

Skin, pip and roughly chop the tomatoes. Cook the seasoned tomato in oil which has been flavoured by frying the garlic for a minute or two and then withdrawing it. Add a little water, if required, to form a purée, and the basil, chopped. In another pan, fry the bread and put it, drained, on a hot dish. Turn the rolled ham, briefly, in hot butter. Meanwhile, slide the eggs, one by one, into the tomato sauce, keeping them separate. Baste constantly and when the whites are set, arrange eggs, sauce and ham on the croûtons and serve.

This dish is excellent accompanied by a purée of spinach or celeriac.

Poached Eggs à la Vierge (from Willy Mucha)

4 eggs ✦ 4 slices white bread without crust ✦ 4 slices foie gras without truffles ✦ 4 tablespoons fresh cream ✦ salt and pepper ✦ paprika

Poach and trim the eggs and put them into a bowl of tepid salted water. Toast the bread lightly and spread it with foie gras. Arrange the eggs on top and leave in a moderate oven for 4 minutes. Season and sprinkle with cream. After ½ minute, dust with paprika and serve.

Œufs en Matelote

¾ pint (½ litre) red wine ✦ bouquet garni ✦ 1 carrot ✦ 1 onion ✦ 1 clove garlic ✦ salt and pepper ✦ a pinch of nutmeg ✦ 4 eggs ✦ 4 rounds white bread ✦ oil ✦ butter ✦ 1 tablespoon flour

Simmer the wine, bouquet, carrot, onion and garlic for 15 minutes and then remove the vegetables. Season the liquid and poach the eggs in it. Brown the bread in a mixture of oil and butter. Put an egg on each croûton and keep hot. Mix the flour with 1 tablespoon of butter and whip it into the wine, stirring until the sauce thickens. Pour over the eggs and serve.

Eggs in Aspic

Pour a little aspic, home-made or otherwise, into the bottom of small egg moulds and arrange in it a pretty pattern of tarragon leaves or strips or small lozenges of tongue or ham. When the aspic has set, put in each mould a poached egg, which you have left for 5 minutes in cold water, trimmed and dried. Cover with aspic and put in the refrigerator to set. When they are firm, turn the moulds out on to a bed of lettuce leaves.

Variations. If any aspic is left over, chop it and use as a garnish, or mix it, while still liquid, with some tinned macedoine of vegetables and a few spoonfuls of mayonnaise and use it for stuffing tomatoes.

Instead of using individual moulds, arrange the eggs in a soufflé dish and separate them with groups of peeled shrimps. Serve with mayonnaise.

Slices of ham or pâté de foie gras can be used instead of eggs.

Œufs Mollet au Gratin

2 oz (50 g) butter ✦ 1½ oz (40 g) flour ✦ 1 pint (6 dl) milk ✦ salt and pepper ✦ 5 oz (125 g) grated cheese ✦ 8 eggs and 2 yolks

Make a white roux (p. 108) and stir in the milk a little at a time. Cook gently for 5 minutes, season and stir in the cheese. As soon as it is melted, beat in the egg yolks. Meanwhile, prepare œufs mollet (p. 36) and lay them in a buttered fireproof dish into which you have poured half the sauce. Cover with the rest and sprinkle with grated cheese. Brown under the grill.

Œufs Mollet with Melted Cheese

7 eggs + ¾ pint (4½ dl) milk +
2 oz (50 g) butter + 3 tablespoons flour + salt and pepper + nutmeg (optional) +
6 oz (150 g) grated Parmesan
cheese + 4 thin slices Cheddar, Emmenthal or Leices-
ter cheese

Cook 4 œufs mollet (p. 36) and peel
them. Meanwhile, make a rather thin
béchamel sauce (p. 108). Season it and
add the grated cheese. As soon as this
has melted, remove the pan from the
fire and when it has cooled a little, stir
in the yolks of the three remaining
eggs and then fold in the whites,
beaten to a snow. Pour the sauce into
a buttered fireproof dish and arrange
the œufs mollet in it. Top each egg
with a slice of cheese and put the dish
into a hot oven for 10 minutes.

Œufs Mollet with Tomato

4 œufs mollet + 4 rounds
buttered toast + 1 tomato +
⅓ cup mayonnaise + ⅓ cup
cream + a few leaves tarragon + 1 small teaspoon
lemon juice + salt and pepper

Allow the eggs to cool and place one on
each round of toast. Remove the skin
and pips from the tomato, chop it and
mix it with the mayonnaise, cream,
tarragon, lemon juice and seasoning.
Pour the sauce over the eggs.

Stuffed Avocados with Œufs Mollet

2 avocados + 1 tomato + 1
small tin of crab + 1 cup
mayonnaise + salt and pepper + 4 œufs mollet + tomato
ketchup

Slice the avocados in half lengthwise
and remove the stones. Spoon out the
pulp and mix it with the roughly
chopped tomato, flaked crab, seasoning and half the mayonnaise and put
the mixture back in the skins. Top
each with an egg covered with mayonnaise coloured with tomato ketchup.

Œufs Mollet Niçoise

1 cup mayonnaise + 2 tablespoons tomato purée + pa-
prika + sugar + 3 tomatoes +
6 œufs mollet + anchovy
fillets + black olives

Mix the mayonnaise and tomato purée
and season with a dash of paprika and
a pinch of sugar. Halve the tomatoes
and scoop out the pips and put an egg
in each. Cover them with mayonnaise
and garnish with fillets of anchovy and
black olives.

This dish can also be made with hard-boiled eggs.

The American Cousin's Ramekin Eggs

4 shallots ✦ ½ pint (3 dl) dry white wine ✦ freshly-milled pepper ✦ 2 teaspoons lemon juice ✦ 1½ oz (40 g) butter ✦ ¼ pint (1½ dl) cream ✦ 6 tablespoons sherry ✦ 8 eggs ✦ 4 oz (100 g) grated Cheddar cheese ✦ nutmeg

Simmer the chopped shallots, wine, pepper and lemon juice until the liquid is reduced to about 2 tablespoons. Stir in half the butter and when melted, divide the mixture between 8 buttered ramekins. Pour over the cream, salted and mixed with sherry. Break an egg into each ramekin, cover with grated cheese and sprinkle with nutmeg. Cook in a moderate oven, standing in a shallow pan of water, for 10–15 minutes until the white is set and the cheese melted.

Œufs en Cocotte Mornay

8 eggs ✦ butter ✦ 1 cup of mornay sauce ✦ ½ small teaspoon paprika ✦ salt and pepper

Butter 8 small ramekins and break an egg into each. Season, cover with mornay sauce (p. 109) and sprinkle with paprika. Cook for 10 minutes in a moderate oven, standing the ramekins in a shallow dish of water.

Ramekin Eggs with Cream and Tarragon

butter ✦ 8 tablespoons cream ✦ 2 tablespoons chopped tarragon ✦ salt and pepper ✦ 8 eggs

Butter 8 ramekins. Mix the cream with the tarragon and season. Pour it into the ramekins and put them, standing in a shallow dish of water, in a hot oven. When the cream is well heated, break an egg into each, top with a small nut of butter, cover with greaseproof paper and cook until the white is firm but soft. Adjust the seasoning and serve.

Œufs à la Tripe

2 large onions ✦ 1½ oz (40 g) butter ✦ 1 tablespoon flour ✦ ½ pint (3 dl) bouillon ✦ salt and pepper ✦ 4 hard-boiled eggs ✦ vinegar

Brown the sliced onions in butter and stir in the flour, allowing it to colour. Add the bouillon, little by little. Season the sauce, which should be rather thick, and pour it over the sliced hard-boiled eggs. Heat through, and sprinkle lightly with vinegar.

Hard-boiled Eggs with Soya Sauce

1 tablespoon oil ✦ 3 tablespoons soya sauce ✦ 4 hard-boiled eggs

Warm the oil and soya sauce in a small pan. Peel the eggs and heat them for 3 or 4 minutes in the liquid, basting all the time so that they turn brown.

Œufs à la Chimay

2 shallots ✦ 4 oz (100 g) butter ✦ 4 oz (100 g) chopped button mushrooms ✦ 3 tablespoons dry white wine ✦ 1½ oz (40 g) cheese ✦ 2 tablespoons flour ✦ ½ pint (3 dl) milk ✦ 3 tablespoons cream ✦ 2 egg yolks (optional) ✦ 8 hard-boiled eggs ✦ cayenne pepper ✦ 4 oz (100 g) grated cheese

Soften the finely-chopped shallots in half the butter. Add the mushrooms and white wine and reduce for 15 minutes. Prepare a mornay sauce with butter, flour, milk and cheese. Off the fire, stir in the cream and egg yolks. Peel the hard-boiled eggs and cut in half lengthwise. Scoop out the yolks and mix them with the mushroom blend. Pile this on the whites, set them on a fireproof dish, which is spread with a little sauce. Pour over the rest, sprinkle with grated cheese and brown under the grill.

Hot Stuffed Hard-boiled Eggs

8 hard-boiled eggs ✦ 2 slices stale white bread, grated ✦ a handful of chopped fresh herbs ✦ salt and pepper ✦ 1½ oz (40 g) butter ✦ 4 oz (100 g) grated cheese ✦ 6 tablespoons cream

Peel the eggs and cut in half lengthwise. Chop the yolks finely and mix them with the breadcrumbs, herbs, seasoning, butter, grated cheese and cream. Pile the mixture on to the whites, spreading what is left over the bottom of a buttered fireproof dish, in which you place the eggs. Put into a hot oven for a few minutes, taking care that the eggs do not become dry.

Eggs Stuffed with Anchovy

4 hard-boiled eggs ✦ 4 fillets of anchovy ✦ 1 teaspoon minced parsley ✦ 1½ oz (40 g) butter ✦ pepper

Slice the eggs crosswise or lengthwise. Remove the yolks and mix them with the pounded anchovy, parsley, butter and pepper. Fill the whites and arrange them in a buttered fireproof dish. Put in a moderate oven for 5 minutes.

These eggs can be used to make a main dish if they are served with tomato, mushroom or mornay sauce or arranged round a cauliflower *au gratin* or a mound of spinach cooked *en branche.*

Fried Eggs with Sweet Corn

1 cup sweet corn ✦ 1 cup béchamel sauce ✦ 2 tablespoons cream ✦ salt and pepper ✦ 4 fried eggs ✦ 4 tomatoes ✦ 4 rashers bacon

Drain the sweet corn, stir it into the béchamel (p. 108) and heat gently. Off the fire, add the cream and season well. Pile the mixture on to a dish and crown it with fried eggs surrounded by halved grilled tomatoes topped with rashers of grilled bacon.

Scrambled Eggs by Candlelight

This is a dish for two, which should be enjoyed by candlelight.

5 eggs ✦ pepper ✦ 1 tablespoon lemon juice ✦ 1 oz (25 g) butter ✦ 2 tablespoons cream ✦ 4 tablespoons—or more—black caviare (Osetrova if possible) ✦ buttered toast

Mix the lightly beaten eggs with pepper, lemon juice, the butter cut in cubes and cream. Cook in a bainmarie, stirring with a wooden spoon. When they are almost done, add threequarters of the caviare and salt if necessary. Stir and spread on buttered toast. Garnish with the rest of the caviare.

Continue this very special meal with a salad of celery or fennel dressed with olive oil, salt and pepper.

Scrambled Egg with Tomato

1 tablespoon olive oil ✦ 1 small chopped onion ✦ 2 tomatoes ✦ a pinch sugar ✦ ½ bay leaf ✦ salt and pepper ✦ 4 eggs ✦ butter ✦ chopped parsley or basil

Melt the onion in oil and add the peeled and pipped tomato, roughly chopped. Season, adding the sugar and bay leaf. Cook, covered, while you prepare the scrambled eggs. If the tomatoes are not very juicy add a little water. Remove the bay leaf, sprinkle with chopped parsley or basil and pour over the eggs.

Stuffed Omelettes

4 raw eggs ✦ a handful fresh herbs ✦ 2 slices white bread, trimmed ✦ milk ✦ 2 hard-boiled eggs ✦ a few mushrooms ✦ butter ✦ salt and pepper

Break each raw egg into a separate cup, season and beat lightly. Scatter with chopped herbs. Soak the bread in milk, squeeze it dry and crumble it into a pan together with the chopped hard-boiled eggs, sliced mushrooms (sauté in butter) and seasoning. Simmer. Make 4 small omelettes with the prepared eggs and stuff them, tucking in the ends of each roll. Arrange them in a fireproof dish, sprinkle with melted butter and put in a moderate oven for 10 minutes.

Omelette with Croûtons

3 slices of white bread, diced ✦ oil and butter ✦ 8 eggs

Fry croûtons of bread in mixed oil and butter. Drain and keep hot. Make two omelettes with the eggs. When half cooked, add the croûtons. Fold and serve while the centre is still a little runny.

Cold Omelette

4 tomatoes ✦ 3 onions ✦ 2 yellow sweet peppers ✦ oil and butter ✦ ½ lb (200 g) French beans ✦ 10 eggs ✦ salt and pepper

Soften the peeled and pipped tomatoes, onions cut in rings and peppers in oil and butter. Drain and put them in a bowl. Cook the French beans for 5 minutes in boiling, salted water. Beat and season the eggs. Pour the eggs into a round fireproof dish or flan mould and arrange the vegetables on them like the spokes of a wheel. Cook in a fairly hot oven until the omelette is set. Cool and turn out on to a round dish.

Crispy Cold Omelette

4 potatoes ✦ oil ✦ 4–5 cloves garlic ✦ ½ lb (200 g) cooked beans or peas ✦ 4 onions ✦ 2 slices stale white bread ✦ 2 tomatoes ✦ oil ✦ 8 eggs ✦ 2 tablespoons water ✦ salt and pepper

Brown the diced potatoes in oil with the chopped garlic. Drain the potatoes, and in the same oil fry the onions, cut in rings, and then the diced bread. Roughly chop the pipped and peeled tomatoes. Arrange all the vegetables and croûtons in a round dish and pour over them the seasoned eggs lightly beaten with the water. Cook in a fairly hot oven until the omelette is set. Cool, and cut in slices like a cake.

Savoury Puffs

In Edwardian days savoury finger-shaped éclairs were called Carolines. Those shaped like cream puffs were known as Duchesses. After stuffing, both were often coated with chaudfroid sauce or brushed with aspic jelly, and just as this was setting, sprinkled with chopped salted nuts or pistacchios. However, both are very good without sauce or trimmings.

To make the choux paste:

½ pint water ✦ 4 oz (100 g) butter ✦ salt ✦ 6 oz (150 g) flour ✦ 4 eggs ✦ 2 tablespoons chopped fresh herbs ✦ 4 tablespoons grated cheese

Boil the water with the butter and salt. Pour in the flour all at once and stir with a wooden spoon until the paste comes away from the sides of the pan. Off the fire, beat in the eggs one by one, and the herbs and cheese. Arrange the choux paste in small teaspoons on a buttered baking sheet, leaving 2–3 inches between. Cook in a moderate oven for 15–20 minutes. When cool, split the éclairs and stuff them.

To make the stuffing:

½ lb (200 g) very soft double-cream cheese mixed with 1–2 chopped shallots and a handful of fresh herbs *or* ½ lb (200 g) herbed cream cheese and 2–3 tablespoons fresh cream

Mix the seasoned cheese with enough cream to make it soft but still firm. Set it to chill.

Portuguese Tomatoes

First prepare a vinaigrette.

1 teaspoon Dijon mustard ✦
2 tablespoons olive oil ✦ 1
teaspoon wine (or cider)
vinegar ✦ 1 teaspoon lemon
juice ✦ salt and pepper

Mix all the ingredients together.

4 fine tomatoes ✦ 4 oz (100 g)
Cheddar, Cheshire or Em-
menthal cheese ✦ a slice
ham ✦ 2 oz (50 g) bacon
✦ 2 tablespoons finely-
chopped herbs

Cut a lid from each tomato and scoop
out the pulp with a spoon. Remove the
pips and cut the flesh in tiny pieces.
Dice the other ingredients. Crisp the
bacon in a frying pan. Lift it off the
fire and mix it with the other things
you have prepared, including the
vinaigrette. Stuff the tomatoes and
serve chilled.

Pancakes Stuffed with Cheese

On pp. 64–66 we have described how pancakes are made.

8 large or 12 small pancakes
✦ ⅓ cup cream ✦ 8 oz (200 g)
grated Cheddar or Emmen-
thal cheese ✦ ¼ teaspoon
paprika ✦ a dash of cayenne
pepper ✦ ¾ cup béchamel
sauce (p. 108)

Lay a portion of cream mixed with half
the cheese, paprika and cayenne pepper on each pancake. Roll them up,
tucking under the ends, and arrange
them in a buttered fireproof dish,
covered with béchamel sauce and
grated cheese. Sprinkle with melted
butter and brown under the grill.

Scrambled Egg Pancakes

Half quantity of basic pancake mixture (p. 65) ✦ 8 eggs
✦ 2 oz (50 g) butter ✦ 1
tablespoon each chopped
tarragon, chervil, parsley
and chives ✦ salt and pepper ✦ 1 hard-boiled egg

Make a single pancake in a large pan.
Beat the eggs lightly together with the
butter, cut in pieces, seasoning, herbs
and 1 tablespoon water. Cook slowly
until they are scrambled but still soft,
and then spread them on the pancake
and roll up. Sprinkle with chopped
hard-boiled egg and serve at once, cut
in slices.

Pancakes Stuffed with Spinach

4 oz (100 g) flour ✦ ½ pint (3 dl) beer ✦ 1 tablespoon oil ✦ 2 eggs ✦ salt and pepper ✦ 10 oz (250 g) cooked spinach ✦ ½ lb (200 g) cottage cheese ✦ ¼ teaspoon powdered mace *or* a little grated nutmeg ✦ cayenne pepper ✦ 2 tablespoons melted butter

Make a batter as on p. 65 using flour, oil, eggs and salt, and beer instead of milk, and stirring in 2 tablespoons of finely-chopped spinach. Leave to rest for 2 hours and then make 8 pancakes. Chop the rest of the spinach coarsely and mix with the cheese and seasoning. Stuff the pancakes, sprinkle them with melted butter and put them into a moderate oven for 5 minutes.

Tunny Fish Pancakes

8 pancakes (p.65) ✦ 4 hard-boiled eggs ✦ medium-sized tin tunny ✦ ¾ cup béchamel (p. 108) ✦ 2½ oz (65 g) butter ✦ 2 tablespoons anchovy paste

Roughly chop the hard-boiled eggs and the tunny. Mix them with the béchamel and stuff the pancakes. Work the anchovy paste into the butter and spread it over the pancakes. Heat in a moderate oven for 5 minutes.

Pancakes with Yoghurt and Smoked Fish

1 cup flour ✦ ½ teaspoonful salt ✦ 2 yoghurts ✦ 1 large egg ✦ smoked salmon or smoked herring fillets in oil for garnish

Put the flour in a bowl and stir in the salt, the yoghurt, and the egg beaten to a froth. The batter must be fairly dense. Make the pancakes on a gentle fire as they must be thick and cooked through. Garnish with smoked salmon or smoked fillets of herring in oil, and pour a little yoghurt over if you wish.

Palatschinken with Chicken

This is an Austrian form of pancake which can be used with different kinds of flavouring and stuffing. To make palatschinken:

8 oz (200 g) flour ✦ 5 eggs ✦ ½ small teaspoon salt ✦ 1½ oz (40 g) butter ✦ ½ pint (3 dl) milk ✦ ¼ pint (1½ dl) cream

Put the flour into a bowl and break the eggs into a hole in the centre, together with the salt and milk. Work these into the flour, using a wooden spoon. Melt the butter in the cream. Stir this into the flour mixture as lightly as possible and leave to rest for an hour. Make pancakes as on p. 65, using 3 tablespoons of the batter at a time.

Prepare the following stuffing and roll some of it in each palatschinken, sprinkle with grated cheese and brown under the grill.

2 oz (50 g) butter ✦ 2 tablespoons lemon juice ✦ 3 cups cold cooked chicken ✦ 6 mushrooms ✦ salt, pepper and a dash of cayenne ✦ 2 tablespoons chopped parsley, chives, chervil, etc. ✦ 2 tablespoons cream ✦ 2 tablespoons sherry ✦ 1½ oz (40 g) grated Parmesan ✦ ½ oz flour

Heat 1½ oz (40 g) of the butter over a low fire, add the lemon juice and the chicken, finely chopped. Cover and simmer for 5 minutes. Add the mushrooms, rather coarsely chopped, seasoning and herbs. Raise the heat and cook 5 minutes more. Uncover the pan and allow the liquid to evaporate a little. Add the cream and sherry. Blend rest of butter with flour and stir gradually into mixture. When the stuffing has thickened, lift it from the fire, divide it between the palatschinken and roll them up. Sprinkle with grated cheese and brown under the grill.

Soufflé Pancakes

8 pancakes (p. 65) ✦ 1½ oz (40 g) butter ✦ 3 tablespoons flour ✦ 1 cup milk ✦ 5 tablespoons grated Parmesan cheese ✦ 3 eggs ✦ butter ✦ salt and pepper

Heat the butter and flour in a small saucepan and stir in the milk, little by little. When the sauce is creamy, add the cheese, season and lift the pan from the fire as soon as it has melted. Cool for a few minutes, then stir in the yolks of egg and fold in the whites, beaten to a snow. Butter a soufflé dish and sprinkle it with flour. Arrange layers of cheese sauce and pancake alternately in the soufflé dish. Finish with sauce and a sprinkling of cheese and put the dish into a moderate oven for 35 minutes. Loosen the sides of the soufflé pancake with a knife, but do not turn it out. Cut in slices like a cake and serve it with tomato sauce, if you wish.

Cheese and Bread and Butter Pudding (Catrien Ariens' Recipe)

4 slices stale white bread ✦ butter ✦ 4 thick slices Cheddar, Leicester, Lancashire or Dutch cheese ✦ 2½ cups milk ✦ 4 eggs ✦ nutmeg ✦ salt and pepper

Butter each slice of bread on both sides, put a slice of cheese on top, and lay them in the bottom of a buttered soufflé dish. Beat the eggs and milk together, season and pour into the dish. Bake in a moderate oven for 30 minutes.

Cheese Loaf

2 onions ✦ 1 bay leaf ✦ 2 cloves ✦ 2 glasses milk ✦ about 2 cups stale bread cut in cubes ✦ 8 oz (200 g) grated Cheddar or Emmenthal cheese ✦ cayenne or freshly-milled black pepper ✦ 2 eggs ✦ nutmeg

Peel the onions, leaving them whole. Attach the bay leaf to one by piercing with the cloves, and leave to infuse in the milk for 10 minutes without boiling. Butter a soufflé dish and fill it with alternate layers of cheese and bread, finishing with the latter. Pepper each layer of cheese well. Let the milk cool and remove the onions. Beat the eggs lightly, stir them into the milk, and season with pepper and nutmeg. Pour the milk over the bread and cheese and allow it to soak in. Bake for 20–30 minutes in a moderate oven and serve hot.

Matefaim Savoyard (from Benoît Braun)

An easy dish to make, popular with the young, whether as cooks or consumers.

2 cups milk ✦ 3 eggs ✦ 1½ oz (40 g) butter ✦ salt and pepper ✦ 4 tablespoons flour ✦ 4 oz (100 g) grated Cheddar or Emmenthal cheese ✦ oil

Cut the butter into small pieces and mix all the ingredients and seasoning in a bowl, using a wooden spoon. A few small lumps don't matter. Lightly oil a shallow fireproof dish and fill it with the mixture. Bake it in a hot oven for 25 minutes. The top must be well browned. If you wish to brown the other side, turn it over for the last 5 minutes. Serve either hot or warm.

Golden Snowballs

5 egg whites ✦ ½ lb (200 g) grated Emmenthal ✦ salt and pepper ✦ flour ✦ oil for deep-frying

Whip the egg whites to a very firm snow. Fold in the cheese and seasoning. Either drop the mixture, a spoonful at a time, into very hot oil, or form balls the size of a small tomato, dip them in flour and fry. When they are golden-brown, drain and serve on a folded napkin.

Croquettes

A croquette mixture can be prepared several hours beforehand. It is then made into balls, ovals, or rolls shaped like a cork. Before plunging the croquettes into deep fat, they should be egg-and-breadcrumbed and left to rest for half an hour. See that the oil is very hot and that the croquettes do not touch one another. They should be crisp outside with a rich creamy centre. When golden-brown, lift them out and drain on kitchen paper. Arrange them on a dish or in a basket lined with a napkin, and keep them hot in the oven with the door open until the last batch is ready.

Either a whole egg or the white alone, lightly beaten with a little water, can be used to attach the breadcrumbs.

Cheese Croquettes

1 oz (25 g) flour ✦ 1 oz (25 g) butter ✦ 1 cup milk ✦ 4 oz (100 g) grated cheese ✦ salt and pepper ✦ 2 eggs ✦ 1 teaspoon water ✦ breadcrumbs ✦ oil for frying

Make a béchamel with the flour, butter and milk (p. 108) and stir in the cheese. Melt the cheese, remove the pan from the fire, season, add one whole egg and one yolk and set to cool in a buttered dish. Form croquettes and dip them in the white of egg, lightly beaten with the water, then in breadcrumbs. Fry as above.

Variations on Croquettes

A simple variation on the above recipe is made by substituting 1½ oz (40 g) of one of the following for the same weight of grated cheese, stirring it into the mixture before it is set to cool: peeled shrimps; minced ham; chopped mushrooms sauté in butter.

Cheese and Meat Croquettes

8 oz (200 g) minced meat ✦ 5 oz (125 g) sausage meat ✦ 5 oz (125 g) diced cheese ✦ 2 eggs ✦ salt and pepper ✦ nutmeg ✦ flour ✦ breadcrumbs ✦ 1 tablespoon water ✦ 1¼ oz (40 g) butter ✦ 1 tablespoon oil ✦ parsley ✦ tomato, mushroom or curry sauce

Mix the meat, cheese, egg yolks and seasoning and form into eight balls. Roll them in flour and then in white of egg beaten with water. Dip in breadcrumbs and leave to rest for ¼ hour. Brown in a frying pan in a mixture of oil and butter. Lower the heat and cook for 5 minutes more. Drain on kitchen paper and serve with fried parsley and tomato, mushroom or curry sauce.

St Paulin, Fontina, Edam or Dunlop cheese is recommended for this recipe.

Raclette

This dish is a speciality of the Valais in Switzerland. Made over a wood fire and eaten with the appetite which comes from the mountain air, it is marvellous.

The cut face of a Valais cheese is held to the flames and as the cheese melts it is scraped on to slices of rough dark peasant bread. It is hard to re-create these conditions, but if you have a suitable source of heat, let the cheese fall into a hot plate and eat it with potatoes in their jackets, gherkins, small onions and rye bread.

Fondues

There are a whole range of dishes, of various nationalities, which consist, basically, of melted cheese. Of these, the most famous is the Swiss fondue. (Incidentally, our own Welsh rarebit belongs to this family.)

A Swiss fondue is not just a food, but a ceremony in its own right. To enjoy it you need a *caquelon* or shallow dish, ideally of earthenware, though enamelled iron or copper will do. Each guest must have a long fork, preferably with an insulated handle, and you will need a hot-plate with an adjustable flame. The whole process may be carried out at table, but you can perfectly well prepare the fondue in the kitchen and just keep it bubbling at table on your hot plate.

The recipe, and the type of cheese used, vary according to the region. We give you a few suggestions and you must take it from there.

175

The Swiss use an acid wine, and even add lemon juice, for their fondue. The French prefer a light dry, but not acid wine. If the fondue is too thick, stir in a little liquid (wine, cider or milk). If it is too thin, add more cheese or a little cornflour mixed with a tablespoon of cold liquid.

For all fondues, first rub the inside of the *caquelon* with garlic. Over a medium heat, pour in the wine, add the cheese, cut in pieces (purists maintain that it should not be grated), and freshly-milled pepper. Stir with a wooden spoon in a figure-of-eight movement. The cheese and wine often show a certain reluctance to blend into a smooth, creamy mixture. To overcome this, draw the *caquelon* aside and stir in a teaspoon of cornflour which you have mixed smoothly with some cold wine or water. Continue to beat. When the fondue is smooth, add a liqueur glass of kirsch. Beat for 3–4 minutes more. The fondue is now ready to go to table where it must be kept very hot, but remember to lower the flame as the *caquelon* empties.

Each guest spears a piece of bread on his long fork and twirls it in the fondue until it is coated. French bread, cut in pieces, is ideal for the purpose, as each piece will have some crust into which the fork can bite. Anyone who drops bread into the fondue must pay a pre-arranged forfeit—perhaps a kiss, or even a bottle of wine. And the wine which you drink with the fondue must be white, and preferably dry. When the *caquelon* is almost empty a crust forms on the bottom which you lift out with the point of a knife. This is usually divided between the guests, while the host may claim the dry, crisp cheese round the edge which is called the *dentelle*.

The fondue may be enlivened by the *trou du milieu* and the *point final*, glasses of kirsch drunk half way through and at the end of the fondue.

Using the same method, here are some local variations:

Fondue Neuchâteloise

This fondue makes use of the excellent white wine of Neuchâtel, which unfortunately does not always travel very well. Use 12 oz (300 g) each of Emmenthal and Gruyère cheese, about 1 pint (6 dl) of Neuchâtel wine, 1 heaped teaspoon of cornflour, 2 teaspoons of lemon juice and a liqueur glass of kirsch. Season with pepper and nutmeg or paprika.

Fondue Fribourgeoise

This fondue, which is called *moitié-moitié*, is made as we have just described, using 12 oz (300 g) each of Gruyère and Vacherin cheese, about 1 pint (6 dl) of Neuchâtel wine, 1 teaspoon of lemon juice, 2 teaspoons of cornflour, and a liqueur glass of kirsch.

The Vacherin, which is cut in cubes, is only added when the Gruyère has already begun to melt.

Appenzell Fondue

This is made as we described above with 8 oz (200 g) each of Appenzell, Emmenthal and Vacherin cheese and cider instead of wine. No kirsch is added.

Fondue Savoyarde

Sometimes, this fondue is made with 20 oz (500 g) of Beaufort cheese. Beaufort is a French type of Gruyère, richer and more buttery than the Swiss version.

A mixture of 7 oz (175 g) each of Comté (another French Gruyère), Emmenthal and Vacherin is also used for this fondue, with about ¾ pint (4½ dl) of dry white wine, 3 tablespoons of kirsch and the usual pepper and garlic.

Fondue Brillat-Savarin

This dish was rather unkindly described by Edouard de Pomiane as 'an excellent dish of scrambled eggs with cheese'.

6 eggs ✦ 5 oz (125 g) grated Gruyère ✦ 2 oz (50 g) butter ✦ pepper ✦ croûtons (optional)

Beat the eggs lightly and put them on a low fire together with the cheese, butter and pepper. Taste to see if salt is required. Stir constantly, and when the fondue has thickened, pour it straight into 4 hot plates. Put croûtons in the plates, if you wish.

Piedmontese Fondue (or *Fonduta*)

8 oz (200 g) Fontina ✦ ⅓ pint (2 dl) milk ✦ 3 egg yolks ✦ 2 oz (50 g) butter ✦ salt and pepper ✦ white truffles (optional)

Cube the cheese and let it stand in an earthenware pan with the milk for 3–4 hours; then cook over a very low fire, stirring with a wooden spoon, until the cheese begins to melt. Add the egg yolks, one by one, and the butter, salt and pepper. On no account let the fondue boil. If you are nervous, stand your saucepan in a shallow pan of water while it is cooking. When it is ready, serve covered with shavings of truffle—or without.

Belgian Rarebit

6 oz (150 g) flour ✦ 1 egg yolk ✦ 1 oz (25 g) butter ✦ pepper and a pinch salt ✦ 5 tablespoons beer ✦ about 1 lb (400 g) Cheddar, Cheshire or Leicester cheese ✦ 2–3 tablespoons Dijon mustard ✦ oil for frying

Make a batter (p. 65) with the flour, egg, butter and a pinch of salt, using beer instead of milk, and leave for 2 hours. Cut the cheese into 8 half-inch slices, then spread the slices with mustard and dip them in the batter. Deep-fry, drain, sprinkle with pepper and serve on a white paper napkin.

Welsh Rarebit

There are as many versions of Welsh Rarebit as there are Welsh accents and all are pleasant. Lancashire cheese is generally held to make the best rarebit, but mature Cheddar or Cheshire will do very well. If you wish to emphasize its relationship with the fondue family, make the rarebit at table in a chafing dish and pour it, bubbling, over pieces of dry or buttered hot toast waiting ready in heated plates. One or two yolks of egg are sometimes added at the last minute to enrich the rarebit and prevent the cheese from hardening so quickly.

4 oz (100 g) cheese ✦ 1 oz (25 g) butter ✦ 5 tablespoons brown ale ✦ salt, pepper, cayenne ✦ plain or hot-buttered toast

Shave or grate the cheese and set over a gentle heat in a shallow saucepan or chafing dish with the butter, ale and seasonings. Stir without boiling and when creamy, pour it over the toast and dust with cayenne pepper.

A quicker version is made by mixing 4 oz (100 g) of grated cheese with 3 oz (75 g) of butter and stirring in seasonings and enough boiling milk to make a thick, creamy mixture. Spread this thickly on toast and brown under the grill. The toast may be previously spread with anchovy paste if you wish.

Golden Bucks (Ninette's recipe)

1½ oz (40 g) butter ✦ 2 tablespoons flour ✦ 1 cup milk ✦ salt, pepper and nutmeg ✦ 2 oz (50 g) grated Parmesan ✦ 2 oz cubed Cheshire or Dutch cheese ✦ vol-au-vent cases ✦ 4 eggs ✦ a small slice ham

Make a béchamel (p. 108) with the butter, flour, milk and seasoning. Off the fire, stir in the grated, and then the cubed cheese. Two-thirds fill vol-au-vent cases with the mixture. Break an egg into each, and top with ham. Put in a moderate oven until the whites are set.

Egg, Tomato and Cheese Toast

½ cup olive oil ✦ 4 fairly thick, trimmed slices bread ✦ 4 slices Cheddar or Cheshire cheese ✦ 2 tomatoes ✦ salt and pepper ✦ 4 eggs

Heat the oil in a large pan, fry the bread, lift out and drain. Place a piece of cheese on each slice and cover with the chopped peeled tomatoes. Place in a hot oven while you fry the eggs. Put these, drained and seasoned, on the fried bread and serve immediately.

If you like the contrast of hot and cold, leave the cheese and tomato raw, and place the hot fried eggs on top.

Milk Rolls Stuffed with Cheese

8 small milk rolls ✦ 2–3 tablespoons milk ✦ 2 oz (50 g) grated cheese ✦ 2 eggs ✦ salt and pepper ✦ oil for frying or 1½ oz (40 g) butter.

The stuffing may be varied by adding to it 2 tablespoons of chopped herbs and shallots or 4 oz (100 g) chopped ham or smoked tongue or shrimps

Halve the rolls horizontally, scoop out the insides and put them, crumbled, into a bowl with the milk, cheese, egg yolks, seasoning and the whites beaten to a snow. Mix lightly. Fill the halved rolls and fry them in deep oil, or brown them, dotted with butter, in a fairly hot oven.

Stuffed Brioches

4 brioches ✦ 1 tablespoon milk ✦ 1½ oz (40 g) butter ✦ 4 oz (100 g) grated cheese ✦ a thick slice of ham (about 4 oz, 100 g)

Slice the tops from the brioches. Remove a little of the insides, crumble them into a bowl and mix with the milk, softened butter, grated cheese and cubed ham. Season, and put the mixture back in the brioches, replacing the tops. Put them on a buttered baking sheet and into a hot oven for 8 minutes.

Ham and Cheese Turnovers

5 oz (125 g) flour and a good pinch of salt ✦ 5 oz double-cream cheese ✦ 2 oz (50 g) butter ✦ 4 slices ham ✦ 6 slices cheese ✦ pepper ✦ 1 egg yolk ✦ ½ teaspoon water

Mix the flour and salt. Beat 3 tablespoons of the flour with the cheese and softened butter, using a fork. Work in the rest of the flour, knead lightly, and roll out the dough. Cut it into 2½-inch (6-cm) squares. Place on each a slice of cheese and a piece of ham and fold over. Damp the edges and firm together. Lay the turnovers on a buttered baking sheet. Brush with egg yolk beaten with the water and bake in a fairly hot oven for 35 minutes.

Cheese and Macaroni Toast

½ pint (3 dl) milk ✦ ½ pint water ✦ a good pinch salt ✦ 1 oz (25 g) butter ✦ ½ lb (200 g) short-cut macaroni ✦ 6 tablespoons cream ✦ 6 oz (150 g) grated cheese ✦ 2 tablespoons Dijon mustard ✦ freshly-milled pepper ✦ 8 slices hot buttered toast

Bring the milk, water, salt and butter to the boil and throw in the macaroni. Cook until the liquid is absorbed, stirring gently. Season and add the cream, cheese, mustard and pepper. Mix well. When the cheese has melted, pile the macaroni on slices of hot-buttered toast and serve immediately.

Croque-Monsieur

There are a number of French recipes for 'toasts', many of which correspond to our own. They are eaten as snacks, or as luncheon and supper dishes, not usually as after-dinner savouries in the English way. The most famous of these *croques* is *Croque-Monsieur*.

8 fairly thin slices bread ✦ butter ✦ 8 slices cheese (Cheddar, Emmenthal, etc.) ✦ 4 large slices ham

Cut the bread into rounds or squares. Butter them and sandwich between each pair alternate layers of cheese and ham. Fry in butter, and when the cheese begins to melt, drain them and serve on a folded napkin.

Before frying, the *Croques-Monsieur* can be dipped in ½ glass of milk, seasoned and beaten with an egg yolk.

Italian Croque-Monsieur

4 fillets of anchovy ✦ 2 oz (50 g) butter ✦ 2 oz (50 g) grated Parmesan ✦ 2 eggs ✦ chopped parsley ✦ salt and pepper ✦ 8 slices buttered bread

Crush the anchovy fillets with a fork and work in the softened butter, Parmesan, egg yolks, parsley and seasoning. Fold in the whites, beaten to a snow. Spread the mixture on the bread, and brown in a hot oven for 8–10 minutes.

Cheese and Tomato Rusks

8 rusks ✦ 8 tablespoons olive oil ✦ 2 tomatoes ✦ chives ✦ salt and pepper ✦ lemon juice ✦ 6 oz (150 g) grated cheese

Soak the rusks in oil. Chop the peeled tomatoes and the chives. Put each rusk in an individual earthenware dish spread with the seasoned tomato mixture. Sprinkle with lemon juice and grated cheese, and brown in a hot oven for 6–7 minutes.

Laurence Reverdin's Cheese Toasts

First:
8 slices white bread ✦ butter ✦ 4 slices Emmenthal cheese ✦ oil for frying ✦ ½ cup béchamel sauce (p. 108)

Cut the bread into 8 rounds and butter them. Sandwich each slice of cheese between two rounds of bread. Fry the sandwiches and when they are crisp and golden-brown, and the cheese is beginning to melt, serve them with béchamel sauce on top.

Second:

2 eggs ✦ 4 oz (100 g) grated cheese ✦ cayenne pepper ✦ 8 slices white bread ✦ oil for frying

Beat the eggs lightly and add the cheese and pepper. Cut the bread into 2-inch squares and spread them with the mixture. Plunge into hot oil, cheese-side down. After a moment or two, lift them out, drain and serve.

Third:

2 eggs ✦ 1 tablespoon kirsch ✦ 4 oz (100 g) grated cheese ✦ pepper ✦ 8 slices white bread ✦ oil for frying

Beat together the eggs, kirsch, cheese and pepper. Sandwich the mixture between squares of bread and fry them golden-brown in deep fat.

Fourth:

8 slices white bread, trimmed ✦ 8 tablespoons white wine *or* kirsch ✦ butter ✦ 8 slices Cheddar or Cheshire cheese ✦ 2 tomatoes ✦ salt and pepper

Soak the slices of bread in wine or kirsch and arrange them in a well-buttered fireproof dish. Cover each with a slice of cheese and a round of tomato. Season, and put in a hot oven until the cheese melts.

Garlic Croque

1 tablespoon oil ✦ 4 oz (100 g) butter ✦ 5–6 cloves garlic ✦ 8 thin slices white bread, trimmed ✦ 4 oz (100 g) grated cheese ✦ salt and pepper

Put the oil and butter in a pan with the garlic and cook gently for 10 minutes. Lift off the fire and leave to stand for 2–3 hours. Remove the garlic. Arrange the bread on a baking sheet and sprinkle it with the garlic butter. Salt the slices, sprinkle with grated cheese and pepper, and put in a hot oven until they are browned and the cheese is runny. Serve very hot with a chilled green salad.

Croque with Egg

4 slices bread, trimmed and buttered ✦ 4 slices cheese ✦ 4 eggs ✦ salt and pepper

Arrange the slices of bread in a buttered fireproof dish with a piece of cheese on each. Put them in a hot oven until the cheese begins to melt. Break an egg on to each *croque*, season and return to the oven until the whites are just set.

182

Crab Toast

4 slices white bread ✦ 1 small
tin crab ✦ ½ cup mayon-
naise *or* béchamel sauce ✦ 4
slices cheese ✦ cayenne pepper

Toast the bread. Mix the crab meat
with the sauce, spread it on the bread
and cover with slices of cheese sprinkled
with cayenne pepper. Brown in a hot
oven or under the grill.

Apple Croque

2 oz (50 g) butter ✦ 8 trimmed slices bread ✦ 1 apple ✦
1 teaspoon lemon juice ✦ 4
slices cheese ✦ 2 tablespoons
white wine ✦ 2 slices ham ✦
cayenne pepper

Melt the butter in a frying pan and fry
the bread. Cut the apple in very fine
slices, sprinkle with lemon juice and
cayenne pepper. Warm the cheese in
the wine, without allowing it to melt.
Sandwich between slices of bread the
ham, apple and cheese. Brown in a hot
oven for 5 minutes and serve very hot.

Hawaiian Croque

4 rounds white bread,
trimmed ✦ butter ✦ 1 cup
grated cheese ✦ 4 table-
spoons cream ✦ cayenne
pepper ✦ 4 slices pineapple
✦ fresh herbs

Butter the bread. Mix the cheese,
cream and pepper and spread on the
bread. Top with a slice of pineapple,
and put under the grill until the pineapple is brown and the cheese melted.
Sprinkle with some chopped fresh
herbs.

Fried Croques

8 slices white bread ✦ 4 oz
(100 g) butter ✦ 1 table-
spoon Dijon mustard ✦ 1
slice ham, minced ✦ 3 eggs ✦
1 cup grated cheese ✦ salt
and pepper ✦ breadcrumbs
✦ oil for frying

Cut the bread into 2-inch squares. Mix
the butter, mustard, ham, 2 egg yolks,
cheese and pepper. Make small sandwiches and dip them first in the remaining egg beaten with water, salt
and pepper and then in breadcrumbs.
Deep-fry until they are golden-brown,
drain on kitchen paper, and serve
them on a napkin folded on a hot dish.

Cheese and Sorrel Quiche

3 oz (75 g) butter ✦ 6 oz (150 g) flour ✦ salt ✦ water ✦ 2 handfuls sorrel ✦ extra butter ✦ 12 oz (300 g) cottage cheese ✦ 3 egg yolks ✦ 4 tablespoons grated cheese ✦ 4 tablespoons fresh cream

Crumble the butter into the salted sieved flour. Add enough water to make a firm dough. Form into a ball without kneading and leave it to rest for 2 hours. Spread the pastry into a tin, without rolling, pressing lightly into place with your knuckles. Meanwhile, melt the sorrel in butter, season, and stir in the cheese which you have beaten with the egg yolks. Fill the pastry case, cover with grated cheese mixed with cream, and bake in a moderate oven for 35 minutes.

This quiche can also be made with spinach.

Cottage Cheese and Tomato Quiche

3 oz (75 g) butter ✦ 6 oz (150 g) flour ✦ salt ✦ water ✦ 12 oz (300 g) cottage cheese ✦ 2 eggs ✦ chives or basil ✦ 3 small tomatoes ✦ 8 fillets anchovy ✦ 2 hard-boiled eggs ✦ 4–5 black olives

Prepare the pastry case as for the cheese and sorrel quiche. Mix the cottage cheese, lightly-beaten eggs, chopped herbs and salt, and arrange the mixture in the pastry case. Cover with peeled, sliced tomatoes and put into a moderate oven for 25 minutes. Lay the anchovy fillets on the quiche like the spokes of a wheel, with a slice of hard-boiled egg between each, topped with a stoned black olive. Put back in the oven for 5 minutes. Serve tepid.

Quiche Lorraine

3 oz (75 g) butter or lard ✦ 6 oz (150 g) flour ✦ salt ✦ water ✦ 6 oz (150 g) smoked bacon ✦ ¼ pint (1½ dl) milk ✦ ⅜ pint (2½ dl) cream ✦ 3 eggs ✦ salt and pepper ✦ 4 oz (100 g) grated cheese (Emmenthal, Sbrinz or Parmesan)

Prepare a pastry case as for the cheese and sorrel quiche. Dice the bacon and cook until crisp. Beat the milk, cream, eggs and seasoning together in a basin and add the bacon and cheese. Pour the mixture into a pastry case and bake for 30 minutes in a hot oven. Serve hot.

Quiche with Œufs Mollet

3 oz (75 g) butter ✦ 6 oz (150 g) flour ✦ salt ✦ water ✦ 1 tablespoon Dijon mustard ✦ 4 tomatoes ✦ seasoning ✦ 4 eggs ✦ 4 oz (100 g) grated cheese ✦ 4 tablespoons cream

Prepare a pastry case as for the cheese and sorrel quiche. Spread the base with mustard and cover it with sliced and seasoned, peeled and pipped tomatoes. Put it in a moderate oven for 25 minutes. Meanwhile, prepare 4 *œufs mollet* (p. 36). Place them on the quiche, cover with grated cheese mixed with cream, and return to the oven for 10 minutes.

Piquant Cheese Tartlets

18 tartlets of flaky pastry ✦ 2 egg yolks ✦ 1 teaspoon Dijon mustard ✦ 1 teaspoon lemon juice ✦ salt ✦ ½ clove garlic ✦ a dash of Worcestershire sauce ✦ ¼ pint (1½ dl) oil ✦ 4 tablespoons cream ✦ 1 teaspoon grated horseradish ✦ 4 firm tomatoes ✦ 4 oz (100 g) Cheddar or Emmenthal cheese ✦ a medium-sized tin tunny ✦ 1 gherkin

Put the egg yolks, mustard, lemon juice, salt, crushed garlic and Worcestershire sauce into a bowl. Stir in the oil, little by little, to form a mayonnaise. When this is thick, continue to stir and add the cream and horseradish. Peel and pip the tomatoes and cut the flesh into pieces. Mix it with the cubed cheese, flaked tunny and sauce. Fill the tartlets with this mixture. Garnish with a round of gherkin and serve cold.

Spaghetti alla Carbonara

1 lb (400 g) spaghetti ✦ 6 oz (150 g) streaky bacon ✦ 1 tablespoon oil ✦ 3 eggs ✦ salt and black pepper ✦ grated Parmesan or Pecorino cheese

Cook the spaghetti in plenty of fast-boiling water. Dice the bacon. If it is very salty, blanch, by putting it in cold water, bringing to the boil, draining and drying. Brown the bacon in hot oil. Beat the eggs. Put the drained spaghetti into a heated salad bowl, sprinkle with bacon and freshly-milled black pepper. Pour over the eggs and mix quickly. Serve with grated Parmesan or Pecorino cheese.

Noodles with Cottage Cheese

4 oz (100 g) flour ✦ 5 oz (125 g) well-drained cottage cheese ✦ 2 egg yolks ✦ ½ teaspoon salt ✦ 1 tablespoon oil ✦ 2 oz (50 g) butter ✦ 2 oz grated Parmesan cheese ✦ freshly-milled black pepper

Put the flour, cottage cheese, egg yolks and salt into a bowl and mix with a wooden spoon. Without kneading too much, form a ball. Cover with a cloth and leave to rest for 1 hour. Roll out to about ⅛-inch thickness (about 2 mm) and cut in strips. Plunge them into a large pan of boiling salted water to which you have added a tablespoon of oil to prevent sticking. After 5–6 minutes, while the noodles are still firm, lift them out, drain and put in a heated bowl. Stir in the butter, sprinkle with cheese and pepper. Serve immediately.

Timbale of Macaroni

1 lb (400 g) macaroni ✦ 1 cup double cream ✦ 3 eggs ✦ 8 oz (200 g) grated Emmenthal or Gruyère cheese ✦ 2 tablespoons grated Parmesan ✦ salt and pepper ✦ nutmeg ✦ breadcrumbs ✦ butter

Cook the macaroni in boiling salted water and drain. Beat together the cream, egg yolks, Emmenthal or Gruyère cheese and seasoning. Fold in the whites, beaten to a snow. Mix with the macaroni and pour into a buttered soufflé mould which you have sprinkled with breadcrumbs. Stand this in a shallow dish of water and cook in a moderate oven for 40 minutes. Dot with butter and sprinkle with grated Parmesan cheese and cook for a further 5 minutes. Serve in the mould.

Cheese Timbale

1½ oz (40 g) butter ✦ 1½ oz flour ✦ ½ pint (3 dl) milk ✦ salt, pepper and nutmeg ✦ 1 tablespoon powdered gelatine ✦ 3 oz (75 g) grated cheese ✦ 2 small eggs *or* 6 tablespoons (1 dl) cream ✦ Cheddar or Cheshire cheese

Make a béchamel sauce (p. 108) seasoned with salt, pepper and nutmeg. Off the fire, add the gelatine, dissolved in water, and the cheese. Heat the mixture without allowing it to boil, and stir in the cream or egg yolks, and the egg whites, beaten to a snow. Pour into individual moulds which you have rinsed in cold water. Chill in the re-

186

frigerator. Just before serving, plunge the moulds in warm water and turn them out on to a bed of shredded lettuce. Decorate each with a small square of cheese.

Regal Fillets of Fish

4 fairly thick fillets of white fish ✦ ¾ pint (4½ dl) dry white wine ✦ 2 oz (50 g) blue cheese ✦ 3 tablespoons breadcrumbs ✦ 3 tablespoons cream ✦ 2 tablespoons lemon juice ✦ 2 tablespoons chopped parsley, chives, and dill ✦ salt and pepper

Put the fillets of fish into cold white wine and heat gently. As soon as the liquid boils, lift out the fish and drain. Mix with a fork the cheese, breadcrumbs, cream, lemon juice, herbs and seasoning. Put the fillets in a buttered fireproof dish. Spread them with the cheese mixture and put them into a very hot oven for 5 minutes.

Fillets of Fish with Yoghurt

4 fillets of white fish ✦ a bay leaf ✦ 1 oz (25 g) butter ✦ 2 tablespoons flour ✦ 2 cartons yoghurt ✦ 3 tablespoons grated Parmesan ✦ ¼ teaspoon curry powder ✦ 2 eggs ✦ salt and pepper

Put the fillets of fish into salted water with the bay leaf. Bring to the boil, lift out and drain. Meanwhile, heat the butter and flour together in a small saucepan, stirring all the time. Add the yoghurt and continue to stir over a moderate fire for 3–4 minutes. Off the fire, blend in the cheese, curry powder, egg yolks, and then the beaten whites. Season. Roll up the fillets and put them in a fireproof dish with the sauce. Cook for 20 minutes in a moderate oven.

Cheeseburger

1 onion ✦ butter ✦ 1 lb (400 g) minced steak ✦ 1 egg yolk ✦ salt and pepper ✦ flour ✦ 4 slices of white bread ✦ oil ✦ 4 slices of cheese

Chop the onion and soften it in the butter. Mix it with the meat, egg yolk, and a little salt and pepper. Form 4 steaks, flour them lightly, and fry them in a mixture of butter and oil for 2–3 minutes on each side. Butter the bread, put a steak on each piece, and a slice of cheese on top. Pepper, and put under the grill until the cheese has melted. Serve immediately.

187

Stuffed Hamburger

1 lb (400 g) minced steak ✦ salt and pepper ✦ 4 slices cheese ✦ butter ✦ oil ✦ 1 anchovy fillet ✦ 2 tablespoons white wine

Season the meat and make 8 small steaks. Sandwich a slice of cheese between each pair, firming lightly to hold them together. Brown in a mixture of butter and oil, turning the steaks carefully so that they do not break. Cover the pan and cook for 2–3 minutes until the cheese melts. Lift out the steaks and put them on a hot dish. Over a slow fire, crush the anchovy in the pan and add a little fresh butter. Sprinkle with white wine, stir well, pour over the meat and serve hot.

Chicken au Gratin

1 chicken ✦ butter ✦ oil ✦ 6 oz (150 g) bacon ✦ 2 onions ✦ 4 oz (100 g) mushrooms ✦ 1 clove garlic ✦ 3 tablespoons tomato concentrate ✦ $\frac{3}{8}$ pint (2$\frac{1}{2}$ dl) red wine ✦ salt and pepper ✦ a pinch sugar ✦ 4 oz (100 g) grated cheese

Cut the chicken into 8 pieces and brown them in a mixture of oil and butter. When they are crisply browned, lower the heat and cook for another 35 minutes, uncovered, moving the pieces from time to time so that they cook evenly. Meanwhile, in another frying pan, brown the diced bacon in a little oil, add the sliced onions and mushrooms, and the garlic, crushed. When they are all lightly browned, pour in the wine mixed with tomato concentrate. Season, and simmer for 15 minutes. Arrange the chicken in a fireproof dish, pour over the sauce, sprinkle with cheese and brown in the oven.

Chicken Gratiné in Sauce

$\frac{1}{2}$ lemon ✦ 1 stalk celery ✦ 2 cloves garlic ✦ salt ✦ a sprig of thyme ✦ 1 large chicken ✦ 3 onions ✦ 2 oz (50 g) butter ✦ $\frac{1}{2}$ pint (3 dl) white wine ✦ $\frac{3}{4}$ pint (4$\frac{1}{2}$ dl) stock ✦ 4 tablespoons flour ✦ 8 oz (200 g) grated Parmesan or Emmen-

Tuck the lemon, celery, garlic, salt and thyme inside the chicken. Soften the finely-chopped onions in 1 oz (25 g) of the butter, using a casserole. Add the chicken, pour over the wine, and let it reduce to half over a moderate fire with the lid off. Add the hot stock and salt, if necessary, and simmer until the

thal cheese ✦ 2 eggs ✦ pepper ✦ 4 tablespoons cream

chicken is done but does not fall apart. Lift it out.

Heat the rest of the butter in another pan. Add the flour, the onions from the casserole and enough of the liquid to make a fairly thin sauce. Off the fire, stir in half the cheese, the egg yolks and pepper. Remove the skin and bones from the chicken and divide it into 8 pieces. Arrange them in a buttered fireproof dish and cover with the sauce. Mix the cream with the rest of the cheese, spread it over the chicken and brown in a moderate oven for 15 minutes.

Tomato Mousse

4 large ripe tomatoes ✦ 4 eggs ✦ ⅜ pint (2½ dl) cream ✦ salt and pepper ✦ paprika ✦ 2 teaspoons lemon juice ✦ a few sprigs parsley or basil

Make a stiff tomato purée by simmering the peeled, pipped and sieved tomatoes. (They can be put through a food mill.) Beat the egg yolks and add the whipped cream and seasoning. Stir in the tomato purée, lemon juice, and the egg whites beaten to a firm snow. Put the mixture into a china bowl and set it to chill for an hour. The mousse should be served in its bowl, sprinkled with chopped parsley or basil.

Lady Birley's Horse-radish Mousse

1½ oz (40 g) butter ✦ 2 tablespoons flour ✦ about ½ pint (3 dl) milk ✦ 4 hard-boiled eggs ✦ 1 oz (25 g) powdered gelatine ✦ ¼ pint (1½ dl) cream ✦ 3 tablespoons grated horse-radish ✦ ½ teaspoon castor sugar ✦ salt and pepper ✦ 1 tablespoon wine (or cider) vinegar ✦ 1 cucumber ✦ French dressing (p. 216)

Make a fairly thin béchamel (p. 108) with the butter, flour and milk. Chop the hard-boiled eggs and dissolve the gelatine in tepid water, stirring well. Off the fire, add to the béchamel all the remaining ingredients but the cucumber and dressing, finishing with the whites of egg beaten to a snow. Verify the seasoning. Pour the mousse into a mould and put it in the refrigerator to chill until set.

Toss the sliced, drained and chilled

cucumber in French dressing (p. 216) and just before serving, arrange it in a border round the mousse.

If the flavour is not strong enough, stir in a little Dijon mustard before folding in the whites of egg.

SALADS

Potato Salad with Cheese

2 large, firm potatoes ✦ 6 oz (150 g) mild Cheddar, Emmenthal or Dutch cheese ✦ 1 fennel root ✦ 1 clove garlic ✦ half an onion ✦ 2 carrots ✦ 4 tablespoons oil ✦ 2 teaspoons lemon juice ✦ a pinch castor sugar ✦ 1 tablespoon cream ✦ salt and pepper ✦ 1 tomato ✦ 4 hard-boiled eggs ✦ a sprig of tarragon (optional)

Boil the potatoes in their jackets. Peel while still warm and cut them, and the cheese, into cubes. Trim the fennel and cut it in fine slices vertically, so that each retains a small plume of green. Grate the garlic, onion and carrots. Beat the oil, lemon juice, sugar, cream, salt and pepper together in a salad bowl. Stir in the vegetables, garnish with tomato quarters and sliced hard-boiled eggs, and sprinkle with chopped tarragon, if you wish.

French Bean Salad

1 lb (400 g) young French beans ✦ salt ✦ 2 tablespoons olive oil ✦ 1 tablespoon lemon juice ✦ 4 oz (100 g) firm cheese (mild Cheddar, Dutch, etc.) ✦ 2 shallots ✦ a few leaves tarragon or mint ✦ freshly-milled pepper

Cook the beans uncovered for 7–10 minutes in boiling, salted water. They should remain slightly crisp. Drain and put in a salad bowl, stirring in the oil while they are still warm. Let them cool, but not chill, and sprinkle with lemon juice. Cut the cheese into matchsticks and mix lightly with the beans. Sprinkle with chopped shallots and tarragon or mint. Pepper, and serve.

Rice Salad

a handful seedless raisins ✦ 1 small onion ✦ 4 oz (100 g) smoked bacon ✦ ½ teaspoon paprika ✦ 4 oz (100 g) soft cheese ✦ 1 tablespoon olive oil ✦ 2 teaspoons lemon juice ✦ salt and pepper ✦ 1 cup cooked rice ✦ 1 green pepper ✦ 1 small tomato

Soak the raisins in tepid water. Slice the onion in rings and put in iced water for half an hour. Slice the bacon and brown it in a teaspoon of oil. Sprinkle it with paprika and cook for 5 minutes more. In a salad bowl, beat the cheese, lemon juice, salt and pepper and the rest of the oil. Add the drained bacon, carefully dried raisins, sliced green pepper and rice, and mix well. Garnish with the onion rings and slices of tomato.

Cucumber Salad

1 cucumber ✦ 1 tablespoon coarse salt ✦ 5 tablespoons yoghurt *or* fresh or sour cream ✦ pepper ✦ 2 teaspoons chopped tarragon

Peel the cucumber and slice finely. Sprinkle with salt and leave the liquid to drain for several hours, washing away the surplus salt. Pat dry with a towel. Put the cucumber into a salad bowl and mix it with yoghurt or cream, pepper and tarragon.

Beetroot Salad

2 cooked beetroots ✦ 3–4 tablespoons wine (or cider) vinegar ✦ 1–2 cloves garlic ✦ 1 egg yolk ✦ 4 oz (100 g) cottage cheese ✦ salt and pepper ✦ lettuce leaves

Slice the beetroot finely, sprinkle with vinegar and leave for half an hour. Meanwhile, mix in a bowl crushed garlic, egg yolk and cheese, stirring well. Season, add the drained beetroot and serve on lettuce leaves.

Lettuce Salad with Cheese

1 large, tight lettuce ✦ 2 oz (50 g) firm cheese ✦ 2 cooked chicken breasts ✦ 1 cup mayonnaise ✦ 3 tablespoons tomato ketchup ✦ 1 hard-boiled egg

Strip off any damaged leaves and, very delicately, remove the heart and the stump of the lettuce, leaving the rest in place. Wash carefully and drain. Shred the lettuce-heart and cut the cheese and chicken in matchsticks. Mix these with half the mayonnaise flavoured with ketchup, and arrange in the centre of the lettuce, sprinkled with chopped, hard-boiled egg. Serve with the rest of the mayonnaise.

Raw Mushroom Salad

1 lb (400 g) mushrooms +
2–3 tablespoons lemon juice
+ 2 teaspoons Dijon mus-
tard + 6 tablespoons (1 dl)
cream + salt and pepper + 2
teaspoons tomato ketchup
(optional)

Clean the mushrooms with a damp paper towel. Slice them finely, sprinkle with lemon juice and leave for 15 minutes. Lightly beat the mustard, cream, salt and pepper, and ketchup if you wish. Mix the mushrooms with the sauce and serve chilled.

Gardener's Salad

1 calf's foot + 2 lb (800 g)
boneless flank of beef + 1
onion + 1 carrot + 2 stalks
celery + a bouquet garni +
2 shallots + a few sprigs
parsley + 3 gherkins + 4
tablespoons oil + 1 tablespoon wine (or cider) vinegar + salt + cayenne pepper
+ French mustard + 1 apple
+ 2 tablespoons lemon juice
+ 1 small lettuce + mayonnaise + 2 hard-boiled eggs +
4 oz (100 g) firm cheese

Put all the meat into a pan of water which you have brought to the boil with the onion, carrot, celery and bouquet garni. Add salt and simmer for $3\frac{1}{2}$–4 hours, skimming the surface from time to time. (This can also be cooked in a pressure cooker.) Chop the shallots and parsley and cut the gherkins in rounds. Slice the beef and the meat from the calf's foot whilst still warm and put it in an earthen-ware dish with the mixed oil and vine-gar, chopped ingredients and season-ing. Mix well and allow to cool. Cut the apple in fine slices and steep it in the lemon juice. Dress the lettuce with mayonnaise and arrange it in six bowls. Heap them with meat salad, cold but not chilled, and top with quartered hard-boiled eggs, the apple drained of juice, and thin slices of cheese.

This salad is really a complete meal.

Gipsy Salad

4 potatoes + 6 tablespoons
oil + 3 tablespoons wine
vinegar + salt and pepper +
a pinch sugar + 2 table-
spoons mayonnaise + 1 small
tin petits pois + $\frac{1}{2}$ cervelat
sausage finely sliced + 6 oz
(150 g) sliced Emmenthal or
Cacciocavallo cheese + 1 cucumber + some diced gherkins

Boil the potatoes in their jackets. Peel and cube them while still warm. Beat the oil, vinegar, salt, pepper and sugar together. Add the mayonnaise and pour over the potato. When quite cold, add the rest of the ingredients, taking care to drain the peas and the sliced cucumber well.

Cabbage Salad

Choose a large, well-rounded smooth white or pale green cabbage or a red cabbage. Soak it in cold, salted water to get rid of any insects and then plunge it for 3 minutes into a large pan of fast-boiling, salted water. Do not cover. Lift out the cabbage, drain and cut the stump flat so that it will stand upright. Gently pull open the outer leaves so that they form a bowl. Remove the centre of the cabbage and shred it. Put the outside in the refrigerator.

For a white cabbage:

1 onion ✦ 2 carrots ✦ 6 oz (150 g) firm cheese ✦ 1 slice pineapple (optional) ✦ ¼ pint (1½ dl) cream ✦ 2 tablespoons wine (or cider) vinegar ✦ 1 teaspoon castor sugar ✦ salt and pepper ✦ 1 teaspoon caraway seeds

Slice the onion, grate the carrot, cut the cheese in matchsticks and mix them with the shredded cabbage heart. Add, if you wish, a slice of pineapple, chopped. Mix the cream, vinegar, sugar, salt, pepper and caraway seeds and stir into the salad.

For a red cabbage:

1 apple ✦ 1 tablespoon lemon juice ✦ 2 tablespoons chopped parsley ✦ 2 hard-boiled eggs ✦ 1 tablespoon Dijon mustard ✦ 1 teaspoon castor sugar ✦ 1 tablespoon oil ✦ 3 tablespoons red wine vinegar ✦ 1 anchovy fillet

Make a salad with the apple (finely sliced) and soaked for 15 minutes in lemon juice, parsley, and the hard-boiled eggs, diced. Mix the mustard, sugar, oil, vinegar and pounded fillet of anchovy, and stir into the salad together with the shredded cabbage heart.

Horse-radish Salad

4 tablespoons oil ✦ 1 tablespoon wine (or cider) vinegar ✦ 1 teaspoon grated horse-radish ✦ 1 tablespoon cream ✦ salt and pepper ✦ 12 oz (300 g) Emmenthal or Gruyère cheese ✦ lettuce leaves ✦ 1 onion ✦ 1 green pepper ✦ 1 gherkin

Make a dressing with the oil, vinegar, horse-radish, cream and seasoning. Cut the cheese in fairly thin slices and then in 1-inch (2½-cm) squares. Mix it with the dressing and arrange in a salad bowl on a bed of lettuce leaves. Garnish with onion rings, strips of green pepper and gherkins cut into small pieces.

N

Italian Hard-boiled Egg Salad

2 fillets anchovy ✦ 1 tablespoon chopped capers ✦ 1
tablespoon chopped parsley
✦ 2 teaspoons lemon juice ✦
6 tablespoons olive oil ✦
pepper ✦ 4 hard-boiled eggs

Crush the anchovies and capers in a
bowl. Stir in the parsley, lemon juice,
oil and pepper. Cut the eggs in quarters and pour over the dressing. Let
stand for half an hour before serving.

Green Pea Salad with Cheese

6 oz (150 g) cottage or
herbed cream cheese ✦ 4
tablespoons cream ✦ 2 tablespoons lemon juice ✦ 1 teaspoon curry powder ✦ salt
and pepper ✦ 8 oz (200 g)
cooked petits pois ✦ 8 oz
(200 g) ham ✦ 2 tomatoes

Beat the cheese with the cream, lemon
juice, curry powder, salt and pepper.
Drain the peas well. Cut the ham into
strips. Mix the peas, ham and dressing
and garnish with sliced, peeled tomatoes.

SWEET DISHES AND CAKES

Ninette's Chocolate Mousse

5 oz (125 g) cooking chocolate ✦ 2 oz (50 g) castor
sugar ✦ 1 tablespoon instant
coffee ✦ 4 egg yolks and 6
whites

Put the chocolate, sugar and coffee into
a saucepan standing in a bain-marie,
and stir with a wooden spoon until the
chocolate has all melted. Off the fire,
work in the egg yolks, one by one, and
then the whites, stiffly beaten. Beat
more vigorously and when quite cool,
put in the refrigerator for $\frac{1}{2}$-hour. Stir
once more before serving.

This basic mousse may be varied in all sorts of delightful ways:

Use milk chocolate instead of plain
Substitute whisky, rum or orange juice for the coffee—or use
no extra flavour at all
Add 1 oz (25 g) of butter to the initial mixture as it is melting
Use lump sugar which will melt slowly, and leave little crisp
pieces in the mousse
Leave out the yolks of egg and serve the light, fluffy mousse
immediately

Add a cup of whipped cream. This mousse will do your figure no good, so why not enjoy it just a little more?

Beat in small pieces of finely-chopped candied orange

Prepare the mousse the day before, using equal quantities of yolks and whites of egg. Put it in the freezing compartment and beat from time to time

Mousse Made in a Bain-Marie

3 whole eggs and 2 yolks ✦ 6 oz (150 g) castor sugar ✦ rind and juice of 2 lemons or 1 lemon and 1 orange or 3 tablespoons well-flavoured fruit purée or ½ teaspoon vanilla essence *or* 1 teaspoon instant coffee

Put the eggs into a saucepan standing in a shallow pan of hot water, and beat over a low fire until they froth. Sprinkle in the sugar and flavouring and continue beating until the mixture is thick and creamy. Pour it into a dish, and stir from time to time as it cools.

Michel Olivier's Mousse

3 eggs ✦ rind and juice of 1 lemon or 1 orange and ¼ lemon ✦ 12 oz (300 g) cream cheese ✦ sugar to taste

Separate the egg yolks and whites. Grate the fruit rinds over the yolks, and stir in sugar, cheese and fruit juice with a fork. Fold in the egg whites, beaten to a snow, and pile the mousse into 4 small bowls. Chill for at least 2 hours.

The citrus fruits can be replaced by 2 tablespoons of strongly flavoured fruit purée.

Rum Mousse

4 oz (100 g) castor sugar ✦ 2 eggs ✦ 6 tablespoons rum ✦ 12 oz (300 g) cream cheese ✦ 4 slices fruit cake ✦ 2 tablespoons powdered chocolate or cocoa powder

Beat the sugar and egg yolks until they are creamy. Stir in 2 tablespoons of the rum and the cream cheese and then fold in the beaten whites of egg. Lay the cake in the bottom of a bowl and sprinkle it with the rest of the rum. Cover with the mousse, sprinkle with chocolate, and chill.

Zabaione

6 egg yolks ✦ 6 oz (150 g) castor sugar ✦ ¾ pint (4½ dl) white wine or Marsala

Beat the egg yolks and sugar in a saucepan standing in a bain-marie, until the mixture falls from the beater like a ribbon. Whisk in the wine, little by little. The zabaione must be thick and frothy.

Zabaione can be eaten warm, and must then be served immediately, or it can be served chilled.

Jam Soufflé

4 egg whites ✦ 2 oz (50 g) castor sugar ✦ 1 tablespoon cognac or whisky ✦ 1 cup of marmalade or apricot jam ✦ butter

Beat the egg whites to a firm snow and add the sugar, little by little, and the cognac or whisky. Carefully stir in the marmalade or jam, and pour the mixture into a mould which you have buttered and sprinkled with sugar. Stand in a shallow dish of water and bake in a moderate oven for 25 minutes.

Venetian Eggs

6 egg whites ✦ salt ✦ 2 oz (50 g) castor sugar ✦ butter ✦ 4 egg yolks ✦ 2 tablespoons gooseberry jelly ✦ 4 teaspoons cream

Whip the whites until they hold a stiff peak, adding a pinch of salt. Whisk in the sugar. Put half the whites into a well-buttered soufflé dish. Place the egg yolks on top, each one surrounded with gooseberry jelly and topped with a spoonful of cream. Cover with the rest of the beaten whites. Cook in a moderate oven for 25 minutes.

Castillian Almond Soufflé

¾ pint (4½ dl) milk ✦ a cinnamon stick ✦ 6 oz (150 g) ground almonds or hazel nuts ✦ 6 egg yolks ✦ 4 oz (100 g) castor sugar ✦ 2 egg whites

Put the nuts in a bowl and gradually stir in the hot milk which you have infused with the piece of cinnamon. Beat the egg yolks and sugar until they are frothy and add to the milk mixture. Fold in the beaten whites of egg, and pour the mixture into a soufflé dish. Bake, standing in a shallow dish of water, in a moderate oven until the soufflé is cooked.

Lilli's Crème Caramel

10 lumps sugar ✦ 1 table-spoon water ✦ a vanilla pod ✦ 1¾ pints (1 litre) milk ✦ 2 whole eggs and 6 yolks ✦ 9 oz (225 g) castor sugar

Make a caramel with the lump sugar and water and run it round the inside of a mould, which you plunge immediately into cold water so that the caramel stays in place. Infuse the vanilla pod, split lengthwise, in the heated milk. Beat the eggs and castor sugar until they are frothy. Remove the vanilla pod, and whisk the milk into the egg and sugar mixture. Pour into the mould. Cook this, standing in a shallow dish of water in a moderate oven for 40 minutes. The water must on no account boil. Allow to cool. Plunge the mould into very hot water for a few seconds and turn out the crème caramel.

Pavlova Pudding (Ninette's version)

4 egg whites ✦ 1 teaspoon vinegar ✦ 1 teaspoon vanilla essence ✦ 6 oz (150 g) castor sugar

Prepare a very hot oven. Beat the egg whites to stiff peak stage, add vanilla essence and sprinkle in the vinegar and the sugar. Oil a baking sheet and cover with oiled greaseproof paper. Turn out the whites on to the paper and form a flat cake. Put it in the oven, turning the heat to low as you do so. Bake for 1½–2 hours. Remove the greaseproof paper and serve cold.

Instead of vanilla one can use coffee extract or powdered chocolate. The Pavlova may be garnished with fresh fruit and whipped cream.

Pineapple Pavlova

6 egg whites ✦ 3 oz (75 g) castor sugar ✦ 1 teaspoon vinegar ✦ 1 tin pineapple pieces

Beat the egg whites to a firm snow and whisk in the sugar, vinegar, and 2 tablespoons of pineapple juice. Pour this into a greased flan tin, dot with pieces of very carefully drained pineapple, and bake in a slow oven for about 45 minutes. Serve hot or cold with vanilla custard sauce.

A Sweet Omelette

6 eggs ✦ 1½ oz (40 g) castor sugar ✦ ½ teaspoon grated lemon rind ✦ a pinch salt ✦ 3 tablespoons cream ✦ 1 oz (25 g) butter ✦ 5 tablespoons jam (optional)

Beat the egg yolks, sugar and lemon rind until they are frothy. Stir in the cream and the egg whites, whipped to a snow with the salt. Melt the butter in a frying pan and cook the omelette over a low fire. Serve immediately.

The omelette may be spread with jam before it is rolled over. To make an attractive finish, sprinkle the surface of the folded omelette with icing sugar, using a red-hot skewer to mark out a lattice pattern.

Palatschinken with Apricot

Make palatschinken as described on p. 171. Fill them with apricot jam, roll them up, and sprinkle with castor sugar and chopped nuts.

Pancakes with Orange

5 oz (125 g) flour ✦ ⅜ pint (2¼ dl) milk ✦ 2 large eggs ✦ 6 oz (150 g) butter ✦ 4 oz (100 g) sugar ✦ 1 orange ✦ rind of 1 lemon ✦ 2–3 tablespoons of mixed cognac and Grand Marnier

Make a pancake batter (p. 65) with the flour, milk, eggs and 2 oz (50 g) each of the butter and sugar. Work the rest of the butter and sugar together with the grated rind of the orange and lemon. Make pancakes and fill them, while still warm, with the butter mixture. Sprinkle them with orange juice. Put the liqueur into a small saucepan, warm it, set it alight and pour it, flaming, over the pancakes. Serve immediately.

Judith Mullen's Buttermilk Pancakes

5 oz (125 g) flour ✦ 1 teaspoon sugar ✦ ½ teaspoon salt ✦ ¾ teaspoon baking powder ✦ ¼ teaspoon bicarbonate of soda ✦ 1 egg ✦ ½ pint (3 dl) sour milk or buttermilk ✦ 2 tablespoons melted butter ✦ oil ✦ maple syrup and extra butter

Sieve the flour, sugar, salt, baking powder and soda into a bowl. Stir in the egg, then the milk and finally, the melted butter. Work the batter as little as possible or the pancakes will be hard. It does not matter if there are a few lumps. Pour spoonfuls into a thick frying pan which you have brushed with oil. The pan must be very hot. As soon as bubbles appear on the surface, turn the pancakes. Serve with melted butter and maple syrup.

Apple Pancakes

If the quantity of sugar is reduced, these pancakes are very good eaten in the Mennonite fashion with grilled pork sausages.

4 apples ✦ 4 tablespoons lemon juice ✦ 6 oz (150 g) sugar ✦ 3 eggs ✦ 6 oz (150 g) flour ✦ ½ oz (15 g) baking powder ✦ ¼ pint (1½ dl) milk ✦ butter ✦ Calvados (optional) ✦ cream

Slice the peeled and cored apples and sprinkle with lemon juice, and 2 table-spoonfuls of the sugar. Prepare a pancake batter (p. 65), working the egg yolks into the mixed dry ingredients. Stir in the tepid milk and leave to rest. Cook the drained apple slices in butter, sprinkling them with sugar and letting it brown. Make pancakes and, as the underneath of each one begins to cook, place apple rings on top. Turn, and when done, serve unfolded and sprinkled with sugar. Sprinkle with Calvados, if you wish, and serve with thick, fresh, chilled cream.

Crêpes Surprise

These pancakes require to be handled with speed, and it is unwise to try them on guests unless your nerves are strong and you have a trial run beforehand.

8 lumps sugar ✦ 2 whole oranges and the juice of another ✦ 10 oz (250 g) flour ✦ a pinch of salt ✦ 1 teaspoon baking powder ✦ 2 eggs ✦ 1 pint (6 dl) milk ✦ 3 oz (75 g) butter ✦ grated rind of 1 lemon ✦ 1 teaspoon lemon juice ✦ 8 portions vanilla ice cream ✦ 3 tablespoons Grand Marnier ✦ 4 table-spoons cognac

Rub the lumps of sugar on the skin of one orange to flavour them and grate the rind of the other. Peel the oranges and quarter them, removing the fine skin. Keep on one side. Sieve the salt, flour and baking powder into a bowl. Stir together the lightly-beaten egg yolks, milk, 2 tablespoons of melted butter, grated orange and lemon rinds, and 1 tablespoon of orange juice. Pour this into the flour, stirring as little as possible. The batter need not be smooth. Fold in the whites of egg, beaten to a firm snow. Make pancakes and keep them hot. Heat the rest of the butter and the orange-flavoured lumps of sugar until they begin to form a caramel. Add the rest of the orange juice and the lemon juice and dip the pancakes in this mixture. Fill them rapidly with quarters of orange and ice cream, sprinkle with liqueur and set alight.

If all your preparations must be done in the kitchen, bring the pancakes flaming to table. It is much more attractive, though, if the butter and sugar are melted in a chafing dish, and the ready-prepared pancakes are dipped, filled and flambé at table.

Simple Bread Fritters

4 eggs ✦ 4 tablespoons milk ✦ 1 teaspoon orange flower water ✦ ¼ teaspoon grated lemon rind ✦ 4 trimmed slices white bread ✦ butter ✦ icing sugar

Beat the eggs, milk, orange flower water and lemon rind in a soup plate. Dip the bread in this mixture and lightly brown each side in butter. Sprinkle with icing sugar and serve very hot.

Cinnamon Bread Fritters

8 slices white bread ✦ 4 eggs ✦ ¼ pint (1½ dl) milk ✦ 3 oz (75 g) sugar ✦ 2 teaspoons powdered cinnamon ✦ 1½ oz (40 g) ground almonds ✦ butter

Cut the bread into rounds. In a soup plate, mix the egg yolks and milk, and stir in the whites of eggs beaten to a snow. In another plate mix the sugar, cinnamon and almonds. Soak the slices of bread in the first plate, sprinkle them with the sugar mixture, and brown them in butter on both sides. Drain on kitchen paper, and lay them on a hot dish. Sprinkle with the rest of the sugar mixture.

Cottage Cheese Tart

½ cup seedless raisins ✦ 3 tablespoons rum ✦ 8 oz (200 g) flour ✦ 4 oz (100 g) butter ✦ a pinch salt ✦ 8 oz (200 g) castor sugar ✦ about 4 tablespoons water ✦ haricot beans ✦ 10 oz (250 g) cottage cheese, well drained ✦ ¼ pint (1½ dl) cream ✦ 4 egg yolks and 2 whites ✦ ¼ teaspoon vanilla essence

Soak the raisins in rum for 2 hours. Mix the flour, butter, salt, 4 tablespoons of sugar and enough water to make a dough, all together in the French manner, working it as little as possible. Cover with a cloth and leave to rest for 2 hours, in the refrigerator if you prefer. Roll out the pastry and line a greased flan tin. Scatter with haricot beans and bake for 20 minutes in a moderate oven. Mix the cheese, cream, egg yolks, vanilla essence, rum-soaked raisins, and the remaining sugar. Add 2 egg whites, beaten to a snow. Remove the haricot beans and fill the tart. Bake for another 25 minutes.

St Bernard's Cakes

5 egg yolks and 6 whites ✦ 5 oz (125 g) castor sugar ✦ ¼ pint (1½ dl) cream ✦ milk ✦ 2 oz (50 g) flour ✦ icing sugar

Beat the egg yolks and sugar until they fall in a ribbon from the spoon. Whip the cream, adding a little milk if it is too thick. Stir the yolks and sugar lightly into the sieved flour and fold in the beaten egg whites. Put the mixture into small paper cases and bake for 3–4 minutes in a hot oven. Sprinkle rapidly with icing sugar and return to the oven for another minute. Serve hot.

Egg Snow and Almond Cake

4 egg whites ✦ 6 oz (150 g) castor sugar ✦ 5 oz (125 g) rice flour ✦ 5 oz (125 g) butter ✦ 2 oz (50 g) ground almonds ✦ flour ✦ some sliced almonds

Beat the egg whites to a snow. Stir lightly together with the sugar, rice flour, just-melted butter and the ground almonds. Put the mixture into a buttered cake tin which you have sprinkled with flour. Cook for 10 minutes in a hot oven, then lay the sliced almonds on top of the cake, lower the heat to 300°F (150°C, Gas 2) and bake for another 25–30 minutes.

Gâteau Poitevin

4 oz (100 g) butter ✦ 5 oz (125 g) flour ✦ a pinch salt ✦ 4 oz sugar (100 g) ✦ 2 tablespoons milk (and a little for brushing) ✦ jam

Cut the butter in pieces and work it rapidly with the sieved flour, salt, sugar and milk. Using your finger tips, fill the mixture into a shallow cake tin, brush the surface with milk and bake for 30 minutes in a moderate oven. Serve with jam.

Small Yoghurt Cakes

Butter ✦ 3 oz (75 g) flour ✦
1½ cartons yoghurt ✦ 2 eggs
✦ 2 oz (50 g) sugar ✦ icing

Butter two dozen patty tins and pre-heat the oven to 350°F (180°C, Gas 4). Sieve the flour into a bowl and mix in the yoghurt, lightly-beaten eggs and sugar. Divide the mixture into the tins and bake for about 25 minutes. Sprinkle with sugar. When cool, turn out the cakes and ice them.

These little cakes, which should be eaten fresh, go very well with bananas, either whole or mashed, and would make an excellent finish to a curry meal.

Country Cake

1 pint (6 dl) cream ✦ 4 oz (100 g) castor sugar ✦ a pinch salt ✦ about 10 oz (250 g) flour ✦ 1½ oz (40 g) butter

Put the cream into a bowl and then stir in the sugar, salt and as much sieved flour as can be absorbed. Spread the dough on a buttered flan tin and sprinkle with flour. Spread it with butter and cook for 20 minutes in a fairly hot oven.

Pineapple Sundae

1 medium tin of pineapple pieces ✦ 4 portions of vanilla and 4 portions of lemon ice cream ✦ cherries

Drain the pineapple and divide half of it between 4 sundae glasses. Put the vanilla and lemon ice, half-and-half, on top of the pineapple. Put the rest of the fruit in the blender or through a food mill, thinning with a little of the syrup, if necessary. Pour into the sundae glasses and top with a cherry.

Rosy Fruit Sundae

4 meringues ✦ orange and vanilla ice cream ✦ fruit ✦ orange juice

In each sundae glass put some lightly crumbled meringue, 2 large spoonfuls of orange ice cream, and a spoonful of vanilla ice. Surround them with red fruit such as strawberries, raspberries or cooked cherries. Cover with crumbled meringue and sprinkle with orange juice.

Coupe Belle Villageoise

Soak 4 Savoy biscuits in port, maraschino or rum. (For children you can use fruit syrup.) Halve these and arrange them in the bottom of four sundae glasses. In each glass put a dollop of vanilla and raspberry ice and surround them with fresh raspberries and wild strawberries. Cover with thick unwhipped cream, lightly sugared.

EGG AND MILK DRINKS

In England, where it originated, egg nog was regarded as an invalid drink. The yolk of egg was beaten to a cream with a dessert-spoonful of sugar, then mixed with a tablespoon of sherry, brandy or rum. Lastly, the white was beaten to a stiff froth and lightly stirred in, and the egg nog was served to the invalid in a glass.

When egg nog crossed the Atlantic, Bourbon became a popular addition, and the egg nog's medicinal function was usually confined to acting as a pick-me-up.

In cold weather, an egg nog party is very welcome. Here are two recipes each making 20 servings, the first simple and the second a little more elaborate.

Quick and Easy Egg Nog

12 eggs ✦ 10 oz (250 g) castor sugar ✦ ¾ pint (4½ dl) milk ✦ 1 pint (6 dl) rum, cognac or Bourbon ✦ nutmeg ✦ ½ pint cream (optional)

Beat the egg yolks and sugar until they are pale and fluffy. Add the milk and the alcohol, little by little, beating all the time. Put in the refrigerator for at least 2 hours. This removes the 'eggy' taste. Serve in a bowl. At the last minute, float on the top egg whites beaten to a snow, or whipped cream sprinkled with nutmeg.

Special Egg Nog

12 eggs ✦ 1 lb (400 g) castor sugar ✦ 1 bottle Bourbon or cognac ✦ 1 glass (3 dl) brown rum ✦ ⅝ pint (4 dl) fresh cream ✦ ¾ pint (4½ dl) milk ✦ nutmeg

Beat the egg yolks and sugar until they form a ribbon (p. 34). Pour them into a punch bowl and add the spirits gradually, beating all the time. Stand the bowl in the refrigerator for at least 2 hours. Whip the cream, adding a little milk if it is too thick, and stir it

and the milk in at intervals. Beat half
the egg whites to a stiff foam and fold
them into the egg nog. Beat the remaining whites, adding a little extra
sugar, and float them on the punch
bowl. Sprinkle with nutmeg, making a
pretty pattern, or tracing a name or
date if you wish.

Grandmother's Milk

This is said to be an excellent cold cure.

Mix a small teaspoon of tincture of iodine with a tablespoon of
sugar. Pour over it ⅜ pint (2½ dl) of hot, not boiling, milk. Stir
well and drink at once, with two aspirins if you like, and go straight
to bed—unless you have someone who is obliging enough to bring
you this rather drastic cure when you are already there.

West Indian 'Lait de Poule'

This curiously named 'chicken's milk'—or could it be 'tart's
treat'—is said to be good for loss of voice and sore throat.

1 egg yolk ✦ a single or
double tot of brown rum ✦
1 tablespoon honey ✦ ½ glass
milk

Put the egg yolk into a bowl with the
rum. Stir the honey into hot, but not
boiling, milk. Beat the egg and rum
and stir in the honey and milk. Drink
at once.

Peach and Ice Cream Cola

1–2 peaches ✦ syrup ✦
vanilla ice cream ✦ whipped
cream ✦ 1–2 tablespoons
rum ✦ cola of your choice

Put into a tall glass a peach poached in
syrup and drained, a dollop of vanilla
ice cream, a tablespoon of whipped
cream, rum, and fill up with cola. The
make is up to you. Serve with a straw
and a long spoon.

If you wish to make this into a meal rather than a drink, put a
second peach and dollop of cream on top of the first.

Treacle Milk

1 pint (6 dl) milk ✦ 2 tablespoons black treacle ✦ cream
✦ cinnamon

Heat the milk and stir in the treacle. Pour into glasses and trickle into each, over the back of a cold spoon, a tea-spoonful of thick double cream. Sprinkle with cinnamon.

Egg Flip

1 egg ✦ 1 teaspoon castor or
brown sugar ✦ 2 teaspoons
sherry ✦ ½ pint (3 dl) milk

Beat the egg and sugar and add the sherry. Warm the milk and stir it in. Heat gently, taking care that the flip does not boil.

Banana Frappé with Rum

This is on the borderline between a drink and a pudding. For teenagers, you may prefer to leave out the rum.

4 bananas ✦ 1½ pints (9 dl)
cold milk ✦ ¼ pint (1½ dl)
cream ✦ vanilla extract to
taste ✦ 2 tablespoons sugar ✦
2 portions vanilla ice cream
✦ 2 portions chocolate ice
cream ✦ rum (optional)

Mix the bananas, milk, cream, vanilla and sugar in a blender and pour into 4 tall glasses. Add to each a large spoon-ful of vanilla ice cream and one of chocolate. Sprinkle with rum.

Honey and Lemon Cup

2 tablespoons clear honey ✦
1 pint (6 dl) milk ✦ 2 teaspoons lemon juice

Stir the honey into hot milk. Off the heat, add the lemon juice and serve immediately.

Almond Whisk

1 oz (25 g) ground almonds ✦
1 oz castor sugar ✦ 1 egg
white ✦ 1 pint (6 dl) milk

Mix the almonds and castor sugar and fold them into the beaten white of egg. Stir lightly into the hot milk and serve at once.

PARTY FOOD

E GGS, cream and cheese all play an important part in cocktail savouries and buffet food. One of the most useful standbys is the hard-boiled egg, either piled into bowls and dipped in sea-salt as it is eaten, or stuffed as we suggest below.

Stuffed Hard-boiled Eggs

For stand-up occasions, choose small eggs, as even half of a large one is apt to stifle conversation for a while. Cut the eggs crosswise, as it is easier to arrange a large number on one dish. Try to vary the colourings of the stuffing. You will find a description of the stuffing process and some suggestions on pp. 40.

To make an attractive dish, garnish the eggs with capers, olive rings, tiny squares of red pepper, chopped parsley or strips of anchovy fillet or smoked salmon.

Cold Canapés

Canapés are made in many different ways and with various bases, which we deal with below. If you are rushed, or taken unawares, then biscuits and one of the cheese spreads we discussed on p. 126 are a useful let-out, but these really must be enlivened with parsley or chopped herbs, or one of the quick garnishes. A useful time-saver which you can prepare at leisure and keep for some time in the refrigerator is potted cheese.

Potted Cheese

This is a good way of dealing with pieces of cheese which may be getting a little dry, or which no longer look attractive on the cheese board. According to Mrs Beeton, potted cheese is 'exceedingly good spread on bread, and is the best way of eating it for those whose digestion is weak'. Not too weak, however, as she suggests adding mixed mustard, cayenne pepper, pounded mace or curry powder to the cheese!

To make potted cheese, first grate the cheese and then pound it with one-third of its weight of butter. Work in 2 tablespoons of white wine or dry sherry to each 4 oz (100 g) of cheese. For Stilton, use the same amount of port or red wine, and for the other blue cheeses, half the quantity of brandy. Flavour the cheese and press it into a jar. Cover it with melted butter. Like this, it will keep a long time in the refrigerator.

Canapés made with White Bread. For this purpose, the uninteresting sliced loaf is a great convenience, especially since it comes in different sizes, and there are varying thicknesses of slice to suit your purpose. If raw or toasted, the bread must be buttered to avoid its becoming soggy. If fried in a mixture of oil and butter it makes an excellent, crisp base, and only requires a simple finish such as cream cheese mixed with chopped parsley. Fried or otherwise, the bread should be cut into 1½-inch squares (4 cm), or other shapes of similar size. Here are some suggestions, using the materials, eggs, cream and cheese, with which this book is concerned:

hard-boiled eggs mixed with mayonnaise or any of its variations; scrambled eggs in any of the forms mentioned on pp. 48–49; a slice of hard-boiled egg lying on a piece of artichoke heart *or* shredded lettuce mixed with mayonnaise and ketchup *or* caviare topped with a slice of lemon (the inexpensive Danish and German caviares are quite adequate for this purposel).

Rye Bread. This needs buttering, and may prove a little awkward to cut and trim. The slices must be small or the canapés will be stodgy. For the top layers try:

blue cheese with a sliver of tongue; a slice of any firm cheese covered with mixed mayonnaise and grated celeriac; cream cheese and flaked tunny fish topped with a black olive; cheese with sliced radish.

Pumpernickel. No slicing problem here, but the robust flavour of the pumpernickel will kill any delicate topping. Cheese with a decided taste like Danish Blue, Münster with caraway seeds, or Provolone Piccante made a good combination.

Biscuits. Large biscuits which require two bites should be avoided; also those which break when you try to spread them. If the biscuit has a delicious flavour of its own, then a very simple finish is sufficient, such as the cream cheese and parsley mentioned above.

Here are a few ideas for canapés made with biscuits:
cottage cheese mixed with chopped cress and lemon juice; skinned sardines mashed with hard-boiled egg yolks, cream, lemon juice and red pepper; cream cheese mixed with pounded walnuts, mustard, and a little tarragon-flavoured vinegar, and garnished with green olives; tunny fish, cream cheese, shredded lettuce or celery, and mayonnaise.

Bridge Rolls. These must be small, and usually have to be ordered in advance. They may be filled with any of the more bulky suggestions above, or with:
sliced Cheddar cheese and a spoonful of chopped celery mixed with rémoulade sauce (p. 76); cream cheese and finely-chopped mushrooms sprinkled with salt, lemon juice and minced parsley; cream cheese mixed with minced ham and Dijon mustard, or horse-radish.

Hot Canapés

Hot canapés are very popular, especially in winter, so it is worth preparing some. In itself, this is not difficult. The only problem is in keeping the canapés warm without drying or burning them.

Large sheets of foil, which can be opened and closed again when you need fresh supplies, will keep your canapés safe in a low oven.

Here are some ideas:

Grate coarsely 4 oz (100 g) of Cheddar or Cheshire cheese and mix it with 2 oz (50 g) of softened butter. Add celery salt and a trace of cayenne pepper. Spread on slices of toast and brown under the grill, or in a hot oven.

Slice 4 oz (100 g) each of Cheddar cheese and thickly-cut ham. Mix them with 4 peeled and sliced tomatoes, season with cayenne pepper and pile on small milk rolls split lengthwise and buttered.

Flavour the same cheese and ham mixture with mustard or horse-radish sauce, and mix it with béchamel. Pile on to split, buttered bridge rolls and put in a hot oven for 10 minutes (425°F, 220°C, Gas 7).

Cocktail-sized sausages browned in the oven and stuck with toothpicks are always popular. Provide small bowls of mustard for dipping. If you cannot obtain these very small sausages, it is possible to make a substitute with chipolatas, by twisting them at intervals. Unless you open them at one end to allow the surplus sausage meat to escape, the chipolatas will burst. Work from the closed end, smoothing gently with your fingers, and make the final twist so that it seals the open end of the sausage. The surplus sausage meat can be used for a stuffing. Bake the sausages in small strings, cutting them apart once they are done and firmly set in their shapes.

Chicken livers, mussels or prunes wrapped in small strips of bacon, speared on cocktail sticks and baked are delicious. Use thinly-cut streaky bacon, smooth each rasher out on a board, divide it in half lengthwise and cut in half again. Brown in a hot oven and serve hot. Small chunks of cheese and ham speared together are also good served hot. See that the cheese is uppermost, so that the ham can catch any which melts.

If you are using prunes, choose the plump American kind. Pour hot water over them and they will be soft enough to dry and stone in a short time. Tough prunes benefit by being soaked in strong tea (remember to save the remains of the pot). They may need a short simmering after this, but it is essential that the prunes remain firm and not soggy. Dry them well.

If the prunes are very large, they can be divided in half before being wrapped in bacon, and you may care to fold the halves round a stuffed olive or an anchovy fillet curled round an almond.

Chicken livers should be tossed in a little hot butter just long enough to make them sufficiently firm to cut in pieces and wrap. If raw, they are inclined to slip out of the bacon roll.

Pierce each roll with a toothpick as you make it, and arrange them close to each other on a fireproof dish so that the little sticks remain upright. These will come to no harm in the oven and provide a clean and convenient approach. Ten minutes in a hot oven are sufficient to brown these savouries. After that, cover them with foil and lower the heat.

Don't forget to accompany the dish, when you serve it, with a bowl for the débris. It is horrid to be left holding a handful of little sticks, and worse still to find them in the dish.

Layered Sandwiches

Trim the crusts from slices of brown or white bread. Butter each slice and spread with different mixtures. Pile one on the other, alternating the colours in an interesting way. Wrap the reconstituted loaf in aluminium foil and put it in the refrigerator for two hours. When it is well chilled, slice it vertically with a sharp knife. Curry powder or saffron, anchovy paste or tomato essence and spinach or parsley juice are all useful for providing colour, though some neutrally-tinted spreads make a good contrast. Any of the mixtures described for white bread or biscuit-based canapés (pp. 207, 208) can be used for layered sandwiches. Here are some more ideas:

minced ham with thick cream and mustard; blue cheese mixed with butter; Camembert mashed with a drop of brandy; cream cheese with fresh herbs; minced shallot and anchovy paste; pâté de foie gras; cod's roe sprinkled with lemon juice
cottage cheese stirred with a little thick cream can be mixed with the whole range of ketchups and chutneys or with minced shallot and anchovy paste; grated apple, curry powder and lemon juice; crumbled crisp-fried bacon; pounded tunny fish mixed into tomato ketchup

The Porcupine

Cocktail sticks loaded with odds and ends and stuck, like the quills of a porcupine, into a grape-fruit or other base, are a familiar sight at a cocktail party. The idea is attractive and convenient, but so often the stereotyped lumps of Dutch cheese, cocktail onions and damp scraps of pineapple are uninspiring. With a little care and originality you can make something really tempting.

Choose a snowy cauliflower, or a glossy white or a gleaming red cabbage and peel off the outer leaves to reveal the clean marble veining and unspoilt bloom inside. Then try to find something different with which to tip the spines of your porcupine.

Cheese truffles. Grated or mashed cheese mixed to a thick paste with butter or cream, can be rolled into small truffles, dipped

in various substances, and chilled in the refrigerator until they are firm enough to impale on cocktail sticks. There are recipes for both parsley and paprika balls on p. 157. Here are some further suggestions:
blue cheese and butter dipped in chopped fresh herbs; soft cheese such as Camembert or Pont l'Evêque dipped in paprika; grated Emmenthal, cottage cheese and butter rolled in caraway seeds; grated Parmesan and cottage cheese and butter rolled in crushed toasted nuts

Other unusual trifles for your porcupine are prunes stuffed with cottage cheese mixed with chopped, salted almonds; cubed salami or strong Spanish *chorizo* sausage; ham and cheese rolled in honey and mustard; pieces of Emmenthal and tongue with pickled onions; cubes of cheese rolled up in smoked raw ham.

Dips
Dips have become very popular and are much quicker to prepare than canapés. They need a little care, however. It is not wise to put out too much dip at a time as the bowl quickly becomes tired-looking and it is better to replace it with a freshly filled one. The mixture must be soft enough to scoop, but firm enough to stay on the biscuit or whatever is used for eating it. Biscuits must be reasonably small, or the dip will vanish too fast, and firm so that they do not shatter leaving trails of crumbs in the bowl.

Vegetables such as pieces of carrot and celery, or cauliflower florets are popular for dipping. They must be chilled until the last moment, free of any water and of a carefully calculated size. The pieces should not bend or break as the dip is scooped up. Each piece must be long enough to keep the finger tips clear but short enough to form a single mouthful. It is annoying to be obliged to chump up a stodgy piece of bare carrot which was too large to get into your mouth the first time, but difficult to dispose of otherwise. As you cut the vegetables, test by dipping to find the ideal size.

Potato crisps taste delicious with a dip, but the bought kind are too fragile for any but family use. The same thing applies to mussels on toothpicks, which leave a trail of devastation. For real luxury, use cooked prawns.

Very thick mayonnaise, on its own or in any of the variations
O*

mentioned on pp. 75–76, makes useful dip. Philadelphia cheese softened with a little sour cream, or cottage cheese mixed with thick fresh cream make excellent dips with any of the following additions adding salt to taste:

2 tablespoons anchovy paste, $\frac{1}{2}$ teaspoon caraway seeds, a chopped sprig of parsley, cayenne pepper; $\frac{1}{2}$ cup drained crushed pineapple, $\frac{1}{2}$ teaspoon chilli powder; 3 oz (75 g) blue cheese, 1 teaspoon cognac, 2 tablespoons chopped fresh herbs; 1 small tin flaked crab, 1 tablespoon Dijon mustard, 2 teaspoons lemon juice, cayenne pepper; $\frac{1}{2}$ unpeeled cucumber, grated and drained, 1 teaspoon Worcestershire sauce, $\frac{1}{2}$ crushed clove garlic, 1 tablespoon lemon juice, a dash of tabasco or cayenne, a little grated onion (optional); one medium-sized tin tunny, drained and flaked, 2 tablespoons capers, coarsely chopped, 1 tablespoon soya sauce, 1 tablespoon grated onion; 1 small peeled and grated apple, 1 tablespoon grated onion, $\frac{1}{2}$ clove garlic, 2 teaspoons curry powder, 1 teaspoon vinegar or lemon juice, a pinch sugar, 3 tablespoons grated beetroot (optional); 1 tablespoon grated onion, a trace of garlic, sieved pulp of $\frac{1}{2}$ tomato, cayenne pepper, 2 teaspoons paprika

WINE AND CHEESE PARTIES

Wine and cheese parties are very versatile. They may be last-minute affairs; a substitute for a cocktail party; a pleasant way of passing the rest of the evening when everyone, supposedly, has dined; or they may even replace a dinner party.

For informal occasions, the simplest solution is to serve cubes of cheese, piled on the most attractive dishes you can find, and a selection of bread and biscuits, all fresh and varied. This basic fare can be made more interesting if you choose half a dozen of the less-known British cheeses and label them, so that people can compare and explore. A rule-of-thumb calculation is 3 oz (75 g) of cheese per person, but this may vary with the age of the guests. However, the British cheeses, all of which can be used up for cooking, are moderately priced, and there is no problem in providing a substantial margin.

This simple basis can easily be upgraded by providing iced butter, jugs of crisp celery, bowls of radishes, watercress and chicory leaves, and dishes of olives, pickled onions, sliced green peppers and gherkins. Piping hot garlic bread is a delight and will probably double your consumption all round. Stacks of soft paper napkins are an essential accompaniment.

Since some cheeses can never achieve a meaningful relationship with certain wines—especially those which are more delicate and expensive—it might be wiser, unless you are well-informed and well-heeled, to choose a Fino sherry (which can be iced in summer) or a South African medium dry, and a good, strong, economical red wine such as a Spanish Rioja. At a party of this sort people are usually more concerned with quantity than quality.

If you are inviting thirty people to a simple party such as this, the following should prove an adequate shopping list:

1 lb each of say, Cheddar, Emmenthal, Caerphilly and Stilton
½ lb each of any three of the other cheeses described in the section on English and Welsh cheeses
4 loaves (rye, French, poppy-seed plait, granary, etc.) and 3 dozen small rolls
2 packets each of rye and wheaten bread and of the large wheels of Swedish crispbread (from the Norway Food Centre, 166 Brompton Road, London S.W.3)
1 dozen packets of crisps (4 each of plain, onion and tomato flavoured)
1½ lb biscuits, the texture and flavours as varied as possible
3 heads of celery, 4 bunches of radishes, 2 heads of chicory, 3 green peppers, 3 bunches of watercress

It is not easy to judge the amount of butter you will need. A rough calculation would be 2 oz (50 g) a head, and 4 oz (100 g) for each long French garlic loaf.

Stuffed Cheese

Choose a whole cheese, suiting the size to the number of guests you are expecting. A Wensleydale or Gouda midget weighs only about 1 lb: an Islay runs from 1½ to 2½ lb; a St Paulin is a little larger and a Tome de Savoie weighs about 3½ lb.

Cut off the top of the cheese and scoop out the centre, leaving a thick layer all round to support the sides. Mash the loose cheese with a little mustard or Worcestershire sauce and add enough beer

213

to make a smooth paste. Put it back into the cheese which you set on a round dish, piling the edge with little squares of buttered rye bread and setting knives at intervals. The cheese, once stuffed, can be kept, covered, in the refrigerator, but must be taken out at least an hour before the party, otherwise the flavour will be muted.

If your wine and cheese party is to be the sole means of subsistence for the whole evening, then it must be carefully planned. The cheeses should be more sophisticated and chosen to form a pleasant contrast of flavour, texture, and even colour. Give a strongly-flavoured cheese a separate dish and serving knives of its own.

Though this type of party is comparatively simple to prepare, it depends for its charm on careful presentation and running repairs are vital. Cheese boards should be whisked away from time to time and tidied; knives washed and replaced; napkins renewed and ash trays emptied. This may sound very obvious, but unless the responsibilities for tidying up are allotted in advance, a party so quickly becomes chaotic.

In cold weather, hot soup makes an encouraging start, or hot canapés such as those described in this chapter. Cold soup is enjoyable in summer. You will need one or two hot dishes, some really interesting salad, and something refreshing like fruit salad or lemon mousse to finish with.

A quiche Lorraine, or one made with cheese and tomato (p. 184), makes an excellent hot dish for a wine and cheese party. Moussaka or baked lasagne are also very good standbys.

Moussaka

There are as many different recipes for this dish as there are ways of spelling the name. The constant elements are meat (usually lamb, cooked or uncooked, though beef or veal can also be used), onions, aubergines, tomatoes and garlic. Tomatoes are not included in Elizabeth David's recipe for Greek *mousaká*, which is covered with a thick egg custard and baked golden-brown.

For about 12 buffet portions, here is a recipe which is useful and adaptable to small variations which may happen to suit you:

Slice about 4 lb (about 1,600 g) of aubergines thinly lengthwise and sprinkle them with coarse salt. Leave them to drain for half an hour, then rinse and dry them in a cloth. Dust the slices with flour and fry in oil until they are browned all over. Drain the aubergines on kitchen paper and keep warm.

Slice 4 large onions, and cream 4 cloves of garlic mixed with salt beneath the broad blade of a kitchen knife. Cook them in oil until transparent, then add 2 lb of meat, chopped or minced, 8 peeled, chopped tomatoes, 2 tablespoons of minced parsley, pepper and salt and enough red wine or rich stock to keep the mixture moist. Cook over a low fire, stirring occasionally, for about 20 minutes. Meanwhile, make a béchamel sauce as described on p. 108, using $\frac{3}{4}$ pint ($4\frac{1}{2}$ dl) of milk.

The meat sauce can if you wish be 'stretched' by the addition of about 4 tablespoons of mixed breadcrumbs and Parmesan cheese. Some people add chopped sauté mushrooms to the sauce. You can also vary the herbs by the addition of a little oregano or thyme, and marjoram or lovage, but use discretion. These herbs should be sensed rather than tasted.

Butter a large, shallow fireproof dish; the moussaka should not be more than about 2 inches deep. Spread the bottom of the dish with slices of aubergine, then a layer of meat sauce, and fill the dish with alternating layers, finishing with aubergine.

Cover the top with a blanket of béchamel perfumed with nutmeg, and sprinkle with grated Parmesan cheese. Instead of the béchamel, one can use two eggs beaten into 4 tablespoons of flour and whisked with two cartons of yoghurt.

This is rather a lengthy dish to prepare, but it can be done the day before. The yoghurt topping would, of course, have to be made and spread just before the moussaka is baked for about $\frac{3}{4}$ hour in a fairly hot oven (400°F, 200°C, Gas 6).

The only snag about moussaka, which in most ways is ideal for the sort of party we are discussing, is that aubergines are not always obtainable. Lasagne, however, are always with us.

Baked Lasagne

Lasagne are wide strips of pasta, either white or coloured green with spinach, which are sold by most good grocers. Like moussaka, baked lasagne can be varied in all sorts of ways and prepared well in advance.

For twelve people, if the dish is for a buffet and not a main course, bring a gallon of salted water to the boil and drop in, one by one, 1 lb (400 g) of lasagne. A tablespoon of oil will help to prevent their sticking to one another. See that the water keeps boiling fast, and at the end of 10 minutes test the lasagne and, while they are still quite firm, turn them into a colander and rinse with plenty of cold water. Lay the lasagne out separately on a clean cloth so that they do not stick together while drying.

Make a rich Bolognese sauce by browning 6 oz (150 g) of chopped streaky bacon with a walnut of butter. Add a large onion and carrot and a small stick of celery, all chopped, and when they are delicately brown, add 1 lb (400 g) of raw minced beef and stir until it too is brown. Add 8 oz (200 g) of chopped chicken livers and, a few moments later, 2 level tablespoons of tomato concentrate and ½ pint (3 dl) of white wine. Season, being careful to allow for the salt which will be contained in the stock if you are using a ready-made one. Add a dusting of nutmeg and then stir in 1 pint (6 dl) of stock. Simmer with the lid on for about 35 minutes keeping the heat very gentle.

Meanwhile make a béchamel sauce as described on p. 108 using 1¼ pints (7½ dl) of milk, and grate 4 oz of Parmesan cheese.

Butter a large shallow fireproof dish and spread a layer of lasagne on the bottom, following with a layer of Bolognese sauce and one of béchamel. Make about three layers in all, finishing with béchamel sauce. Up to this point, everything can be prepared in advance.

When you are ready to finish the lasagne pre-heat the oven to 350°F (180°C, Gas 4). Cover the dish with a generous blanket of grated Parmesan cheese (about 4oz, or 100 g) and bake for about half an hour. The top should be golden-brown, so raise the heat of the oven towards the end, if necessary.

If you are holding the lasagne back for consumption later on in the evening, lower the heat of the oven once the dish is browned, and cover it with foil.

The sauce for the lasagne can be varied by the addition of ham, chicken giblets or mushrooms. Use also different herbs such as basil, marjoram or lovage to make a subtle variation.

When preparing a salad, wash all the greens well beforehand, shake them as dry as possible, and put them in a plastic box or bag for several hours, preferably in the refrigerator. Mix French dressing in the proportion of 1 spoon of vinegar to 3 of oil. Add sea salt, freshly-ground black pepper, a pinch of sugar, a dash of Accent or Aromat, and some mustard if you like. Stir in the pale inner leaves of the celery and spring onions, finely chopped, and minced fresh herbs.

Choose a bowl which is large enough to allow you to toss the salad comfortably, and rub it with garlic before you begin. The dressing can be made well beforehand. Toss the salad greens at the last minute, making sure that there is no water clinging to the leaves.

For an all-evening party it is better to have one really large bowl and re-fill it from time to time with fresh, crisp salad rather than having several bowls of salad which will gradually wilt. The dressing can be ready-mixed in a bottle and tossing only takes a moment.

To make salad for thirty people you will need, approximately:

6 lettuces, 3 bunches of watercress, 2 cucumbers, 3 bunches of spring onions, 1 lb chicory, 2 green peppers, all the fresh herbs you can find (chives, mint, tarragon, parsley, chervil, marjoram and a little thyme or sage)

For this more elaborate party you may be tempted to offer a wider selection of wine, but this would require more glasses and more washers-up, and we feel it is better to stick to a straight choice. A cool Beaujolais or a sturdy Mâcon, and a medium-dry Riesling or a rosé will see a party through.

Allow an absolute minimum of half a bottle per person. This is very near the danger line, and everyone, including you, will have a happier evening if there is a generous reserve. Sale-and-return arrangements are as a rule easily made with a wine merchant. If not, you may have some wine to enjoy afterwards.

NOTES

INDEX

Main recipes, appearing on pages 156 to end of book, are here shown in capitals. Since all three sections contain other descriptions of preparations and cooking, sufficiently detailed to rank as recipes, the reader's attention is called to these by use of an asterisk. All cheeses are listed under the head 'Cheeses', not elsewhere.